Colección Támesis

SERIE A: MONOGRAFÍAS, 323

CONTEMPORARY HISPANIC CINEMA

INTERROGATING THE TRANSNATIONAL IN SPANISH AND LATIN AMERICAN FILM

CONTEMPORARY HISPANIC CINEMA

INTERROGATING THE TRANSNATIONAL IN SPANISH AND LATIN AMERICAN FILM

Edited by

Stephanie Dennison

TAMESIS

First published 2013 by Tamesis, Woodbridge

ISBN 978 185566 261 2

Tamesis is an imprint of Boydell & Brewer Ltd
PO Box 9, Woodbridge, Suffolk IP12 3DF, UK
and of Boydell & Brewer Inc.
668 Mt Hope Avenue, Rochester, NY 14620–2731, USA
website: www.boydellandbrewer.com

A CIP catalogue record for this book is available
from the British Library

The publisher has no responsibility for the continued existence or accuracy of
URLs for external or third-party internet websites referred to in this book,
and does not guarantee that any content on such websites is,
or will remain, accurate or appropriate

Papers used by Boydell & Brewer Ltd are natural, recyclable products
made from wood grown in sustainable forests

Printed in Great Britain by
CPI Group (UK) Ltd, Croydon, CR0 4YY

For Libia, Deborah, Tamara, Nuria, Marvin,
Sarah, Catherine and Alessandra

CONTENTS

ACKNOWLEDGEMENTS

I would like to thank the School of Modern Languages and Cultures of the University of Leeds, the School of Media at the University of Lincoln, the Instituto Cervantes, the Instituto Camões and the Brazilian Embassy in London for their financial support for either the symposium upon which this edited collection is based (*Transnational Film Financing in the Hispanic World*, June 2009, University of Leeds) or for the cost involved in bringing this book project to fruition.

At the Instituto Cervantes in Manchester I am grateful to Kepa González for his support for this project, and for tirelessly answering my questions about the Viva film festival and Cine en Construcción. A number of contributors have benefitted from the opportunity to interview directors, producers and other industry professionals: our heartfelt thanks go to them.

In the School of Modern Languages and Cultures and beyond I would like to thank a number of colleagues who have supported this venture in one way or another: Cristian Aliaga, Stuart Green, Sofia Martinho, Lúcia Nagib, Thea Pitman, Rob Rix, Laura Rodríguez Isaza, Antônio Márcio da Silva, Duncan Wheeler, and the very smart and engaged undergraduate students on my Latin American Film Industries module.

Thanks to Stephen Hart for his encouragement at the initial stages of the book project and to Scott Mahler at Tamesis Press for his support, advice and patience.

Thanks finally to Fernando for all the childcare and to Anna, for forgoing mummy's company at weekends for the sake of 'the book'.

CONTRIBUTORS

Sarah Barrow is Head of the School of Media at University of Lincoln, UK. She has published numerous articles on British and Hispanic cinemas and has a particular interest in Peruvian cinema. She co-edited *50 Key British Films* (Routledge, 2008), was a contributor to *50 Key American Films* (Routledge, 2009), and is co-editing a project for Routledge on world cinemas (2014).

Stephanie Dennison is Reader in Brazilian Studies at the University of Leeds. She is co-author of two monographs on Brazilian cinema (*Popular Cinema in Brazil*, MUP 2004 and *Brazilian National Cinema*, Routledge 2007). She co-edited *Remapping World Cinema: Identity, Culture and Politics on Film*, Wallflower 2006 and *Latin American Cinema: Essays on Modernity, Gender and National Identity*, MacFarland 2005. She was co-editor of cinema journal *New Cinemas* (Intellect) 2010–11.

Marvin D'Lugo is Professor of Spanish and Screen Studies at Clark University (Worcester Massachusetts) where he teaches courses on Spanish and Latin-American cinemas. His primary areas of film research include theories of authorship and the aesthetics of transnational cinema. He is author of *The Films of Carlos Saura: The Practice of Seeing* (Princeton 1991); *Guide to the Cinema of Spain* (Greenwood 1997); *Pedro Almodóvar* (Illinois 2006) and co-editor of *Companion to Pedro Almodóvar's Cinema* (Wiley-Blackwell 2013). Since 2008 he has been principal editor of *Studies in Hispanic Cinema*. His current research involves auditory culture in the development of transnational Hispanic films.

Tamara L. Falicov is an associate professor and department chair of film and media studies at the University of Kansas. Professor Falicov's specialty is Latin American Cinema, with particular focus on the film histories of Argentina and Cuba. Her book *The Cinematic Tango: Contemporary Argentine Film* (London: Wallflower Press, 2007) was named an "Outstanding Academic Title" by CHOICE, the premier source of reviews of academic books, electronic media and Internet resources for higher education. She has researched numerous topics such as the Ibero-American film production fund Programa Ibermedia and issues related to multi-country co-production, the role of Hollywood in Latin American film production, young videographers in Patagonia, the film industry in Uruguay, and US-Argentine film exchange relations under the Good Neighbour Policy. She is the co-editor of the book series *Framing Film Festivals* by Palgrave MacMillan.

Catherine Leen is a lecturer in the Department of Spanish, National University of Ireland, Maynooth. She has published articles and book chapters on Chicana/o cinema and literature, Latin American cinema and the work of Luis Buñuel and Guillermo Gómez-Peña. She was a Fulbright Scholar at the University of California, Santa Barbara, in 2008 and is an affiliate member of the Hispanic Research Center, Arizona State University. She is currently completing a monograph on Latina/o Filmmakers and Mexico and her volume *International Perspectives on Chicana/o Studies: "This World is my Place,"* co-edited with Niamh Thornton, will be published by Routledge, New York, in 2013.

Alessandra Meleiro is Associate Professor of Cultural Production at Universidade Federal Fluminense, in Rio de Janeiro (Department of Arts and Cultural Studies). She has a PhD in Cultural Politics from the University of São Paulo. She holds a Post-Doctorate at the Media and Film Studies Programme (University of London). She is Scientific Coordinator of the Center for Analysis of Cinema and Audiovisual and Cebrap (Brazilian Center for Planning and Analysis). She is President of the Cultural Initiative Institute. She is editor of Escritura's multi-volume book series World *Cinema: Industry, Politics and Market* and Editor of Escritura's multi-volume book series *Brazilian Film Industry*.

Deborah Shaw is Reader in Film Studies at the University of Portsmouth. She has published widely on Latin American film and cultural studies. She is the author of *The Three Amigos: The Transnational Films of Guillermo del Toro, Alejandro González Iñárritu, and Alfonso Cuarón* (Manchester University Press, 2013), *Contemporary Latin American Cinema: Ten Key Films* (Continuum: 2003) and editor of *Contemporary Latin American Cinema: Breaking into the Global Market* (Rowman and Littlefield: 2007). She is co-founding editor of *Transnational Cinemas* (Intellect).

Nuria Triana Toribio is Professor of Hispanic Studies at the University of Kent. She is the author of *Spanish National Cinema* (Routledge, 2003) and co-author of *The Cinema of Álex de la Iglesia* (Manchester University Press, 2007). She is co-editor of the series *Spanish and Latin American Filmmakers* for Manchester University Press. She has published on film festivals, contemporary Spanish film cultures, and new strategies of auteurism, particularly in relation to transnational financing, production and dissemination strategies. Her most recent work has appeared in *Screen, Secuencias* and *Studies in Hispanic Cinemas*. She is currently developing a manuscript entitled *Spanish Film Cultures*.

Libia Villazana specialises in Latin American Cultural Politics and Policy and Transnational Cinemas with a particular focus on films co-produced between Latin America and Europe. She is the author of *Transnational Financial Structures in the Cinema of Latin America: Programa Ibermedia in Study*, 2009 and has published in numerous cinema and media journals including *Framework* and *Journal of Media Practice*. She is an independent documentary filmmaker: her most recent film, *Latin America in Co-production* (UK/PE 2007) was screened at the Tate Modern, London. She was also the Director of the 8th Discovering Latin America Film Festival, one of the largest film festivals of its kind in London. Her recent research is informed by the fields of migration and transnational studies; she is currently developing a cross-disciplinary research project at the Institute for the Study of the Americas, University of London, and preparing her next monograph (co-authored), *Latin Americans Abroad: Constructing Transnational Cultural Spaces in London* (Palgrave 2014).

PREFACE

One of the results of the quite dramatic changes in twenty-first-century film production and funding is the veritable boom in academic publications on the transnational features of contemporary filmmaking.[1] But despite the dependency of many film cultures of Latin America on international funding for their very survival, and despite the fact that they have, at least by scholars in the USA and UK, been traditionally subjected to a kind of supranational lumping together, scant attention has been paid to date to the transnational quality of filmmaking in the region. A number of very recent texts have sought to examine the contemporary cinema of Latin America beyond the rubric of the national, but on closer inspection we see that only a handful of chapters spread over these books are in any way comparative in nature.[2] Very few texts analyse the *film industries* of Spain, Portugal or the nations of Latin America, and none to date has considered all three in relation to each other. And while a number of article-length works have helped to pave the way in terms of analysing the transnational links between Spanish and Latin American cinema, only two scholars (both contributors to this volume) have dealt with these links in any detail: Marvin d'Lugo edited a special double issue of the film journal *Studies in Hispanic Cinemas* in 2009 entitled 'Beyond the Hispanic Atlantic: Cinema and its Symbolic Relocations', while in the same year Libia Villazana published *Transnational Financial Structures in the Cinema of Latin America: Programa Ibermedia in Study*.[3]

---

[1] See, for example, Natasa Durovicová and Kathleen E. Newman (eds), *World Cinemas, Transnational Perspectives* (Abingdon: Routledge, 2009); Elizabeth Ezra and Terry Rowden (eds), *Transnational Cinema: The Film Reader* (London: Routledge, 2006). More significantly for this study, two scholars of Latin American cinema, Deborah Shaw (a contributor to this volume) and Armida de la Garza founded in 2010 and edit the academic journal *Transnational Cinemas*.

[2] See, for example, Deborah Shaw (ed.), *Contemporary Latin American Cinema: Breaking into the Global Market* (Lanham: Rowman and Littlefield, 2007); Cacilda Rêgo and Carolina Rocha (eds), *New Trends in Brazilian and Argentine Cinema* (Bristol: Intellect, 2010); Nayibe Bermúdez Barrios (ed.), *Latin American Cinema: Local Views and Transnational Connections* (Calgary: University of Calgary Press, 2010).

[3] Marvin D'Lugo, 'Across the Hispanic Atlantic: Cinema and its Symbolic Relocations', *Studies in Hispanic Cinemas*, 5.1–2 (2009), 3–7; Libia Villazana, *Transnational Financial*

One of the striking features of twenty-first-century filmmaking in Latin America, then, is the increase in co-operation between 'Hispanic' (Spanish- and Portuguese-speaking) countries. Evidence of this can be seen in the growth, for example, in the number of co-productions between or among Spain, Portugal and Latin American film-producing nations, the formal pooling of Spanish, Portuguese and Latin American film production resources under the umbrella of Ibermedia, and the post-production funds available through the San Sebastian film festival aimed at Spanish-speaking America and Brazil (Cine en Construcción/Films in Progress). Such late twentieth- and early twenty-first-century 'processes of Hispanisation' are part of a larger picture: they can also be witnessed in the penetration of Spanish business interests in Latin America (including Brazil) and Portugal, the two-way flow of people across the Atlantic and the development of a number of regional economic blocs in Latin America (the Mercosur/Mercosul [the Southern Common Market], CAN [the Andean Community of Nations], and more recently, the Unasur/Unasul [the Union of South American Nations], for example).

The impact of such economic and cultural shifts is therefore ripe for exploration. It was thus as a result of a certain frustration at the lack of discussion of the transnational nature of the funding of much of contemporary Latin American film that I organised in 2009 a symposium at the University of Leeds entitled 'Transnational Film Financing in the Hispanic World'. This volume contains a number of chapters based on presentations at this symposium,[4] together with specially commissioned pieces (chapters by Libia Villazana, Marvin D'Lugo and Catherine Leen). Our discussions focused on the following key questions:

- What place do initiatives such as Ibermedia and Cine en Construcción have within national film industries, some of which have their own, albeit limited local sources of support?
- What is the impact (perceived or otherwise) on the scripts, choices of cast and film aesthetics of films supported by such initiatives?
- Have such initiatives helped to forge a cinema that is instantly recognisable as 'Hispanic'?

Structures in the Cinema of Latin America: Programa Ibermedia in Study (Saarbrucken: Verlag Dr Muller, 2009). Two other recent texts are worth mentioning here in terms of rethinking filmmaking in Latin America in relation to national boundaries: Miriam Ross's book-length study *South American Cinematic Culture: Policy, Production, Distribution and Exhibition* (Newcastle: Cambridge Scholars, 2010) and Dolores Tierney's article 'Alejandro González Iñárritu: Director without Borders', *New Cinemas*, 7.2 (2009), 101–17. Ross's otherwise insightful and very useful text limits itself to an analysis of the film cultures of Argentina, Bolivia, Chile and Peru.

    4 I would like to thank Paulo Filipe Monteiro and Mar Binimelis, who also attended and gave papers at the symposium.

It is hoped that this book can serve as a starting point to begin to provide answers for these and other pertinent questions.

As well as overviews of the workings of key 'Hispanic' film-financing initiatives such as Programa Ibermedia and Cine en Construcción (chapters 4 and 5 respectively), the volume includes two key chapters that interrogate the transnational from the perspective of Latin American cinema (chapters 2 and 3). The different chapters contained in this volume focus on the film cultures of Spain, Portugal, Mexico, Venezuela, Argentina, Brazil, Peru and Paraguay. While mention is made in the text of world-wide financing initiatives such as the Hubert Bals fund in Rotterdam, Sundance in the USA and the World Cinema Fund in Berlin, initiatives that many of the film cultures discussed in this volume regularly take advantage of, our focus will be on those that are aimed at Spain, Portugal and Latin America. As we see it, initiatives such as Programa Ibermedia and Cine en Construcción facilitate a more focused discussion of a range of meanings afforded to the term transnationalism: these range from the workings of those driven by economic imperatives, such as co-productions and 'Hispanic' film festivals, to the cultural, for example the invention of a marketable 'Latinamericanness' in Spain, or a 'Hispanic aesthetic' elsewhere.

As Chris Berry has observed, no transnational cinema exists without encountering and negotiating national spaces and cultures.[5] This volume thus includes chapters that deal with a specific 'national' film industry: Sarah Barrow on Peruvian cinema – chapter 7; Catherine Leen on Paraguayan cinema – chapter 8; and Alessandra Meleiro on Brazilian cinema – chapter 9, but the focus of these chapters is on transnational film financing strategies, and the extent to which these 'national' film industries have come to rely upon both international co-production partners and foreign capital. Our focus is thus the transnationalisation (as in the increasing organisation of production on a cross-border basis by multinational organisations) of film production in the Hispanic world. While we undoubtedly concentrate on Latin American cinema in this volume, we include a chapter (chapter 6) that focuses on Spanish cinema, and in particular, the Latin American dimension of both the filmmaking of Pedro Almodóvar, and of his production company El Deseo.

Stephanie Dennison

---

5   Chris Berry, 'What is Transnational Cinema? Thinking From the Chinese Situation', *Transnational Cinemas*, 1.2 (2010), 111–27 (p. 112).

1

National, Transnational and Post-national: Issues in Contemporary Filmmaking in the Hispanic World

STEPHANIE DENNISON

The purpose of this chapter is to map out new ways to think about contemporary Latin American cinema that take us beyond both the traditional close reading of national films within national contexts, and the dismissive notions of new trends in co-production as signifying nothing more than commercially driven expressions of global capital in movement. First I explore the transnational cultural links between Spain, Portugal and Latin America, the historical and cultural basis for these links, and the extent to which such links are affecting notions of 'the national' within Latin American film production. The second part of the chapter then focuses on two Brazilian co-productions, Ruy Guerra's *Estorvo* (*Turbulence*, 2000) and Henrique Goldman's *Jean-Charles* (2009), by way of providing a case study of filmmaking from a national industry that tends to be read as somehow set apart from filmmaking in other regions of the Hispanic world.

What do we mean by Hispanic and Latin American?

I take as my starting point an interrogation of the meanings of loaded terms such as 'Hispanic' and even 'Latin American', in the light of recent shifts in economic and cultural relations between Spain, Portugal and their American former colonies, and in the context of ongoing debates on the meaning of such terms among, for example, the influential Latino community of the USA. Part of the difficulty in discussing their meanings stems from the fact that the terminology shifts, depending on one's location (the UK, the USA, Spain, Portugal or Latin America) and on one's locus of enunciation. On this issue it is worth stating that when films circulate with the label 'Hispanic', 'Ibero-American' and even 'Latin American' it is almost exclusively beyond the confines of their home territory, so an international market is readily implied by such labels. Thus, while I make every effort not to fall into the trap of exoticising Hispanic cinema, an issue discussed later in this chapter, I do admit to a form of 'othering' that, as I see it, is part of the experience of viewing films beyond the borders in which they are made.

It is also hard not to be influenced by the rather singular usage that such terms have been afforded in academia over the years. For example, although the term Hispanic has been used in the US census since 1980, more often than not it is an adjective associated with academia, given its still widespread use in institutions of Higher Education, with a variety of meanings being afforded the term: in the UK it can refer exclusively to the study of Spanish and Spanish culture; it can also signify the languages of Spain and occasionally of the ex-Spanish colonies of America (e.g. Castilian, Catalan, Galician, Basque, Quechua), or it can refer to the languages and cultures of the Iberian Peninsula as a whole (in other words, it can include Portuguese). In US academia, however, Hispanic does not usually include Portuguese or Brazilian (although occasionally one can find Departments of Hispanic Studies where Portuguese and Brazilian Studies are taught). The most common definition for the Hispanic world, for example, would appear to be Spain, Latin America, and the Latino USA.[1]

With regard to the term Latino, Paul Allatson explains:

> Latino and not Hispanic is preferred by many Latinos/as because it avoids the Spanish European shadow that makes Hispanic the attractive option for Latino conservatives, government apparatuses and business interests alike. Unlike Latino/a, Hispanic is widely regarded by Latinos/as as an imposed identity marker, one that homogenises diverse Latino/a communities and privileges the Spanish and European imperial, cultural and racial heritage. (*Key Terms*, p. 122)[2]

---

[1] Paul Allatson, *Key Terms in Latino/a Cultural and Literary Studies* (Malden, MA and Oxford: Blackwell, 2007), p. 91. By way of illustration, the film journal *Studies in Hispanic Cinemas* is dedicated almost exclusively to Spanish-language cinemas.

[2] María DeGuzmán confirms that the term Latino excludes Spain, thus avoiding

Terms such as Hispanic and Hispanic-American are therefore used in an academic context, in a non-uniform way and are increasingly regarded as old-fashioned and neo-colonial in pretensions.[3] Take, for example, Ilan Stavans' influential *The Hispanic Condition* published in 1995, in which the Mexican-American cultural commentator places emphasis on the Spanish language as the bedrock of this so-called 'condition'.[4] As a result of doing so, critics argue, Latin American indigeneity is erased. To be sure, it is difficult not to think of projects that emphasise the Spanish language as anything other than colonialist, because the danger is that issues relating to race, class, gender and sexuality get forgotten.

The term that appears to be preferred by academics in the USA, and by supra-national government bodies, is Ibero-America.[5] Within the academic context, Ibero-American studies

> encompass the history, cultures, and affairs of the American territories conquered by the Spanish and Portuguese between the 15th and 18th centuries. It also focuses on all the subsequently independent Spanish-speaking republics, Brazil, and all the Caribbean, taking into consideration each region's preexisting indigenous cultures. By the same token, Iberian studies encompass the same study areas for Spain and Portugal from the Early Middle Ages to the present.[6]

the putative 'double bind of colonization by both Spaniards and Anglos: *Spain's Long Shadow: The Black Legend, Off-Whiteness and Anglo-American Empire* (Minneapolis: University of Minnesota Press, 2005), p. 295.

3   Consider, for example, the academic journal *Hispanic American Historical Review*, founded in the USA in 1916 and dedicated to publishing scholarly articles on Brazil and the ex-Spanish colonies of America. A respected journal, its title betrays its neo-colonial origins: see I. R. Lavretskii, 'A Survey of the Hispanic American Historical Review 1956–1958', *Hispanic American Historical Review* 40.4 (1960), 340–60 (pp. 341–2). See also Leslie Bethell, 'Brazil and "Latin America"', *Journal of Latin American Studies*, 42 (2010), 457–85 (pp. 475–6).

4   Ilan Stavans, *The Hispanic Condition: The Power of a People* (New York: Harper Collins, 1995).

5   An anecdotal aside: the prefix Ibero does not appear to be as clearly understood in the UK, even within academic circles and among students. At my own institution (the University of Leeds) the undergraduate degree programme title Ibero-American Studies was replaced with Hispanic and Latin American Studies, given that many prospective students were unsure of its meaning. As it happens, this same degree programme and the academic unit that delivers the programme were recently renamed Spanish, Portuguese and Latin American Studies (SPLAS), a trend that can be identified up and down the UK. It is for this reason that I am loath to adopt the Ibero-American label when discussing the cinemas of Spain, Portugal and Latin America.

6   University of Wisconsin library website: http://www.library.wisc.edu/guides/Ibero/ (Last accessed 1 December 2011).

Meanwhile we have, by way of example of the official use of the term, the Ibero-American Summit (the Cumbre Iberoamericana and Cúpula Ibero-Americana in Spanish and Portuguese respectively), a yearly meeting, organised by the Iberoamerican Community of Nations, of the heads of government and state of the Spanish- and Portuguese-speaking nations of Europe and the Americas, and, of course, Programa Ibermedia.

Regarding the term's use in the Spanish language, Susanne Gratius alerts us to potential pitfalls:

> [E]l término Iberoamérica crea confusiones, ya que algunas veces incluye España y otras no. Pese a los esfuerzos por construir una comunidad de naciones, sigue siendo un concepto unilateral que no calará hasta que algún ciudadano al otro lado del Atlántico diga que se siente iberoamericano.[7]

> The term Ibero-America causes confusion, given that sometimes it includes Spain and sometimes not. As a result of efforts to create a community of nations, it continues to be a unilateral concept that won't be resolved until a citizen on the other side of the Atlantic says that s/he feels Ibero-American.

The frustration and potential confusion over such labels has been addressed, but only partially, in the latest US census (2010), which included the new question: 'Are you of Hispanic, Latino or Spanish origin?' Critics can easily argue that while the question recognises the desires of the USA's non-Anglo populations to be offered more culturally and ethnically specific labels, the yes/no nature of the answer means that, for the purposes of data collection, the Hispanic, Latino and Spanish will continue to be lumped together as one group of 'ethnic others'. And while Brazilians may recognise themselves in terms such as Hispanic or, what is much more likely, Latino, it is not clear how, if at all, those of Portuguese origin might situate themselves within this 'Hispano-family'. Tensions, therefore, continue to exist in relation to all of the terms put forward to date to describe this grouping of nations, tensions that are invariably glossed over in official discourse relating to film. My contention is that given that certain nations/regions/social groups have a more tenuous place within the Hispano-family, it is worth giving due attention

---

[7] Suzanne Gratius, 'La vocación iberoamericana de España', *El país*, 17 May 2010. I am grateful to Nuria Triana Toribio for drawing this news article to my attention. English translation is mine.

to how they position themselves, in order to fully appreciate how this 'family' operates.

The Hispanic Atlantic

Spain is currently the second largest investor in Latin America after the USA.[8] 'Spanish' culture is aggressively marketed throughout the world by the Instituto Cervantes, a Spanish public institution founded in 1991 to promote Spanish language teaching and knowledge of the cultures of Spanish-speaking countries. The Instituto Cervantes plays a significant role in the Cine en Construcción film funding programme, while Spain is the majority financier of the Programa Ibermedia, whose headquarters are notably located in the Spanish capital.

The domination of the Spanish-American markets by Spanish business interests is being increasingly mirrored in Brazil, where big businesses such as the Banco Santander[9] and telecommunications company Telefónica have quickly established themselves in the Brazilian market in the last 10 years or so. Demand for Spanish language classes has also been promoted by the gradual growth in importance for Brazil of the Mercosur/Mercosul customs union, with the Instituto Cervantes currently heading up the race to provide Spanish-language training.

Conversely, there has been a considerable increase in immigration from Africa but especially from Latin America to Spain: 'This immigration has gained a quantitative and qualitative importance that has probably never been known before in modern Spain.'[10] There are between 650,000 and 700,000 Latin Americans living in Spain at a conservative estimate, many of whom are employed in low-paid jobs such as cleaners, maids and occasionally entertainers.

---

[8] 'Spanish Companies in Latin America: A Good Bet? Investments in Latin America Offer Protection against Spain's Slowdown', *The Economist*, 30 April 2009. Available at http://www.economist.com/node/13579705 (Last accessed 19 December 2011).

[9] Curiously enough, the Banco Santander currently offers financial support to nearly 50 universities in the UK. Much of the funding offered to UK universities (and those elsewhere) is to support travel to, and to bring students from, what have come to be termed 'Santander countries' (namely Spain, Portugal and the countries where the Banco Santander has a presence in Latin America: Argentina, Brazil, Chile, Colombia, Mexico, Peru, Puerto Rico, Uruguay and Venezuela).

[10] Joseba Gabilondo, 'Introduction', *Arizona Journal of Hispanic Cultural Studies*, 5 (2001) 91–113 (p. 91)

This two-way flow of capital and bodies across the Atlantic brings to the fore a host of political and historical problems that have not been fully addressed by neither (sic) Latin Americanists nor Hispanists. Is this new development an unprecedented and unexpected emergence of a 'new' Spanish (neo) imperialism? Is it simply a distorted and anachronistic twist to a more global and less specifically Spanish economic reorganisation? Or to put it otherwise, is it global capital disguised as Spanish? (Gabilondo, 'Introduction', p. 92)[11]

Joseba Gabilondo, and other cultural commentators, thus draw our attention to a seeming pattern of re-colonisation by Spain of Latin America (this time including Brazil) as witnessed in both recent economic penetration, 'Hispanic' cultural initiatives being led by Spain, and the 'subaltern' position being assumed by a new wave of immigrants arriving in Spain from Latin America seeking work.

But Gabilondo himself realises that there is more to Spanish and Latin American cultural exchanges than a straightforward case of twenty-first-century neo-colonialism, despite all of the above: hence his promotion of the idea of the Hispanic Atlantic. Concepts such as the Hispanic Atlantic which, like the Francophone and Lusophone (Black) Atlantics, serve in part to challenge historical and cultural Anglocentrism (of the kind espoused, perhaps unwittingly, by Paul Gilroy's well-intentioned original conception of the Black Atlantic), are useful in that they encourage us to think beyond the binaries metropole/(ex) colony, or centre/periphery. As Marvin D'Lugo explains:

The notion of a Black or Hispanic Atlantic is designed, of course, to challenge the sacrosanct category of the nation and its corollaries in national culture and national cinema. But, as well, the idea of the Atlantic is a metaphor for 'movement across' and an opaque allusion to the multiple levels of migration, those of people, of cultural artefacts, and finally of audiovisual technologies like cinema that have

---

[11] In an interesting contemporary twist to the picture presented by Gabilondo in 2001, in 2010 17,600 Brazilians left Spain to return home, while only 12,900 left Brazil for Spain. According to the same source, the number of foreign workers arriving in Brazil has increased by 57%: many of these workers come from Spain and Portugal. See 'Brasil endurece exigências para entrada de espanhóis', *Exame*, 12 February 2012. Available at: http://exame.abril.com.br/economia/brasil/noticias/brasil-endurece-exigencias-para-entrada-de-espanhois-2?page=2&slug_name=brasil-endurece-exigencias-para-entrada-de-espanhois-2 (Last accessed 12 September 2012).

transformed the spatial, political and cultural consciousness of their audiences.[12]

He continues: 'there is no single fixed "place" occupied by Spanish-language cinema, thus the allusion to an imprecise geographic term, the Hispanic Atlantic' (p. 5). Hence the need for a more nuanced approach to understanding contemporary cultural relations between Spain and Latin America, one which views, for example, the relationships forged by Latin American directors with European producers/funders as symbiotic.

In what strikes me as a deliberatively provocative, but still nonetheless interesting observation, Gabilondo elsewhere takes this 'evening out' of cultural power relations suggested by the concept of the Hispanic Atlantic one stage further by arguing that

> nowadays, for the global production and consumption of power/knowl-edge, both mass-oriented and academic, Spanish culture is a subset of Latin America, or to put it boldly: *culturally speaking Spain is a region of Latin America.* Spain is part of the Latin American area of studies.[13]

For sure, Spain is frequently, and then nearly always negatively, lumped together with Latin America in the US and European imaginary. María DeGuzmán, in her analysis of the representation of Spain and Spaniards in US fiction of the nineteenth and twentieth centuries, argues that 'American' identity has been posited 'either overtly or implicitly and without ironic distance, in contradistinction to the one figured as "Spanish"' (DeGuzmán, p. 243), which reminds us of contemporary commonplace assumptions about Latin America from abroad. Meanwhile Baltasar Fra-Molinero reminds us of Edmund Spenser's description of Spain as a 'mingled nation' (that is, less than white).[14] Thus the Spanish (and the Portuguese) in Europe are often seen to share the 'suspect whiteness' (Fra-Molinero, p. 147) of the Latin Americans,[15] in a process succinctly

---

[12] Marvin D'Lugo, 'Across the Hispanic Atlantic: Cinema and its Symbolic Relocations', *Studies in Hispanic Cinemas*, 5.1–2 (2009), 3–7 (p. 5).

[13] Joseba Gabilondo, 'One-Way Theory: On the Hispanic Atlantic Intersection of Postcoloniality and Postnationalism and its Globalizing Effects', *Journal of Iberian and Latin American Literary and Cultural Studies* 1 (2001). Available at: http://arachne.rutgers.edu/vol1_1gabilondo.htm (Last accessed 12 May 2012).

[14] Baltasar Fra-Molinero, 'The Suspect Whiteness of Spain', in *At Home and Abroad: Historicizing Twentieth-century Whiteness in Literature and Performance*, ed. La Vinia Delois Jennings (Knoxville: University of Tennessee Press, 2009), pp. 147–69 (p. 147).

[15] See, for example, Ana M. López, 'Are All Latins from Manhattan? Hollywood,

described by Román de la Campa, whereby negative alterity becomes readily applicable to all nations and regions from a distance.[16] The irony is that the 'otherness by dint of non-whiteness' of the 'Hispanics' as it was understood by Anglo-Saxon America and Europe, and frequently portrayed by Hollywood, went against official versions of most 'Hispanic' nations in the nineteenth century, and at least those of Spain, Portugal and Argentina in the twentieth century.[17]

At the same time as unequal patterns of development have helped to sustain the idea of the secondary (or even tertiary) status of Latin America in relation to the North, the Iberian Peninsula has long held a peripheral status in Europe, a status which is still in evidence today and invites a pejorative othering: consider, for example, the abusive term PIGS, recently used (and only later half-heartedly denounced) in the English-language media to describe the economically troubled countries of Western Europe (Portugal, Ireland, Greece and Spain).

Many, if not all, of the stereotypes identified by DeGuzmán as being associated by Americans with the Spanish in the past, are also frequently applied by Anglos to Latinos.[18] And with the peripheral, unruly and not-quite-whiteness of Hispanics and Latin Americans came an association

Ethnography and Cultural Colonialism', in *Mediating Two Worlds: Cinematic Encounters in the Americas*, ed. John King, Ana M. López, Manuel Alvarado (London: BFI Publishing, 1993), pp. 67–80; Isabel Molina-Guzmán, *Dangerous Curves: Latina Bodies in the Media* (New York and London: New York University Press, 2010).

[16] Román de la Campa, 'Comparative Latin American Studies Literary and Cultural Theory', in *Comparative Cultural Studies and Latin America*, ed. Sophia McClennen and Earl Fitz (West Lafayette: Purdue University Press, 2004), p. 62. Quoted in Victoria Ruetalo, 'Border-crossings and Textual Gaps: A "Globalized" Mode of Production in *Profundo carmesí* and *Terra estrangeira*', *Studies in Hispanic Cinemas* 5.1–2 (2009), 57–71 (p. 69).

[17] For example, Amy Kaminsky references the international exposition of 1900 in Paris and suggests that Argentina tried to efface any sign of an Indigenous presence, despite the fact that Europeans expected evidence of racial difference: 'They wanted the thrill of the exotic, a personal contact with the undifferentiated Latin American from which Argentina was trying to extricate itself': 'Argentina White', in *At Home and Abroad: Historicizing Twentieth-century Whiteness in Literature and Performance*, ed. La Vinia Delois Jennings (Knoxville: University of Tennessee Press, 2009), pp. 1–28 (p. 20).

[18] 'the country of Inquisition, darkness, sadists, "Oriental blood", outlaws, brigands, violent passions (fuelled by the imbibing of wine and sherry and the consumption of garlic and peppers), laziness, primitivism, timelessness and/or stagnation, tragedy, mystics, morbidity, and death (p. 278)'. Elsewhere DeGuzmán (*Spain's Long Shadow*, p. 248) describes the tendency to 'Black Legendise' and orientalise Spain, to argue for the existence of a collective Spanish soul, and to tally it with pride, cruelty, sensuality and irrationality'.

with 'dark, libidinal urges', a 'sexually marked latinity',[19] which informed early Hollywood representations of the Mediterranean[20] and (later) Latin America, and which continue to influence the consumption of Spanish and Latin American culture elsewhere in the world.[21]

In relation to Hollywood and specifically the so-called Good Neighbour films of the 1930s and 1940s, Philip Swanson describes 'the beginnings of a process in which Latinity, in film and consumer culture more widely, would come to stand for the unconscious of the North or the West, the necessary other side of the discipline of capitalism and Protestant morality' (Swanson, 'Going Down', p. 3). The Good Neighbour films' 'negligent undifferentiation' (López, p. 70), whereby Hollywood revealed its inability and/or unwillingness to distinguish ethnically and culturally between Cubans, Brazilians and Argentines, for example, finds a kind of parallel in the roles played by 'Hispanic' stars in contemporary Hollywood. Take, for example, the CVs of the most high profile of contemporary Spanish actors: Antonio Banderas and Penelope Cruz. As well as Spaniards, both have played Mexicans, Brazilians, Italians and undifferentiated 'Latins' on screen.

Luso-exceptionalism

Interestingly enough, Portugal and Brazil are excluded from Joseba Gabilondo's mapping out of the so-called Hispanic Atlantic. In what, for scholars of Luso-Brazilian Studies, is an all-too-familiar tone and excuse, Gabilondo remarks in an endnote: 'Here the issue of Portugal and Brazil will not be addressed for reasons of space. However, I am fully aware that

---

[19] Philip Swanson, 'Going Down on Good Neighbours: Imagining *América* in Hollywood Movies of the 1930s and 1940s (*Flying Down to Rio* and *Down Argentine Way*), *Bulletin of Latin American Research* 29.1 (2010), pp. 71–84; first published online 15 July 2009 DOI: 10.1111/j.1470–9856.2009.00318.x, pp. 1–14 (quote p. 3).

[20] Ana M. López reminds us that in the first decades of the twentieth century the appellation Latin always connoted Mediterranean rather than Latin American: 'Are All Latins from Manhattan?', p. 71.

[21] Consider, for example, Justin Chang's final line in an otherwise sensible review of Alejandro Lande's remarkable 2011 film *Porfirio* about the hardship of Colombia's disabled poor: 'The palpably warm Latin American temperatures and abundance of full and semi-nudity lend the film a relaxed, earthy sensuality': 'Porfirio'. Available at: http://www.variety.com/review/VE1117945262/. (Last accessed 31 January 2012).

the problem is complex and requires its own theorization' (Gabilondo, 'Introduction', p. 111, endnote 1).

Part of the 'complexity' of this 'problem' doubtless stems from the fact that concerted efforts to distinguish itself from Spain mark much of Portugal's modern and even contemporary cultural history. By way of illustration, we have the widely held belief, theorised on both sides of the Atlantic (that is, in Portugal and perhaps even more so, in Brazil) in *Luso-exceptionality* – 'the putative set of abilities possessed by the Portuguese to accommodate and incorporate cultural and racial diversity that led to Lusotropicalism'.[22] The legacy of Lusotropicalism can be found in twenty-first-century relations between Portugal and the PALOPS (the Portuguese-speaking former colonies in Africa), which perhaps bear more similarities to Spanish relations with Spanish America than does Portugal's relationship with Brazil.

Unlike the Instituto Cervantes, the Portuguese equivalent organisation, the Instituto Camões does not see its role as including *América* in any meaningful way. In fact the difference in relationship between Brazil and Portugal, and Spanish-American countries and Spain is worth stressing here. The size of Brazil's population (190 million compared to Portugal's 10 million), along with its growing economic might, has much to do with this difference in relationship. Spanish America's population of 375 million, along with its attendant economic and cultural strength, is diffused among 19 nations, most of which have inexpressive population sizes and economies. This difference is worth bearing in mind when considering the relevance for Brazil of, for example, observations on 'colonial legacies' in relation to Latin America.

The Instituto Camões' promotion of Lusophone culture is concentrated instead on the Portuguese language and cultures of Portugal and the PALOPS (Angola, Mozambique, Cape Verde, Guiné-Bissau and São Tomé e Príncipe). In fact the Instituto Camões supports the promotion of culture and the dissemination of knowledge regarding all eight of the member states of the Comunidade de Países de Língua Portuguesa (the Portuguese Commonwealth) *except* Brazil. Perhaps as a result of this,

---

[22] Miguel Bandeira Jerónimo, 'An Enduring Global Imperial Imagination: Lusotropicalism, Lusophonia and the Remnants of the Third Portuguese Empire', paper given at *London Debates 2010: How does Europe in the 21st Century Address the Legacy of Colonialism?* Available at: http://commonwealth.sas.ac.uk/events/event-details. html?id=7431. (Last accessed 4 January 2012).

Lusophone or Portuguese-language cinema is frequently interpreted as meaning the cinemas of Portugal and Portuguese-speaking Africa. [23]

In international marketing terms Portuguese cinema arguably finds its place more naturally within World Cinema (auteurist art-house) perhaps partly as a result of its frequent omission from Hispanic film festivals and retrospectives,[24] and because of the domination of the scene by *auteur* filmmakers such as Manoel de Oliveira, João César Monteiro and Pedro Costa. Portuguese co-producers of films made with Hispanic partners tend to serve as minority stake-holders in films that are rarely read as 'Portuguese'.[25] When films do have something of interest to say about Portugal from a transnational perspective, they tend to explore the impact of the historical relationship with Portugal's former colonies on contemporary Portuguese society.[26] That said, the body of Portuguese filmic work that can usefully be examined from a 'Hispanic' transnational perspective is steadily growing.[27]

[23] A notable exception to this rule is Cineport, a small but not insignificant annual film festival based in João Pessoa in the northeast of Brazil that screens Portuguese-language films from around the world, including both Brazil and Portugal, and with some funding from the Instituto Camões. A longer running Luso-Brazilian film festival in Santa Maria da Feira in Portugal (now in its 13th year) notably receives no such funding from the Portuguese government.

[24] Ibermedia is gradually making an impact on Hispanic film festivals and film series, in the sense that Portuguese cinema is increasingly finding a place in such festivals. Consider, for example, the annual film series entitled 'Iberoamérica Images' at the Museum of Modern Art in New York. The 2011 edition of the series, which began in 2009, highlighted Manoel de Oliveira's *O estranho caso de Angélica* (*The Strange Case of Angelica*, 2010), a Portugal/Spain/France/Brazil co-production.

[25] A good example of this would be Vicente Ferraz's forthcoming Brazil/Italy/Portugal co-production *A montanha* (*The Mountain*), a big-budget Brazilian World War II drama set in Italy. Portugal's Stopline production company has provided 20% of the funding for this film.

[26] Even a film such as the eagerly awaited *O grande Kilapy* (*The Great Kilapy*), a co-production between Brazil, Portugal and Angola, filmed in João Pessoa (Brazil) with a predominantly Brazilian cast by award-winning Angolan filmmaker Zezé Gamboa, is set during the Angolan colonial war. Rather than considering the nature of relations between Brazil, Portugal and Africa, the film will repeat the venture of the Brazil/Portugal/Cape Verde co-production *O testamento do Senhor Napumoceno* (*Napumoceno's Will*, 1997), whereby Brazilians can 'stand in for' Africans under Portuguese rule.

[27] Consider, for example, *José e Pilar* (Miguel Gonçalves Mendes, 2010), whose working title had been *União Ibérica* (Iberian Union, a reference to the historical period 1580–1640, after the Portuguese crisis of succession, when the Spanish monarchy ruled in Portugal). In 2000 Manoel de Oliveira made *Palavra e utopia* (*Word and Utopia*), a Portugal/Spain/Italy/France/Brazil co-production dealing with the life of Father Antonio Vieira, a seventeenth-century priest based in Brazil. To date the most discussed Portugal/Brazil co-production, and one of an inexplicably small number of films dealing with the

If anything it is Portuguese fiction that has made the most notable contribution to twenty-first-century Hispanic filmmaking to date. Take, for example, *El crimen del padre Amaro* (*Crime of Father Amaro*, 2002), a co-production between Mexico, Spain, Argentina and France, and one of the most successful 'Mexican' films of all time at the Mexican box office. The film is based on a nineteenth-century novel by the Portuguese Eça de Queirós (*O crime do Padre Amaro*). The relationship between Nobel prize-winning Portuguese writer José Saramago and his Spanish wife has produced one of the most interesting collaborative efforts between Portugal and Spain (and Brazil) of recent times, the documentary *José e Pilar* (Miguel Gonçalves Mendes, 2010). And while Fernando Meirelles' big-budget 2008 *Blindness*, a Canada/Brazil/Japan co-production, may be the most well-known film adaptation of Saramago's work, in 2010 António Ferreira adapted the short story 'Embargo' with funding from Portuguese, Spanish and Brazilian producers. Perhaps more significantly in the context of 'Hispanic' transnational filmmaking is George Sluizer's *A jangada de pedra* (*The Stone Raft*) a 2002 Spain/Portugal/Netherlands co-production based on Saramago's novel of the same name that tells the tale of what might happen if the Iberian Peninsula were to be cut adrift from the rest of Europe.

As the only Portuguese-speaking country in Latin America, Brazil too has both suffered and benefitted from its 'exceptionalism'. Brazil has been systematically excluded, and its cultural and political élite has systematically excluded itself from any notion of Latin or South American unity until relatively recently. In the nineteenth century its government was proud to declare itself 'a única exceção na América' ('the only exception in America', in a reference to its monarchy, an offshoot of the Portuguese Braganza dynasty that ruled in independent Brazil from 1822 until the declaration of the Republic in 1889). Simón Bolívar omitted imperial Brazil from his vision of a nineteenth-century confederation of South American republics, and even after 1889 and the declaration of the Brazilian Republic Brazil's growing links with the USA were a source of suspicion on the part of its neighbours. They believed, and not without reason, that Brazil's Panamericanist phase at the turn of the twentieth

---

contemporary relationship between Brazil and its former colony, is Walter Salles and Daniela Thomas's *Terra estrangeira* (*Foreign Land*, 1995). The film offers quite a unique and sophisticated analysis of the relationship between not just nations and citizens of the contemporary Lusophone world, but of the 'Hispanic' world more broadly speaking, and specifically, the place of Brazilians and Portuguese in this 'Hispanic' world.

century was inspired by a desire not only to strengthen ties with the USA, but also to assume the role of diplomatic leadership in Latin America.[28]

From the 1980s onwards, and in particular in the twenty-first century, what amounts to a seismic shift has taken place in Brazil's relations with its South American neighbours, witnessed in increased commercial links with Latin American governments and businesses via the various customs unions mentioned above, and the growth of so-called 'Multilatinas'.[29] But perhaps one of the most expressive examples of Brazil's new-found Latinamericanness in what has been dubbed the 'Latin American Decade'[30] is Brazilian Bank Itaú's recent international marketing strategy of selling itself as a 'global' Latin American business.[31] At the same time, Brazil's growing economic might, and its evident growing determination to reap the benefits of promoting culture as a form of 'soft power' mean that the potential neo-colonial intentions of Spain serve as much less of a threat within Brazil's socio-economic landscape.

With regard to filmmaking it is easy to forget that, while Brazil was really never a member of the club of Latin American nations that met to discuss the fortune and future of the region in the nineteenth and first half of the twentieth century,[32] Brazilian avant-garde filmmakers in the 1960s and 1970s played a central role in forging the notion of a 'shared cultural heritage', via the connections between *cinema novo*, Third Cinema and Imperfect Cinema. And while in Brazil State financing policies are in place which enable films to be made without recourse to international funding, and while the domestic market is large enough to financially

---

[28] A century on, and Brazil is once again being seen to lead, or at least to seek to lead, in Latin America. Consider, for example, the Brazilian government's enthusiasm for UNASUL, which it helped found, and its lukewarm reception of the decidedly anti-American CELAC (Community of Latin American and Caribbean States), led by Hugo Chávez: see Manuel Barcia, 'A Star is Born: Enter the CELAC', *The Huffington Post*, 28 December 2011. Available at http://ww21st century w.huffingtonpost.co.uk/manuel-barcia/a-star-is-born-enter-the-_b_1172484.html#es (Last accessed 15 January 2012).

[29] Multilatinas are 'firms that [have] leveraged domestic positions to expand their operations throughout Latin America'. See Lourdes Casanova (ed.), 'From Multilatinas to Global Latinas: The New Latin American Multinationals'. Available at: www.iadb.org/intal/intalcdi/PE/2009/03415.pdf (Last accessed 10 February 2012); Lourdes Casanova, *Global Latinas: Latin America's Emerging Multinationals* (London: Palgrave Macmillan, 2009).

[30] 'A Latin American Decade?', *The Economist Special Report on Latin America*, 11 September 2010, p. 14.

[31] See Banco Itaú website. Available at: www.itau.com. (Last accessed 31 January 2012).

[32] For a fascinating account of Brazil's sustained omission from the notion of 'Latin America', see Bethell, 'Brazil and "Latin America"'.

support (commercially successful) Brazilian films,[33] there is a growing interest on the part of the Brazilian Culture Ministry in making international co-productions, and particularly with Hispanic countries.[34]

Hispanic and Latin American cinema abroad

The international trajectory of films is gradually becoming an increasingly significant subject of interest for scholars, partly as a result of the formal disavowal of the 'strictly national' paradigm, and partly because of the growth in importance of international box offices and TV audiences for contemporary films. For Latin American filmmakers and producers, the main impetus for collaborating with producers from Spain, for example, is to increase a film's chances of entering both/either the Spanish TV market, and/or the European cinema circuit. And many of the transnational funding initiatives that Hispanic or Latin American films tap into are linked to international film festivals, such as the link between Cine en Construcción and the festivals of San Sebastián and Toulouse. Furthermore, for all the rhetoric surrounding the goal of fostering local markets in Latin America for Latin American products, as espoused by the Programa Ibermedia, for example, the fact remains that many Latin American films are still restricted to film festivals and their relatively small audiences.[35]

While much has been made of the recent boom in critically acclaimed Hispanic and Latin American film production[36] and the growth in interest in Spanish- and Portuguese-language films abroad, it is perhaps worth recalling that the 1960s witnessed a similar boom, which lasted well into

[33] Consider, for example, the phenomenal commercial success of *Tropa de Elite 2: O enemigo agora é outro* (*Elite Squad 2: The Enemy Within*) and other films produced by Globo Filmes, the film arm of the mighty Brazilian Globo corporation.

[34] See National Film Agency (ANCINE) website. Available at www.ancine.gov.br (Last accessed 10 February 2012).

[35] A notable exception to this rule is the Havana film festival, which is very well supported by local audiences, and which offers 'a discursive space in which films and festival participants are taken beyond their national space and made part of a wider regional cultural sphere': Miriam Ross, *South American Cinematic Culture: Policy, Production, Distribution and Exhibition* (Newcastle: Cambridge Scholars, 2010), p. 179.

[36] Consider, for example, the increased interest in Portuguese cinema provoked by the work of Pedro Costa, the sustained domination of European Art-house cinema by Spanish Pedro Almodóvar, and the interest in Mexican cinema spurred by the so-called three amigos: Alejandro González Iñárritu, Alfonso Cuarón and Guillermo Del Toro. It is worth noting, of course, that a similar (but smaller-scale) 'boom' was recognised by Euro-American critics as having taken place in the mid 1990s.

the 1970s, that was categorised by a desire to see Latin American avant-garde cinema. Michael Chanan suggests, however, that contemporary European critics are suffering from a form of cultural amnesia, and that they have forgotten how developed, as opposed to underdeveloped, Latin American cinema was aesthetically and politically in the 1960s:[37] '[W]e now live in a (screen) world where striking films from Latin America are [heralded] like exotic rarities, orchids in a world of postmodernism' ('Latin American Cinema', p. 42). Alejandro González Iñárritu's *Amores Perros* (Mexico, 2000) is an excellent case in point. With its then unknown cast and crew, the film offered critics the opportunity to usher in the new millennium with 'something new' in film terms. Thus, regardless of the existence of a clear development in Latin American film history, from the point of view of film programmers and foreign film critics 'quality' Latin American cinema seems destined to be forever associated abroad with novelty. As well as the novelty value perennially associated with inter-nationally marketable Latin American cinema, Chanan recognises that it is possible that the Latin American filmmakers of the 1960s 'served for the European as an imaginary other' (p. 42).[38] *Cinema Novo* filmmaker Glauber Rocha for one was acutely aware of the way Brazilian films were consumed in Europe at that time, and of Europeans' habit of turning to the culture of the underdeveloped world to satisfy their nostalgia for primitivism.[39] Such primitivising, or exoticising, can, of course, be traced back to the times of first contact between the Europeans and the continent of America. In film terms it is present in early documentaries featuring indigenous peoples and as we have already seen, in the Good Neighbour films, for example. In many ways cinema was a continuation of travel writing and the organisation of universal exhibitions in terms of a desire on the part of Europeans and Americans to display the exotic other. Amy Kaminsky, on the subject of the exposition in Paris in 1900 writes that Europe longed to 'consume the Indigenous, exotic other, a tasty morsel for a jaded palate' (p. 20).[40]

---

[37] Michael Chanan, 'Latin American Cinema: From Underdevelopment to Postmodernism', in *Remapping World Cinema: Identity, Culture and Politics in Film* ed. Stephanie Dennison and Song Hwee Lim (London: Wallflower, 2006), pp. 38–54 (p. 38).

[38] See also Lisa Shaw and Stephanie Dennison, *Brazilian National Cinema* (London: Routledge, 2007), p. 87.

[39] See Glauber Rocha, 'An Aesthetics of Hunger', in *New Latin American Cinema: Theory, Practices and Transcontinental Articulations*, ed. Michael M. Martin (Detroit: Wayne State University Press, 1997), pp. 59–61.

[40] For more information on the stereotyping created by travel writers in Latin America,

One of the expressions of this 'exotic other' are films that portray levels of violence and poverty unknown to the bulk of European and US audiences. Hence the continuation of what has been described as *porno-miseria*, a term popularised in Colombia in relation to 1970s filmmaking: hard-hitting, gritty films that more often than not depict street children, child prostitution, gang violence and so on. At the other extreme of this 'exotic othering' process we find the kind of films that frequently travel to Instituto Cervantes's sites in Europe via the Cine en Construcción initiative: for example, international co-productions that portray quirky characters in exotic locations experiencing the post-modern or post-national in a dramatic or entertaining way. Here, the list is seemingly endless: from the light-hearted *El baño del Papa*, (*The Pope's Toilet*, 2007) via Walter Salles' big-budget bio-pic *Diarios de motocicleta* (*The Motorcycle Diaries*, 2004) – an 8-country co-production, to small films that deal with complex sexual identities, such as Lucía Puenzo's powerful *XXY* (2007).

Distributing and exhibiting Hispanic films

Lest we assume erroneously that Hispanic and, more specifically Latin American film production can be reduced to those (predominantly co-produced and commercially driven) films that make it to our local art-house cinema or film festival, or are screened on Spanish TV (the principal TV outlet for Hispanic film), it is useful to detail here some of the initiatives being taken to deal with the twin issues of distribution and exhibition.

Mary Douglas and Baron Isherwood posit that it is consumption that makes culture visible and stable.[41] And it is precisely this question of visibility that exercises cultural policy-makers across the Hispanic world. It is no longer enough that Peruvians and Paraguayans, for example, *make* films (a difficult enough process for many smaller film industries): these films must be *seen* (and ideally by local, national and international audiences).

Beyond the traditional (and potentially lucrative) distribution and exhibition circuits such as those discussed above, we should not underesti-

see Gareth A. Jones, 'Latin American Geographies', in *The Companion to Latin American Studies*, ed. Philip Swanson (London: Arnold, 2003), pp. 5–25 (pp. 9–14).

[41] Mary Douglas and Baron C. Isherwood, *The World of Goods: Towards an Anthropology of Consumption* (New York: Basic Books, 1979), p. 38. Reprinted with a new introduction (London: Routledge, 1996).

mate the role played by national cultural institutions in the dissemination of Hispanic film abroad. The Instituto Cervantes, as well as sponsoring Cine en Construcción, promotes the dissemination of successful films in Europe through its local branches and contacts with schools and universities. It is also very active in organising and sponsoring retrospectives, Q&As with directors and film study activities linked to movie theatres and university film and language programmes (as is the Instituto Camões, and the embassies of Brazil and Mexico in the USA and Europe, for example).

A number of these cultural institutions work in conjunction with a growing number of private initiatives being set up to promote Hispanic film, and with diehard cinephile emigrés. For example, Inffinito runs a number of events promoting Brazilian culture abroad, with support from local Brazilian embassies and consulates, including annual Brazilian film festivals in cities such as London, Rome, New York, Miami, Madrid and Vancouver. The two main Latin American film festivals in London, the London Latin American Film Festival and the Discovering Latin America film festival, are run not for profit, and again, rely on the cinephilic enthusiasm of their founders, Cuban Eva Tarr Kirkhope and Mexican Mauricio Davila respectively.

Meanwhile, Latin American filmmakers, producers and distributors are actively and creatively engaging in new modes of production, distribution and exhibition which are designed to challenge the traditional domination of the US majors. There are many examples to be found across the region of 'alternative' distribution networks, ranging from travelling cinema initiatives led by well-intentioned industry professionals (the Mexican Ambulante project linked to Gael García Bernal and his Canana production company,[42] for example) to Brazil's Vídeo nas Aldeias project and Peru's Caravana Documental, the purpose of which is to take film (making and viewing) to indigenous communities. Brazilian company RAIN is leading the way in digital cinema and cinema on demand (COD) in the region, with the express purpose of doing away with the need for expensive 35mm film copies; Brazilian Carlos Gerbase's *3 efes* (*3 Fs*, 2007) was the first feature film to be simultaneously released on digital and DVD formats and simultaneously screened in cinemas (via RAIN), on television and on the internet; and Argentine filmmaker Alexis dos

---

[42] Canana was formed in 2005 by Bernal and fellow Mexicans Diego Luna and Pedro Cruz and has been behind a number of critically acclaimed Latin American feature films.

Santos, with his film *Random Strangers* (2011), took part in the Cinema Reloaded crowd-funding programme of the Rotterdam film festival.[43]

Filmmakers and viewers are increasingly turning to the short film format, given its affinity with the internet. [44] As Debra Castillo argues:

> [G]iven the inherently conservative nature of feature films, which increasingly need to respond to the requirements of international cooperative agreements, it can no longer surprise us that some of the most exciting and innovative work in cinema in contemporary Latin America will never be found in cinemas; instead, it is available for viewing and downloading, on thousands of sites, to a wide, appreciative, if highly segmented, potential audience.
>
> ('The New New Latin American Cinema', p. 35)

An interesting (but singular) example of successful showcasing of Latin American 'product' on the internet is the young Uruguayan filmmaker Federico Alvarez and his 2009 short film *Ataque de pánico* (Panic Attack). Alvarez uploaded his four and a half minute video about a robot invasion of Montevideo onto YouTube in 2009. The short has received over 6.5 million views on YouTube, making it one of the most seen Latin American films of the decade.[45] The Mexican film *Revolución* (*Revolution*, various, 2010), made up of a series of 10 short films by Mexican directors, was viewable on YouTube for 48 hours, and reportedly took 100,000 hits outside of Mexico alone.[46]

---

[43] Only €4,400 of the €15,000 cost of the short film was raised through crowd-funding, thus falling considerably short of expectations.

[44] Websites that host short films from Latin America include www.tech-mex.mx.org; www.solocortos.com; www.tuminuto.com (in Mexico), www.videometraje.com.ar (in Argentina) and www.portacurtas.com.br (in Brazil). For more information, see Debra A. Castillo, 'The New Latin American Cinema: *Cortometrajes* on the Internet', in *Latin American Cyberculture and Cyberliterature*, ed. Claire Taylor and Thea Pitman (Liverpool: Liverpool University Press, 2007), pp. 33–49.

[45] Alvarez has in many ways become the poster boy for the phenomenon of the digital CV: two weeks after posting the film he reportedly received a phone call from Warner offering him a job (as told by Aya Mironi, Strategic Partner Manager for YouTube in the UK at Branding Latin American Cinema event in London, May 2011).

[46] In chapter 7 Catherine Leen draws our attention to the success of Paraguayan filmmaker Joaquín Baldwin, whose digital short feature *Sebastian's voodoo* won the Short Film Corner award at Cannes in 2009.

Case study: two Brazilian co-productions[47]

One of the dangers, of course, in attempting to chart out a new or at least reconfigured cultural space is the trap of essentialising, whereby one ends up confirming the erroneous notion that 'systems of production and distribution collude to create mutually exclusive aesthetic cultures'.[48] It is thus important not to over-emphasise the uniformity of contemporary Latin American film production.[49] For a start, Latin American filmmakers are still capable of eschewing the commercial impetus and making challenging/indulgent films.[50] We also need to guard against over-emphasising the 'trading on the exotic' argument,[51] or at least of not recognising such films' potential to address (trans/post)national concerns. The first film to be analysed here, *Estorvo*, serves as an illuminating example of both of the above points. First of all, in relation to the question of commercialism versus challenge/indulgence, the veteran transnational film director Ruy Guerra quite openly rejected the 'narratives and aesthetics that international film festivals privilege',[52] having proudly declared that in his adaptation of singer-songwriter Chico Buarque's widely translated, international best-seller of the same name, he made no attempt whatsoever to pander to audience expectation or taste. *Estorvo*, a Brazilian/Cuban/Portuguese co-production, is quite a faithful adaptation of Buarque's disturbing portrayal of post-modern society which follows the journey of an unnamed man through an unnamed city to meet his tragic end. It

---

[47] What I describe as Brazilian co-productions are films whose Brazilian producers are majority stake-holders.

[48] Janet Harbord, *Film Cultures* (London: Sage, 2002), p. 117.

[49] That said, in the view of Lúcia Nagib, it is possible to identify a formula to certain 'new cinemas' that 'offer an intermediate product between art and entertainment', such as the presence of local colour, realism, a private hero and an improbable but convincing event: 'Going Global: The Brazilian Scripted Film', in *Trading Cultures: Global Traffic and Local Cultures in Film and Television*, ed. Sylvia Harvey (Eastleigh: John Libbey, 2006), pp. 95–103.

[50] Consider, for example, two recent and frankly 'difficult' musicals made by film directors better known for a more accessible story-telling style: Lucia Murat's *Maré, nossa história de amor* (*Another Love Story*, Brazil, France, Uruguay, 2007) and Pablo Stoll's *Hiroshima* (*Hiroshima: A Silent Musical*, Uruguay, Argentina, Colombia, Spain, 2009). Consider also the award-winning Carlos Reygadas and his 2012 film *Post Tenebras Lux* (Mexico/France/Netherlands/Germany) which was booed by audiences in Cannes.

[51] Chanan, 'Latin American Cinema', p. 46.

[52] Miriam Ross, 'Film Festivals and the Ibero-American Sphere', in *Film Festival Yearbook 2: Film Festivals and Imagined Communities*, ed. Dina Iordanova and Ruby Cheung (St Andrews: St Andrews Film Studies/College Gate Press, 2009), pp 171–87 (p. 187).

was shot on location in both Rio de Janeiro and Havana, filmed predominantly in Portuguese and the protagonist, Buarque's unnamed first-person narrator (referred to as Eu or I/me in the film) is played by Cuban film star Jorge Perugorría.

Some Latin American international co-productions come in for fierce criticism, given their failed attempts to reconcile the series of demands made upon them by the nature of co-productions themselves:[53] I like to think of these failed attempts as 'Hispano-puddings', rather than Euro-puddings, or, using Tamara Falicov's term, a Latin American mole with a sprinkling of Spanish manchego cheese.[54] On the surface, *Estorvo*, a three-way co-production, smacks of 'Hispanopudding'. For a start, there does not seem to be any logic and very little continuity, with regard to location. Secondly, the rather disturbed, first-person narration of Buarque's book is translated by three different voices in the film version: the thick Cuban accent of actor Jorge Perugorría (who speaks Portuguese in the film, despite the confusion of many Brazilian critics who mistook him to be speaking a mixture of Spanish and Portuguese, or *portunhol*); the intertitles made up of first-person extracts from Chico Buarque's text written in Brazilian Portuguese, and, perhaps more disorientating still, a voiceover supplied by the Mozambican-born Portuguese-accented Ruy Guerra himself. Thus the bad accents and social decontextualisation, the commonest criticisms aimed at Hispanopuddings, are present in *Estorvo*. But what is clear when viewing the film is that, rather than failing to accommodate co-production demands, in *Estorvo* Guerra is playing with notions of the transnational (in terms of location, language and choice of actors), as if consciously reflecting on the cinematic implications of making co-productions. The transnational tropes present in *Estorvo* are thus very effectively used to translate the post-modern concerns of the source text.

Such a reflection on the implications of the process of making co-productions can be seen in a number of more recent films. The 2010 Spanish, French, Mexican co-production *También la lluvia* (*Even the Rain*), directed by Iciar Bollaín, is the most striking example of this

---

[53] '[P]erhaps one of the most open debates arising in Latin America within the practice of coproduction – on the part of the filmmakers and producers but also on the part of scholars – is related to the aesthetic value of those films made with Spain. A great number of these films suffer – in one way or another – from social decontextualisation': Libia Villazana , 'Hegemony Conditions in the Co-production Cinema of Latin America: The Role of Spain', *Framework* 49.2 (2008), 65–85 (p. 70).

[54] See chapter 4 in this volume.

phenomenon to date. In the film Sebastián played by Gael García Bernal arrives in Cochabamba, Bolivia, accompanied by a cast and crew to make a film about Christopher Columbus's first voyage to the New World and the subsequent subjugation of the indigenous population. Filmmaker Sebastian wants to focus on the experience of Bartolomé de las Casas, who was so distraught over the treatment of the natives that he dedicated the rest of his life to their cause. The irony here is that his producer Costa has chosen Bolivia, the poorest country in South America, because it makes sense economically to do so. Extras in Bolivia are willing to work long hours for just two dollars a day.[55]

A further example of this phenomenon can be found in César Charlone and Enrique Fernández's El baño del Papa (The Pope's Toilet, 2007), a Uruguayan/French/Brazilian co-production. David Martin-Jones and Soledad Montáñez argue that, with its plot revolving around the imminent arrival of the Pope in the Uruguayan village of Melo in 1988, El baño can be read as a 'mannered disavowal of the film's own attempts to reach beyond the nation for profit.'[56] I would take this idea one stage further and suggest that in the film the imminent arrival of thousands of Brazilians to witness in turn the arrival of the Pope works as a comment on the then imminent Treaty of Asunción and the economic promises that greater co-operation with Brazil within the Mercosul/Mercosur would supposedly bring.

But returning to Ruy Guerra's Estorvo, I see a similar process taking place of both a reflection on Brazil's place in a post-modern, post-national Latin America, and a disavowal of the financial advantages to be gained from transnational filmmaking. For a start, we have the jarring effect of language in the film, seemingly a timely intervention on the issue of the presence of 200 million Portuguese-speakers in the 'Hispanic' family of nations. The dialectologist John Lipski writes of the widespread belief that cross-language communication between native speakers of Spanish and Portuguese speakers can easily be effected by 'faking' an approximation to the non-native language without actually having learned it (a process which we witness taking place in Estorvo). Lipski also describes

---

[55] See also Habana blues as discussed by Tamara Falicov in chapter 4 of this volume. Miriam Ross (South American Cinematic Culture, pp. 118--19) discusses Alex Bowen's Mi mejor enemigo (My Best Enemy, Argentina/ Chile/ Spain, 2005) as another example of a co-production whose plot mirrors co-productions.

[56] David Martin-Jones and Soledad Montáñez, 'Bicycle Thieves or Thieves on Bicycles? El bano del papa 2007', Studies in Hispanic Cinemas 4.3 (2007), 183–98 (p. 186).

a more recent (if very fanciful) belief that is beginning to emerge in Brazil in particular: that, as a result of both Brazil's strengthening of economic ties with its neighbours and of the increased presence of Spanish businesses and industry in Brazil, it will eventually cease to be a Portuguese-speaking country, but will rather speak only *portunhol*.

In the world of *Estorvo* authenticity is pointless and language is rendered meaningless as a marker of identity. Not so for the Brazil/UK co-production *Jean-Charles*, Henrique Goldman's 2009 film based on the true story of Jean-Charles de Menezes, the young Brazilian mistaken for a terrorist and shot dead by police in London in 2005. The bulk of Goldman's film depicts Brazilians at work and play in the British capital, home to between 70,000 and 100,000 Brazilians. There is no code-switching here, no hybrid language being used, but instead we have a veritable celebration of Brazilian Portuguese (everyone in London, it seems, speaks Portuguese). It is as if the whole socio-economic experience of migration, and the political context that often provokes migration, can be reduced to a festival of laid-back conversation, food, beer, dance, music and so on.

Brazilians are left to their own devices until post-national forces denominated global terrorism spoil this slice of Brazilian life in London, and Jean-Charles is shot dead. At this point the language focus shifts to English. Without the safe haven of Portuguese, whereby language stands in for nation,[57] the surviving characters are quite simply lost. English is depicted as the language of patronisation, of racism, of unwieldy bureaucracy, and of bad news. Given the well documented difficulties that Goldman experienced in getting this co-production made (there is no formal co-production agreement between the UK and Brazil), and given the film's failure to secure distribution within the UK, it is tempting to read *Jean-Charles* in a similar light to *El baño del Papa* and *Estorvo*, in the sense that it works in part as a reflection on the nature of post-national filmmaking practices. *Jean-Charles* forces us to question the likely commercial success of certain types of transnational film ventures by Brazilian filmmakers, given that the overwhelming 'Brazilianness' of the film seems to have worked against it in terms of finding a market in the UK.

---

[57] As Carolin Overhoff Ferreira reminds us, the celebrated Portuguese poet Fernando Pessoa once declared 'My nation is the Portuguese language': 'The Limits of Luso-Brazilian Brotherhood: Fortress Europe in *Terra Estrangeira* by Walter Salles and Daniela Thomas', *Third Text*, 20 (2006), 731–41.

As Michael Chanan argues, 'cinema inevitably constitutes a site of ideological contestation over definitions of nation, state, people and country' ('Latin American Cinema', p. 43). As we have just seen, there is evidence in contemporary Latin American co-productions that while transnational film financing imperatives do not necessarily translate into overnight commercial success for films, the good news is that, far from being aesthetically constrained by such imperatives, filmmakers are actively contributing to debates on the meaning of 'the national' through their problematisation of notions of the transnational.

Conclusion

As Chanan reminds us, 'cinema was transnational from the very start, and global in reach and operation by the 1930s' ('Latin American Cinema', p. 41). From early on in the history of Latin American film industries Italians, for example, were working in Brazil and North Americans were working in Mexico. Popular Latin American genre films such as melodrama and exploitation films were distributed throughout Latin America, with (Golden Age) Mexican cinema dominating the Latin American film market in the 1940s. Spain and Portugal were co-producing short films together as early as 1919, with the first feature film co-production between the two countries being made in 1936. They had already co-produced 34 films together before the founding of the Programa Ibermedia.[58] Meanwhile prolific filmmakers such as Ruy Guerra and Manoel de Oliveira have been making international co-productions since at least the 1980s.[59]

Therefore it is not so much the recourse to transnational film financing that is new to the Spanish, Portuguese and Latin American film industries, it is the sheer volume of films, particularly those from Latin America, that now rely on such film financing mechanisms. The festivals, competitions and transnational funding initiatives that can be identified as favouring, or even nurturing Latin American films (as well as Programa Ibermedia and Cine en Construcción, there is the Hubert Bals fund linked to the

[58] Paulo Filipe Monteiro, 'International Film Financing in Portugal: How? When? And with what Results?', paper given at the symposium *Transnational Film Financing in the Hispanic World* (University of Leeds, 29 June 2009).

[59] Most of Manoel de Oliveira's films released from the 1980s onwards are European co-productions. Among Ruy Guerra's many co-productions are three adaptations of the work of Colombian author Gabriel García Márquez.

Rotterdam film festival, Fonds Sud in France, even Sundance to an extent, and the World Cinema fund linked to the Berlin Film festival) are contributing to the latest reconfiguration of Hispanic and Latin American cultural space. What this chapter has sought to do is chart twenty-first-century transnational film practices, in order to paint a more complete picture of this space. It has also provided a reading of films which reveals their potential both to reflect on the nature of this new cultural space, and at the same time to continue to make a meaningful contribution to interpretations of national culture.

2

Redefining Transnational Cinemas:
A Transdisciplinary Perspective

LIBIA VILLAZANA

Introduction: transnationalism and cinema, crisscross parallels

Transnationalism as a research field is highly transdisciplinary; it has been mainly developed in university departments of Migration Studies, Anthropology, Sociology, Political Science, Geography, International Relations, History, Cultural Studies and Film Studies. Consequently, although the theoretical foundations of the term have been primarily related to the dynamics of migration, the meaning of transnationalism is nowadays extremely loose. Initially the term was concomitant with the transnational movement of bodies; however, communication and technological development such as the Internet and the World Wide Web have propelled multivalent forms of interconnectedness across national borders, giving rise to a transnational virtual mobility.[1] Cinema has naturally been absorbed by the macro- and micro-dynamics of the migration

---

[1]   Arjun Appadurai and Carol Breckenridge, 'On Moving Targets', *Public Culture*, 2, (1989), i–iv; Manuel Castells, *The Rise of the Network Society* (Oxford: Blackwell, 1996); Robin Cohen, 'Diasporas and the Nation-State: From Victims to Challengers', *International Affairs*, 72 (1996), 507–20; Alejandro Portes, *Globalization from Below: The Rise of Transnational Communities*, Working Paper Series, Oxford University. Transnational Communities: An ESRC Research Programme; WPTC–98–01 ([Oxford]: Transnational Communities Programme, 1997), pp. 1–26; Gayatri Spivak, 'Who Claims Alterity?', in *Remaking History*, ed. Barbara Kruger and Phil Mariani (Seattle: Bay, 1989), pp. 269–92. Reprinted in *Art in Theory 1900–1990: An Anthology of Changing Ideas*, ed. Charles Harrison and Paul Wood (Cambridge, MA: Blackwell, 1992), 1119–24; Steven Vertovec, 'Conceiving and Researching Transnationalism', *Ethnic and Racial Studies*, 22.2 (1999), 447–62.

processes and it has consequently enticed the emergence of new narratives and collaborative forms of production. Transnational cinemas is one
of the emergent fields of research within Film Studies which has devoted
attention to the study of, particularly, film collaborations across borders.[2]
In order to grasp the conceptual permutations that transationalism has
been subjected to, this chapter will briefly outline the genesis of the term
and its fluctuating historiography, including Film Studies approaches to
it. Furthermore, one of the contributions of this chapter to the literature
on transnational cinemas is the opportunity it presents to reify the interconnectedness of transnationalism, as used in Film Studies, to its roots in
Migration Studies, Anthropology and Sociology. With this in mind, this
chapter intends first to make use of and take advantage of the transdisciplinary approaches to transnationalism so as to offer a holistic view
of the theoretical formulations and practices of transnational cinemas.
The rationale behind selecting a holistic approach lies in the possibilities
that this method offers to clarify some common misleading assumptions
about transnational cinemas, particularly those concerning international
film co-productions. Since this chapter is informed by the manifold
conceptual formulations of the term transnationalism, it proposes a study
of transnational cinemas from three critical approaches articulated by
transnationalism so as to further understand the multi-vocal character of
transnational cinemas. These approaches are: the debates surrounding the
conceptual blurring between 'transnational', 'international' and 'multinational'; the interstitial and liminal sites between 'transnationalism from
above' and 'transnationalism from below', and the conceptual formulations of 'transnational communities'.

Secondly, the chapter seeks to demonstrate the usefulness of transnationalism as a vastly transdisciplinary research method for Film Studies.
Most of the literature on transnational cinemas does not address one of the
fundamental characteristics of the term '*trans*national', which is precisely
its *trans*disciplinary nature (see Bergfelder; Ezra and Rowden; Durovicová

---

2   See Tim Bergfelder, 'National, Transnational or Supranational Cinema?: Rethinking
European Film Studies', *Media, Culture & Society*, 27.3 (2005), 315–31; Elizabeth Ezra
and Terry Rowden (eds), *Transnational Cinema: The Film Reader* (London: Routledge,
2006); Libia Villazana, *Transnational Financial Structures in the Cinema of Latin America:
Programa Ibermedia in Study* (Saarbrucken: Verlag Dr Muller, 2009); Natasa Durovicová
and Kathleen E. Newman (eds), *World Cinemas, Transnational Perspectives* (Abingdon:
Routledge, 2009); W. Higbee and Song Hwee Lim, 'Concepts of Transnational Cinema:
Towards a Critical Transnationalism in Film Studies', *Transnational Cinemas Journal*, 1.1
(2010), 7–21.

and Newman; Higbee and Lim).[3] Spanning disciplinary borders beyond Cultural Studies and making use of approaches to transnationalism by Migration Studies, Anthropology, Sociology and Geography, for instance, is still an under-developed area and as such a challenge for Film Studies scholars. Transnationalism is transdisciplinary because its approaches transcend the borders of conventional disciplines and incorporate the methods of other disciplines to its subject/object of study, while maintaining as much as possible the framework of those disciplines. Transnational cinemas can be better studied from a transdisciplinary perspective rather than from an interdisciplinary one, since the latter tends to adapt other disciplines' methods to its theoretical and/or methodological frameworks, whereas the first maintains the methods of other disciplines.[4] Thus, transdiciplinarity is a valuable methodological tool to theorise and to further develop the concept and applications of transnational cinemas.[5] In this respect, the study and the potential contributions of transnationalism to transnational cinemas are still to be exploited.

Transnationalism first surfaced in a discussion of migration and identity in the USA in 1919 as a way to consciously 'internationalise' US politics 'within the framework of the wider world'.[6] Thus, the term transnationalism is not a new one; it has been studied and theorised since it first appeared in the political arena. In the 1980s, the term was used

---

[3] See also Hamid Naficy, 'Phobic Spaces and Liminal Panics: Independent Transnational Film Genre', in *Global–Local: Cultural Production and the Transnational Imaginary*, ed. Rob Wilson and Wimal Dissanayake (Durham, NC and London: Duke University Press,1996), pp. 119–44; Hamid Naficy, *An Accented Cinema: Exilic and Diasporic Filmmaking*. (Princeton: Princeton University Press, 2001).

[4] For an in-depth insight into the dynamics of transdisciplinarity as a research method see Gertrude Hirsch Hadorn, Holger Hoffmann-Riem, Suzette Biber-Klemm, Walter Grossenbacher-Mansuy, Dominique Joye, Christian Pohl, Urs Wiesmann and Elizabeth Zemp (eds), *Handbook of Transdisciplinary Research* (Bern: Springer, 2008). Transdisciplinary research has also been defined as the collaborations between different academic disciplines and non-academic researchers. As Jill Jäger has pointed out, the uniqueness of the transdisciplinary approach 'lies in the partnership between members of different disciplines and stakeholders'; 'Forward', Hirsch Hadorn, Hoffmann-Riem *et al.* (eds), p. vii.

[5] An example of applied transdisciplinarity in Film Studies is the use of the ethnographic research method Participant Observation in the study of practice and theory of documentary filmmaking, for example, the work of Vertov's *The Man with a Movie Camera* (1929); Rouch and Morin's *Chronicle of a Summer* (1960); Ross McElwee's *Sherman's March* (1985); Enrica Colusso's *ABC Colombia* (2007); Libia Villazana's *Latin America in Co-Production* (2007).

[6] Patricia Clavin, 'Defining Transnationalism', *Contemporary European History*, 14.4 (2005), 421–39.

as a synonym for 'inter-states relations' or to replace 'multinational' corporations for 'transnational' corporations, since the first term was associated with greed and inequality (Clavin, p. 433). Nowadays, transnationalism refers to non-governmental organisations which encourage non-state relationships. Instances of these transnational institutions are the market, the Catholic Church and networks of human rights activists.[7] The creative applications, transformations and ultimately usefulness of the term have been discussed and contested by the numerous disciplines which have appropriated it (see, for example, Waldinger and Fitzgerald; Naficy; Bergfelder; Ezra and Rowden; Durovicová and Newman; Villazana; Higbee and Lim).[8] As a result the literature produced on the study of transnationalism together with the debates surrounding the validity of

---

[7] Roger D. Waldinger and David, Fitzgerald, 'Transnationalism in Question', *American Journal of Sociology*, 109.5 (2004), 1177–95.

[8] See also, Michael Kearney, 'Borders and Boundaries of State and Self at the End of Empire' *Journal of Historical Sociology*, 4.1 (1991), 52–74; Michael Kearney, 'The Local and the Global: the Anthropology of Globalization and Transnationalism', *Annual Review of Anthropology*, 24 (1995), 547–65; Roger Rouse, 'Making Sense of Settlement: Class Transformation, Cultural Struggle and Transnationalism among Mexican Migrants in the United States', in *Towards a Transnational Perspective on Migration*, ed. Nina Glick Schiller, Linda Basch and Cristina Blanc-Szanton (New York: New York Academy of Sciences, 1992), pp. 25–52; Roger Rouse, 'Thinking Through Transnationalism: Notes on the Cultural Politics of Class Relations in the Contemporary United States', *Public Culture*, 7.2 (1995), 353–402; Robert Smith, 'Changing Practices of Citizenship, Membership and Nation within the Context of Transnational Migration: Comparative Insights from the Mexican and Italian Cases', paper presented to ICCCR International Conference on Transnationalism, Manchester, 16–18 May 1998; Robert Smith, 'Comparing Local-level Swedish and Mexican Transnational Life: An Essay in Historical Retrieval', in *New Transnational Social Spaces: International Migrations and Transnational Companies in the Early Twenty-first Century*, ed. Ludger Pries (London: Routledge, 2001), pp. 37–58; Michael Smith and Luis Guarnizo (eds), *Transnationalism from Below* (New Brunswick, NJ.: Transaction Publishers, 1998); Nina Glick Schiller, 'Terrains of Blood and Nation: Haitian Transnational Social Fields', *Ethnic and Racial Studies*, 22.2 (1999), 340–66; Nancy Foner, *From Ellis Island to JFK: New York's Two Great Waves of Immigration.* (New Haven: Yale University Press, 2000); Peggy Levitt, *The Transnational Villagers* (Berkeley and Los Angeles: University of California Press, 2001); Luis Guarnizo, 'On the Political Participation of Transnational Migrants: Old Practices and New Trends', in *E Pluribus Unum? Contemporary and Historical Perspectives on Immigrant Political Incorporation*, ed. Gary Gerstle and John Mollenkopf (New York: Russell Sage Foundation, 2001), pp. 213–63; Robert C. Smith, 'Mexicans: Social, Educational, Economic, and Political Problems and Prospects in New York', in *New Immigrants in New York*, ed. Nancy Foner (New York: Columbia University Press, 2002), pp. 275–300; Andrew Higson, 'The Limiting Imagination of National Cinema', in *Cinema and Nation,* ed. Mette Hjort and Scott MacKenzie (London: Routledge, 2000), pp. 63–74. Sheldon Hsiao-peng Lu, 'Historical Introduction: Chinese Cinemas (1896–1996) and Transnational Film Studies', in *Transnational Chinese Cinemas: Identity, Nationhood,*

what the term includes are considerably varied and somewhat puzzling to comprehend as a whole. However, there are convergent points between the diverse approaches, which are useful for this chapter's proposals, as we will see later. One of the most quoted concepts of transnationalism – the first contemporary attempt to define the term – is provided by three social scientists, Linda Basch, Nina Glick Schiller and Cristina Szanton-Blanc:

> We define 'transnationalism' as the process by which immigrants forge and sustain multi-stranded social relations that link together their societies of origin and settlement. We call this process transnationalism to emphasize that many immigrants today build social fields that cross geographic, cultural, and political borders.[9]

The rationale of the above concept requires outlining inasmuch as it jettisons a classical theoretical formulation on migrancy, namely the assimilation approach.

Transnationalism, as a re-visited theoretical approach on migration, re-emerged by the end of 1980s. It maintains that the act of migrating requires analysis at both ends (the leaving and receiving country); thus, it is not necessarily tied up with a single nation-state as proposed by the migration perspective. Migration theory, and within it the assimilation approach, has had the tendency to study the country of origin of migrants and their host country separately and it has not delved into how migrants' activities unfold between the two ends. The reason for this is the assumption that migrants needed to incorporate themselves fully into the host culture; this involved distancing from their birth culture. In other words, migrants were asked virtually to be re-born. Instead, transnationalism recognises the web of connections that exist with the birth country (via for instance, the countless remittances sent back and forth, the numerous informal commercial exchanges between the two ends, the impact on the birth country of émigrés' political movements, and so on). In so doing, transnationalism sees migration as a dynamic system of construction and reconstruction of social spaces which affects – economically, socially, politically, and culturally – both ends, those who migrated and their fami-

Gender, ed. Sheldon Hsiao-peng Lu (Honolulu: University of Hawaii Press, 1997), pp. 1–31.

9   Linda Basch, Nina Schiller Glick and Cristina Szanton-Blanc, *Nations Unbound: Transnational Projects, Post-colonial Predicaments, and Deterritorialized Nation-States*, (Langhorne: Gordon and Breach, 1994), p. 6.

lies, relatives, and friends who remain in the birth country. In this way, transnationalism seems to contest the principles of the assimilation theory and instead nourish the proposal of migrant 'integration', which promotes multiculturalism and, with it, cultural diversity. Furthermore, the contrast between transnationalism and assimilation seems more apparent when studying the assimilationist's approach to culture. It has been pointed out (Ralph Grillo paraphrasing Thomas Faist) that assimilation exercises a 'container concept of culture'; assimilation conceives 'culture as a fixed and essential phenomenon [...] This container concept sees culture as essentially territorial, based on a shared language and somewhat static'.[10] Culture does not only go beyond territories but it is also in constant transmutation. Culture travels, it crosses borders, since culture is not only embedded in individuals who are in continuous territorial mobility but it is also globally widespread by communication developments, which have strongly facilitated cultural exchanges. Thus, the assumption that culture is tied up with territories and it is static is nowadays unsustainable. From the above rationale it is not difficult to establish parallels between transnationalism – as supposed to assimilationism – and cinema. Contemporary film production, for instance, which is to a great extent characterised by collaborations across borders, cannot be tied up anymore to a single territory because films nowadays tend to acquire, for financial and exhibition purposes, more than one national identity. The film *Basic Instinct II*, for example, is technically speaking a British, American, Spanish and German film, partly because it received financial support from film bodies which were linked to these countries. This example, however, gives rise to a series of questions such as: what establishes the nationality(ies) of a film? Its production (financial) means? Its theme? The nationality of its director? Is the UK–USA production *The Constant Gardener*, directed by Brazilian Fernando Meirelles, a British, American or Brazilian film, or all of these nationalities at the same time? Fernando Meirelles, director of *Cidade de Deus* (*City of God*, 2002), worked with the Uruguayan-born and naturalised-Brazilian cinematographer César Charlone on the film *The Constant Gardener*. Charlone and Meirelles's work created in *The Constant Gardener* an enticing atmosphere, contrasts, colours and pace that are similar to those found in *Cidade de Deus*. This is not surprising,

---

[10] Ralph D. Grillo, 'Transnational Migration and Multiculturalism in Europe', in *Oxford: ESRC Transnational Communities Working Paper*, WPTC-01–08, 2001, p. 15; Thomas Faist, *The Volume and Dynamics of International Migration and Transnational Social Spaces* (Oxford: Oxford University Press, 2000), p. 287.

since a cinematographer becomes a sort of painter of a film, shaping the composition of the film's mise-en-scène, mixing colours, creating different atmospheres with the lighting; a cinematographer is in essence responsible for the artistic composition of a film. Thus, unavoidably the duo Meirelles–Charlone was prone to produce both films in an arguably similar style. But what is relevant for this chapter are the dynamics and mechanisms of the 'in-between' processes of production and the mobility of the film in all its forms, once it is produced. It is the transnational geography or what happens between the many producing territories that concerns this chapter.

Film co-production and its 'international' and 'transnational' features

In Film Studies the cinematic practice that has been closely related to, and fundamentally concerned with, transnationalism is film co-productions (Villazana, *Transnational Financial Structures*, p. 3; Higbee and Lim, pp. 7–21); as such herein co-production will be taken as a component of transnational cinemas, in the spirit of transnationalism. That is, this section – and the chapter as a whole – does not include co-productions organised, for instance, within the same country because the transnational features of these types of films are arguably weak. What remains to be clarified here is why co-productions have been largely positioned within the international arena instead of the transnational one. A simple Google search confirms the widespread use of the term 'international co-productions' with 6,200,000 results as supposed to 'transnational co-productions' with 58,520. Moreover, when inputting the term transnational next to co-production in the above search only a few results referred to cinema.[11] So what are transnational co-productions? What are the transnational qualities of the film co-production practice? And ultimately, what is the relevance of the co-production prefix? This section will attempt to analyse the above questions using transnationalist approaches.

The numerous conceptual blurrings which have emerged between 'transnationalism' and terms such as 'international' and 'multinational' are worth considering here since they are transferred to approaches on

[11] Search conducted on 11 March 2011.

transnational cinemas.[12] The conflation used which baffles the above terms may find its roots in the constant metamorphosis that transnationalism has been subjected to since it first surfaced. Historian Patricia Clavin provides an illustrative example of the bewildering use of 'international' and 'transnational':

> [T]he development of a single trading area under the auspices of the European Economic Community falls under the heading 'international' [...] while the European Union's educational programmes come under the heading of 'transnationalist' initiatives. (p. 425)

In this example, however confusing it might seem, it is possible to identify a difference between the use of both terms, international and transnational. Transnationalism seems to be used here as tantamount to cultural exchange and border erasing processes, which are promoted by European initiatives such as the Bologna Programme. This programme intends to create a European Higher Education Area with the aim of adopting 'a system of easily readable and comparable degrees'.[13] In other words, students from the Bologna countries would benefit from freedom of mobility in their educational and professional preparation within at least the European Higher Education Area. In contrast, international is merely used in the above example as a commercial exchange.

The border-crossing between the terms 'multinational' and 'transnational', within international banking, offer a further example:

> J.P. Morgan and Co. was a multinational company comprising J.P. Morgan & Co. in New York; Drexel & Co. in Philadelphia; Morgan Grenfell in London, Morgan & Cie in Paris. This bank has a multinational structure but beyond that it sustained its relationship to a transnational community of businessmen, financers, and government officials.

---

[12] Transnationalism has similarly been indistinctively used to signify globalisation as in the case of Grillo, 'Transnational Migration', p. 6. There also seems to be a cross-disciplinary debate concerning 'international migration', 'transnational migration' and transmigration or 'transmigrants', as in the cases of Grillo, p. 5; Portes, *Globalization from Below,* p. 16; and Schiller, Basch and Szanton-Blanc, *Towards a Transnational Perspective,* p. 52. In this respect, the relevant distinction is between immigrants (people who migrate) and transmigrants (immigrants who keep alive the connections between home and host country). Thus, transmigration is a concept commonly used in transnationalism.

[13] See The Bologna Declaration of 19 June 1999. http://www.bologna-bergen2005. no/Docs/00-Main_doc/990719BOLOGNA_DECLARATION.PDF. (Last accessed 25 February 2011).

> This transnational community while working across borders profited from the existence of national frontiers since financial gain lay precisely in exploiting different national circumstances. (Clavin, p. 430)

The J.P. Morgan and Co. instance not only serves to illustrate the uses of 'multinational' and 'transnational' but it also helps to clarify how 'international', as employed in the first example, is connected to transnationalism.[14] That is, the international processes of commercial exchange are propelled and frequently supported by a 'transnational community of businessmen, financers, and government officials'.

In his research on transnationalism, Social Anthropologist Steven Vertovec provides a rather variegated view on the manifold uses of the term.[15] In his words: 'For the United States Department of Defense, transnationalism means terrorists, insurgents, opposing factions in civil wars conducting operations outside their country of origin, and members of criminal groups (Secretary of Defense 1996)' (Vertovec, p. 450). According to debates held among International Relations scholars since the 1960s, *inter*national concerns 'relations *between* states' and *trans*national refers to 'institutions *extending beyond* and even *encompassing* states' (Waldinger and Fitzgerald, p. 7). This distinction is particularly relevant to our conceptual approach to cinemas with transnational characteristics (holding connections between two or more countries). The rationale for placing 'international' next to film co-productions is surely to do with the involvement of the constant commercial and aesthetic exchanges between the two or more participant countries in the production of these films. However, the International Relations' theoretical references to international and transnational could lead us to conclude that film co-production is not necessarily international or its international feature is weak and hollow. Co-productions are rarely agreements *between* states, co-productions are rather transnational inasmuch as the agreements are outlined *beyond* state control and can at the same time flexibly encompass the state, mostly for financial purposes. The reality is that in commercial trading, which is commonly denoted as 'international', as we saw in the example above, private contracts dominate the final agreements even if

---

14 J.P. Morgan and Co. is currently named JPMorgan Chase & Co., following the merger between 'J.P. Morgan & Co' and 'Chase Manhattan Corporation'.

15 Steven Vertovec directed the ESRC research programme on Transnational Communities based at the University of Oxford. For further information on this project see http://www.transcomm.ox.ac.uk/wwwroot/drsteve.htm. (Last accessed 24 February 2011).

the budget partially relies on state(s) financing (Villazana, *Transnational Financial Structures*, pp. 55–93). The International Relations' distinction between 'international' and 'transnational' is helpful, however, inasmuch as it differentiates the initiatives organised between states and those with partial or non-state control. This feature applies to transnational cinemas and it is pertinent to study, since it allows us to pinpoint the particularities and differences between those films co-produced under strong influence of agreements between states and those productions supported by private enterprises and bodies with only small participation of states. Programa Ibermedia (a film fund devised by the government of Spain, Portugal and several Latin American countries to back the production of these coun-tries financially – see chapter 3) and Fonds Sud Cinéma (a fund provided by the French Ministry of Culture and Communication, National Center of Cinematography (CNC) and the French Ministry of Foreign Affairs) fall into the first scenario,[16] and the Hubert Bals Fund (an initiative of the Rotterdam Film Festival) illustrates the second.[17] I have already dealt with the study of the mechanisms of the above two differentiated types of film funds and the films resulting from their productions (Villazana, *Transna-tional Financial Structures*, pp. 31–93).[18] However, it is relevant to stress here that in the cases where state programmes and subsidies participate in the productions, those productions require private funds in order to receive state support. This is in fact one of the explicit conditions of the great majority of state programmes and also private subsidies.[19] In other words, for co-producers to apply for/be granted funds from film bodies

[16] For an in-depth insight into the working dynamics of Ibermedia see Libia Villazana, *Transnational Financial Structures in the Cinema of Latin America: Programa Ibermedia in Study* (Saarbrucken: Verlag Dr Muller, 2009); Libia Villazana, 'Hegemony Conditions in the Co-production Cinema of Latin America: The Role of Spain', *Framework*, 49.2 (2008), 65–85; Teresa Hoefert-Turégano, 'The International Politics of Cinematic Coproduction: Spanish Policy in Latin America', *Film and History: An Interdisciplinary Journal of Film and Television Studies*, 34.2 (2004), 15–24.

[17] For an extensive analysis on the mechanisms of film co-production, particularly those involving Latin American countries, Spain and Portugal, see Villazana, *Transnational Financial Structures*.

[18] Francisco Lombardi's *Ojos que no ven* (*What the Eye Doesn't See*, 2003) and *Mariposa Negra* (*Black Butterfly*, 2006). Both films are contextualised using similar political references – Alberto Fujimory's corrupted presidency – but the stories are treated differently. As a result, the first film did not obtain funds from Ibermedia and the second did: Villazana, *Transnational Financial Structures*, pp. 61–2.

[19] See the eligibility criteria of some of the funds that provide financial aid for film co-productions: Programa Ibermedia, www.programaibermedia.com; Hubert Bals Fund, http://www.filmfestivalrotterdam.com/en/about/hubert_bals_fund/; Fond Sud Cinéma, http://www.diplomatie.gouv.fr/en/france-priorities_1/cinema_2/cinematographic-

supporting developing countries' productions, such as the Fonds Sud Cinéma and Hubert Bals Fund described above, producers would need to have already secured a certain percentage of the total funds of the production. Furthermore, the transnational feature of those films co-produced by more than one country is apparent in the subsequent processes of distribution and exhibition, with only few exceptions where states have control over cinema exhibition. Most of the financial aid offered to co-productions is poured into the actual production of the films rather than into distribution and exhibition. This is because Hollywood blockbusters have dominated a great part of cinema distribution and exhibition worldwide since around the end of the First World War;[20] hence competing with Hollywood's distribution networks has proved to be a difficult task. States, then, have little control over and participation in distribution and exhibition, two of the most complex processes of film production.[21] The transnational features of film co-productions become apparent when one acknowledges the cultural inflection of the co-production practice and the transnational community of filmmakers and film industry professionals and enthusiasts that this practice generates. As in the examples of the European Union's educational programmes (i.e., the Bologna Programme) and J.P. Morgan and Co. (its transnational community component), the transnational ingredient of film co-production is most likely to be found in the study of the mechanisms that unfold in the process of co-production which serves to conflate different cultural film practices. This is very visible when a film involves collaborations between dissimilar cultures such as, say, Venezuelan and French or Spanish technicians and actors. It is not enough, then, to study, for instance, the effects of a co-produced film on the participant countries separately (i.e. audience research), for this practice to be called transnational; it is not even enough to study the different countries and bodies' legislations that regulate such collaborations to celebrate transnationalism in these films unless these regulations

---

cooperation_9/production-support-funding_10/fonds-sud-cinema_11/index.html. (Last accessed 18 February 2011).

20 Michael Chanan, 'Economic Conditions of Early Cinema', in *Cinema 1900–1906, FIAF 1982*; revised version in Thomas Elsaesser and Adam Barker (eds), *Early Cinema: Space Frame Narrative* (London: BFI, 1990) p. 179.

21 The Spanish film market share in Spain is around 6% and the remaining market is taken by the Motion Picture Association of America's (MPAA) films. The MPAA comprises the largest distribution companies in the USA, including Twentieth-Century Fox, Miramax and Universal. In Britain the market share is 8.6%; in Italy it is 10.5%; France generally reaches the highest percentage of all European countries with 34.5%; Villazana, *Transnational Financial Structures*, p. 60.

are positioned within a transnational geography (i.e., Ibermedia; Fonds Sud Cinéma; Hubert Bals Fund and so on). Film co-production is transnational when the study veers towards what happens during the actual process of the production chain (production, distribution and exhibition) and when the 'in-between' processes are explored and acknowledged.

Film piracy: a transnational cinema practice from 'below'

Transnationalism has not only become multi-vocal, through the diverse approaches provided by a variety of academic disciplines, but it has also been studied from multi-directional perspectives. In other words, transnationalism has commonly been examined from the movement from below to the upper layers of social stratifications and vice versa. These multi-directional perspectives are recognised as 'transnationalism from above' and 'transnationalism from below'.[22] The first refers to the élite migration and transnational capitalist class.[23] The example of J.P. Morgan and Co. given earlier serves as an illustration of this category. This class is formed by, for instance, transnational corporation executives, 'globalizing state bureaucrats, politicians and professionals, and consumerist elites in merchandizing and the media' (Vertovec, p. 454). Transnationalism from below is depicted instead by the lion's share of immigrants, who have propelled the growth in informal economies. However, as Michael Smith and Luis Guarnizo warn us,

> [i]n investigating the 'above' and the 'below' of transnational action, we should guard against the common mistake of equating 'above' exclusively with global structures or agents. Categorizing transnational actions as coming from 'above' and from 'below' aims at capturing the dynamics of power relations in the transnational arena. (p. 29)

Although transnationalism from below could seem to produce less of an economic impact on the world economy as compared to migrants within the category of 'above', it is worth acknowledging the existence of the so-called 'transnational nation-state',[24] which to some extent turns the

---

[22] See, for example, Portes; Michael Smith and Guarnizo; Waldinger and Fitzgerald.

[23] Leslie Sklair, 'Transnational Practices and the Analysis of the Global System', in *Globalization in the Twenty-first Century*, ed. Axel Hulsemeyer (Basingstoke: Palgrave Macmillan, 2003), pp. 15–32.

[24] Peggy Levitt and Nina Glick Schiller, 'Conceptualizing Simultaneity: A Trans-

aforementioned assumption on its head. Transnational nation-states are sending states which retrieve their émigrés living abroad by conceding them dual nationality and by virtue of this they re-instate their national membership. Social Anthropologist Nina Glick Schiller and her associates have called this process 'deterritorialized' nation-states formation (Smith and Guarnizo, p. 8). The reason for re-establishing connections with their émigrés is greatly related to the impact of remittances sent by these émigrés on the economy of the corresponding transnational nation-states. According to Peggy Levitt and Nina Glick Schiller, '[s]tates such as El Salvador, Mexico, Portugal, the Dominican Republic, and Brazil fall into this category' (p. 1023). Furthermore, in 2010, the Inter-America Development Bank (IDB) estimated that in Haiti, Guatemala, Honduras, Nicaragua and El Salvador remittances represent over 10 per cent of these countries' gross domestic product.[25] The aforementioned examples not only show the unquestionable relevance for these states to re-instate their émigrés but also the need to recognise, in academic research, the economic, political and social importance of these remittances sent from 'below' to the economic stability of the 'above' want-to-be globalising states.

The category of 'below' in particular composes the second critical reference of this chapter, since the study of informal economies emerging from transnational cinema practices can be connected to the approach of transnationalism from below. Smith and Guarnizo maintain that despite the different theoretical approaches to transnationalism, there are concurring points, and one of them is conceiving transnationalism as a subversive and popular resistance force 'from below' against the 'hegemonic logic of multinational capital' (p. 5). When drawing crisscross parallels between cinema and the aforementioned converging use of transnationalism, some questions inevitably arise. For example, is the practice of film co-productions a subversive and popular resistance force 'from below' against the 'hegemonic logic of multinational capital'? If so, in what ways? Can we think of any other ways within the transnational cinematic practices that correspond to the description of the aforementioned converging point? Film co-production is not necessarily subversive and

national Social Field Perspective on Society', *International Migration Review*, 38.3 (2004), 1002–39.

  25 'Remittances to Latin America Stabilizing after 15% Drop Last Year – MIF', on Inter-American Development Bank website. Available at: http://www.iadb.org/en/news/news-releases/2010–03–04/remittances-to-latin-america-stabilizing-after-15-drop-last-year-mif,6671.html. (Last accessed 18 February 2011).

it is not necessarily a force from 'below'. However, those co-productions outside of the Hollywood circuit can be said to have been organised as a force 'from the middle' – if one is allowed to create this category – against precisely the hegemony of the global distribution and exhibition networks commanded by Hollywood. The consequences of these co-productions' 'middle' force are the emergence of transnational film blocs; a good example of this phenomenon is the Programa Ibermedia, which works within the Ibero-American region. This and other such programmes offer film distribution and exhibition funds to aid member countries. From this perspective, Ibermedia represents an alternative – albeit a limited one – that partly assists producers with the recovery of the films' production costs. The proviso here is the focus of Ibermedia, which prioritises funding film production rather than film distribution and exhibition (Villazana, *Transnational Financial Structures*, pp. 43–8; Villazana, 'Hegemony', pp. 65–85). Within Europe – with global reach in some cases – other film bodies operate with the aim of promoting European cinema by aiding film production, distribution, exhibition and training. These funds include the MEDIA Pogramme, Eurimage Fund and EUROPA Cinemas (available only to those EU member countries of these programmes); MEDIA International (which aims at promoting exchange between non-EU member states and EU states' film production); EUROMED cinemas (offering support to the distribution and exhibition of Mediterranean and European films); and Outside Media (devoted to third countries' support in the promotion of European films).[26] These initiatives are clearly tantamount not only to protectionism of European cinemas against Hollywood's distribution hegemony but also – and as consequence of the above – European cinemas' need for expansion. The setting up of these film bodies offers some insights into the types of resistance of non-Hollywood cinema to Hollywood cinema in terms of the absorption of new markets. One way to exercise this market extension is by spanning European cinema's audiences to developing countries. This is the case, for instance, of the Outside Media programme, whose purpose is to financially support film distributors from third-world countries to distribute and exhibit *only* European films in their home market. Film audiences in developing countries are enticed mostly by Hollywood's productions (with few exceptions such as India).[27] Thus, programmes

---

[26] See Europa Cinema's website. Available at: http://www.europa-cinemas.org/en/index.php. (Last accessed 21 February 2011).

[27] See Villazana, *Transnational Financial Structures*, p. 60.

such as Outside Media attempt to compete with Hollywood for a share of the world's film market. From the example of Outside Media it is possible to assert that film co-production and distribution, for instance, do not necessarily come 'from below', since the aforementioned types of organisations seem hegemonic themselves. Programa Ibermedia offers a compelling example: its preference for funding a selective group of film directors and producers has not gone unnoticed.[28]

If cinematic co-production is not fundamentally a subversive force from below, there is room for arguing that the transnational practice of film piracy may be a subversive resistance force from below. This assertion falls somewhat into an ongoing debate related to whether film piracy is seen as a reaction against abusive capitalist practices or whether it is rather a terrorist action which is combined with an organised crime system.[29] Given the relevance and the effects of this debate, this section proposes to incorporate the study of film piracy as an integral component of transnational cinemas, particularly in the transdisciplinary fashion. This is because for film piracy to become sustainable it needs to build strong social networks of businesses across borders. Otherwise, how would a DVD copy of a film which has not yet been released in a country reach the streets and household TVs of that country? These networks have not only managed to destabilise large digital film distribution companies such as Blockbuster and as such make history in the global film industry, but they have also modified the film-viewing experience. The following testimony of an anonymous film piracy buyer in Mexico provides a case in point: '[W]e couldn't see all these movies in the theatre [...] The sodas, the parking, the candy, the popcorn. How much would it all cost?'[30] The large film distribution chain Blockbuster has been forced to close in many countries not only in Latin America but also in South Korea and Europe,

---

[28] Hoefert-Turégano, 'The International Politics of Cinematic Coproduction', pp. 15–24.

[29] See, for example, Gregory F. Treverton, Carl Matthies, Karla J. Cunningham, Jeremiah Goulka, Greg Ridgeway, Anny Wong, *Film Piracy, Organized Crime, and Terrorism* (Los Angeles, CA: RAND Corporation, 2009); 'Piracy and the Long Term of the Film Marketplace'. Available at: http://shoana63roach.jimdo.com/2011/01/22/piracy-and-the-long-term-of-the-film-marketplace/ (Last accessed 22 January 2011); 'Extortion-like Mass Automated Copyright Lawsuits Come to the US: 20,000 Filed, 30,000 More on the Way', 30 March 2010. Available at: http://www.techdirt.com/articles/20100330/1132478790.shtml (Last accessed 21 February 2011).

[30] Oscar Avila, 'Movie Piracy in Mexico', *Chicago Tribune*, 21 February 2009. Available at: http://www.pvscene.com/3287/movie-piracy-in-mexico/ (Last accessed 22 February 2011).

for example. In Spain, 86 Blockbuster-owned stores closed, leaving the country in 2006 virtually free from this digital film provider. According to Blockbuster representatives, around 60 per cent of the DVDs viewed in Spanish households were pirated.[31] In the USA, film piracy 'deprives the American government of £570 billion in lost tax revenue every year'.[32] As the current US Vice President, Joe Biden, has put it, '[t]o state it very bluntly, piracy hurts.' No wonder the US President Barak Obama has declared war on the illegal practice.[33] Similar stories are extended to Latin America; in Brazil, for instance, allegedly 50 per cent of the films sold on DVD are pirated copies.[34] In Mexico, film piracy has cost $483 million in 2005 to the US film industry, 'more than any other foreign country, according to the most recent data from the Motion Picture Association of America' (Avila, 'Movie Piracy', n. p.). The Mexican government is changing the country's legislation favouring the fight against counterfeiting movie piracy. It is doing so by, for instance, targeting as a crime the recording of films in cinema theatres; before it was only unlawful if the owners of these copies showed intention to distribute them.[35] The rocketing film piracy industry – and it goes without saying that music piracy is just as rife – has led to the organisation of government and private agencies devoted to the study of this sector. However, for academic research it seems that fieldwork is required to dig into the dynamics of this vast industry. The problem is how to break into those illegal networks – one or two anonymous case studies using Participant Observation, for instance, might suffice to provide some hints on how they operate. The illegal nature of the film piracy practice makes it difficult to access and gather data from any of these networks; understandably as they are highly protective of their practice. However, the practice has become so regular that it is openly exposed and greatly accepted by the public, particularly in many countries of the developing world. For instance, the counterfeiting activities of DVDs and tapes are significantly visible on the streets of

[31] DGA Quarterly. Available at: http://www.dgaquarterly.org/BACKISSUES/ Spring2010/PiracyByTheNumbers.aspx (Last accessed 21 February 2011).

[32] 'President Obama "Declares War" on Film Piracy' in NME Movie News. Available at: http://www.nme.com/filmandtv/news/president-obama-declares-war-on-film-piracy/176965 (Last accessed 21 February 2011).

[33] 'President Obama "Declares War" on Film Piracy', in NME Movie News.

[34] Andrew J. Barden and Katia Cortes, 'Brazil's Piracy under Fire as Lula Caught with Contraband Film', 14 November 2005. http://www.bloomberg.com/apps/news?pid= newsarchive&sid=aiVz7vok1v5A (Last accessed 22 February 2011).

[35] Avila, 'Movie Piracy'.

Seoul, São Paulo and Mexico City, to mention only a few of the allegedly highly active film piracy cities. In any case, film piracy practice resembles the effects of the transnationalisation of labour, since it weakens 'a fundamental premise of the hegemony of corporate economic elites and domestic ruling classes' (Portes, *Globalization from Below*, p. 18).

The evident political and economic implications of this practice, together with the changing dynamics of the global film industry caused by the effects of film piracy, and the study of how this practice affects film viewing requires imperative attention in academic research. Transnational cinemas seem to be one of the growing fields capable of incorporating this study.

Transnational Latin American cinema: a community in motion

There is another dimension to the concept of transnationalism, which becomes our third convergent axis with transnational cinemas. This dimension is the so-called Transnational Communities and is one of the most popular concepts within transnationalism. It was initially proposed by Sociologist Alejandro Portes in 1997 and extensively studied later by, among other scholars, Steven Vertovec and his associates at the University of Oxford. For Portes the concept of transnational communities is twofold; there are those communities which retain ties to their communities of origin (in the birth country) but establish new communities in the host country. There is also another type of community formed by 'return immigrants' who maintain strong connections with their former host country. In the outlining of his concept, Portes briefly incorporates the effects of the migration processes on the cultural sphere by stating that 'The phenomenon [transnationalism] acquires a cultural veneer as borne [sic] performers and artists use the expatriate communities as platforms to break into the First World scene and as returnee artists popularize cultural forms learned abroad' (Portes, *Globalization from Below*, p. 16). Historically, there have been extensive transnational communities of Latin American artists and, most relevant for this chapter, filmmakers, who have left their countries of origin for different reasons such as political persecution, lack of film production prospects or just in search of better opportunities. Many of these Latin Americans émigrés fall into the two categories analysed by Portes. The filmmakers this chapter takes as instances to refer to the conceptual connections between transnational community and transnational Latin American cinemas are what could seem at first glance a paradox, those pioneers of the New Latin American Cinema (Nuevo Cine Latinoamericano). Part of these filmmakers project was – and arguably still is – to unite Latin America culturally and politically to confront imperialism and defend national and regional identities. Delimiting and decolonising their cultures and nations was then part of the project. Some of the filmmakers and artists who took part in this new cinematic wave are part of a community in 'fast motion'; they are, the Argentinean Fernando Birri, Cubans Julio García Espinosa and Tomás Gutiérrez Alea, Colombian Gabriel García Márquez; all of whom studied at the Centro Sperimentale di Cinematografia in Rome (Experimental Film Centre); the Brazilian Glauber Rocha, who also spent time in Italy; Argentinean Fernando 'Pino' Solanas, who took refuge in France together with Chilean Patricio Guzmán; Chilean Miguel Littín who went into exile in Mexico; Octavio Getino, a Spanish-born and naturalised Argentinean filmmaker, and Bolivian Jorge Sanjinés. These and many other Latin American filmmakers of the 1950s, 1960s, and 1970s spent time abroad in close contact with (and significantly influenced by) the European cinematic trends of the time, particularly Italian Neorealism (1940s and 1950s), Free Cinema (1950s and 1960s), the French Nouvelle Vague (1950s and 1960s), Griersonian social documentary, and American Independent Cinema (1970s and 1980s), among other film waves.[36]

These filmmakers searched hard for a cinematographic language that would better identify national characteristics and spirits; they have long pursued a cinema that could better represent them, that could tell the world that these countries are taking part in the world historiography. They have searched for a non-complacent cinema; a non-Hollywood cinema; a non-European cinema; ultimately, a national and regionally (meaning, a Latin American) united cinema. The New Latin American Cinema was then born in 1967 in Chile during the Viña del Mar Film Festival. A series of meetings were held during the festival where they 'discussed with passion the definitions and future [cinema] plans'.[37] Some of the purposes of these meetings, and of the festival as a whole, were

---

[36] Julio García Espinosa, 'Cuban Cinema: A Long Journey toward the Light', in *When was Latin America Modern?*, ed. Nicola Miller and Stephen Hart (New York and London: Palgrave Macmillan, 2007), pp. 167–76. See also Mariluce Moura, 'A Constructor of Utopias', *Pesquisa online*, September 2006. Available at: http://revistapesquisa.fapesp. br/?art=1778&bd=1&pg=5&lg=en (Last accessed 22 February 2011).

[37] Aldo Francia, *Nuevo Cine Latinoamericano en Viña del Mar* (Santiago, Chile: CESOC, Ediciones ChileAmerica and ARTECIEN, 1990), p. 23.

[i]nvestigar nuevas formas de lenguaje cinematográfico a través de una expresión latinoamericana auténtica y propia, fundamentando la problemática del hombre y de la raza; redescubrir lo autóctono e incorporarlo a nuestro cine [...] Reunir a la gente de cine latinoamericano en sus diferentes actividades y manifestaciones, con el fin de intercambiar experiencias y posibilitar la asociación de esfuerzos comunes.

to investigate new forms of cinematographic language through a genuine Latin American expression accounting for the problematic of men and race; to re-discover the autochthonous and to incorporate it in our cinema [...] To bring together everyone working on cinema and its different activities in Latin America with the aim of sharing experiences and making it possible to form associations united in our common effort. (Francia, p. 23, my translation)

The Viña del Mar Film Festival gathered a wealth of Latin American filmmakers supportive of the construction of national/regional cinemas. These filmmakers established – spontaneously – one of the first Latin American Cinema Communities ever formed in the region – if not the first one – with an extraordinarily enduring impact on the ways cinema will be defined in Latin America. This historical cinema meeting in Chile in 1967 was followed by many more enthusiastic gatherings, which helped to transform the cinema of Latin America.[38]

In their effort to re-construct national/regional cinemas, these filmmakers launched a group of cinema manifestos and cinematic theoretical reflections to catapult innovative aesthetic and production approaches which would expose and celebrate cultural specificity and whose films would intentionally distance themselves sharply from the commercial and hegemonic forms of cinematic production. This is the case of Fernando Solanas and Octavio Getino and their aesthetically radical film experiment *La hora de los hornos* (*The Hour of the Furnaces*, 1965–68), and their

[38] For insights on these filmmakers' styles, film aesthetics and Third Cinema theories see Fernando Solanas and Octavio Getino, 'Towards a Third Cinema' in *Movies and Methods. An Anthology*, ed. Bill Nichols (Berkeley: University of California Press, 1976), pp. 44–64. See also Octavio Getino, 'Some Notes on the Concept of a "Third Cinema"', in *New Latin American Cinema. Vol. 1: Theory, Practices, and Transcontinental Articulations*, ed. Michael T. Martin (Detroit: Wayne State University Press, 1997), pp. 99–107; Julianne Burton, *Cine y cambio social en America Latina* (Mexico: Diana Editorial, 1991); Michael Chanan, 'The Changing Geography of Third Cinema', *Screen*, 38.4 (1997), 372–88; Michael Chanan (ed.), *Twenty-five Years of the New Latin American Cinema* (London: BFI and Channel Four Television, 1983); Mike Wayne, *Political Film: The Dialectics of Third Cinema* (Sterling, VA: Pluto Press, 2001).

pioneering 'Towards a Third Cinema' manifesto, first published in 1969. Also, Glauber Rocha with his 'An Aesthetic of Hunger', published in 1965; Julio García Espinosa and his 1969 groundbreaking cinema theory, 'For an Imperfect Cinema'; Jorge Sanjinés and his writings on 'Problems of Form and Content in Revolutionary Cinema'; and years later, in the 1980s, Tomás Gutiérrez Alea and his reflections on 'The Dialectic of the Spectator'. These are only a few of the new cinema theorists emerging from Latin America during the 1960s, 1970s and 1980s. Many of these filmmakers still maintain relevant (aesthetic and commercial) connections with European cinema circuits. This is so for Fernando Birri, who has lived in Italy since 1964 with some prolonged visits to Cuba, Mexico and Venezuela and Patricio Guzmán, who has lived in exile in France, Cuba and Spain after the 1973 Chilean coup d'état (Burton, pp. 23, 91). Similarly, Solanas and Sanjinés have produced some of their films with European production houses and TV channels.

These Latin American filmmakers, although promoters of the re-creation of both national and regional cinemas, can yet be identified as being transnational filmmakers/theorists and to a great degree belonging to a transnational cinema community. The transnational features of their work and of their careers as filmmakers are unequivocal. First, they have been actively engaged in aesthetic and production exchanges with Europe and the influence of European cinema trends is apparent in their work.[39] Secondly, and departing from the first point, their theoretical formulations and empirical cinema exploration have in turn influenced other cinemas, most notably African and Asian but also European and Russian cinemas. One instance of the influencing power of the aforementioned Latin American Cinema Community is the theoretical proposal formulated by scholar Hamid Naficy in his publication entitled *An Accented Cinema*: *Exilic and Diasporic Filmmaking*. In his words, 'The accented cinema is one of the offshoots of the Third Cinema, with which it shares certain attributes and from which it is differentiated by certain sensibilities' (Naficy, *An Accented Cinema*, p. 30). Naficy has extensively studied the aesthetics and production implications of those films made by diasporas and exilic filmmakers. Accented Cinema is a cinema made by displaced filmmakers living in exile or in diaspora, many of whom work in 'interstitial and artisanal modes of production, distribution and consumption',

---

[39] See, for example, Michael Chanan (ed.), *Twenty-five Years*; Burton, *Cine y cambio*; Fernando Birri, *Por un nuevo cine latinoamericano 1956–1991* (Madrid: Ediciones Cátedra, 1996).

resulting in a hybridity of style, identifications and ideologies (Naficy, *An Accented Cinema*). Moreover, Third Cinema theory became a transnational theory inasmuch as its proposals are not limited to the national/regional borders within which it was created. Its categories can embed other cinemas. As Teshome H. Gabriel stated, 'although Third Cinema films are made chiefly in the Third World, they may be made anywhere, by anyone, about any subject, and in a variety of styles and forms, as long as they are oppositional and liberationist' (Hamid Naficy paraphrasing Teshome H. Gabriel).[40] From this perspective, transnational cinema practices could seem directly opposed to definitions of national cinemas. However, in the case of the New Latin American Cinema movement, for instance, transnational cinema practices have served to emphasise the thrust that galvanised the New Latin American Cinema movement to propose a change to the Latin American political scenario. This is certainly concomitant with approaches to transnationalism whereby transnational practices (i.e., the dynamics of the migration of labour) are believed to be potentially contrahegemonic (Smith and Guarnizo, p. 5) in that they tend to attenuate the international inequalities of wealth and power (Portes, *Globalization from Below*, p. 18). The pioneers of the New Latin American Cinema created, very possibly without knowing it, a timeless cinema spreading from the continent to the world.

Some final reflections

This chapter proposes what in many ways is a methodological experiment whereby a multitude of academic disciplines – fundamentally Film, Transnationalism and Migration Studies – endeavour to work together in an attempt to uncover innovative conceptual frameworks within the field of transnational cinemas. This is manifest through the application of a transdisciplinary method to our subject of study. One of the benefits of this approach is to be able to dissect the studied topic with a rather different scalpel revealing in turn significant results. One of the potential pitfalls of the approach is the need to either take knowledge for granted so as to avoid revisiting some rather well-known concepts and thoughts from one or more of the disciplines in question or to fall into the reiterative mode. In the case of this chapter and in the insertion of Film

---

[40] Teshome H. Gabriel, *Third Cinema in the Third World: The Aesthetics of Liberation* (Ann Arbor: UMI Research Press, 1982) pp. 2–3, in Naficy, *An Accented Cinema*, p. 30.

Studies' approaches to transnationalism, it was imperative to include conceptual formulations widely used in the literature of Hispanic and Latin American Cinemas (i.e., Third Cinema and the New Latin American Cinema movement). In the case of Transnationalism and Migration Studies, it was essential to incorporate recognised theories and models such as 'internationalism', 'transnationalism from below' and 'transnational community'. What is intriguing, however, about these reiterations from various disciplines is the emergence of valuable knowledge unfamiliar to those disciplines involved in the study. This is precisely the virtue of the method. For Film Studies research it is rather unusual to refer to transnationalism from a social sciences perspective: the theorisation of this term has primarily used a Cultural Studies approach. Similarly, transnationalism as researched by social sciences is unfamiliar with notions of film co-production processes or film piracy across borders for instance. The study of transnational cinemas through other disciplines' lenses contributes greatly to a deeper appreciation of the micro-dynamics of this field. Thus, in film co-production by replacing the more commonly used term international for transnational, one stresses the cultural inflection and the in-betweenness of this practice. Similarly, the incorporation of film piracy as an imperative research topic for transnational cinemas and the exploration of the formation, activities and effects of transnational cinema communities on cinema historiography are largely possible almost exclusively through the transnational theories formulated within social sciences. In this respect, this chapter is only a starting point in the attempt to expand the horizons of transnational cinemas research, regardless of the geographical positioning of the research. This is a cinema rich in identities but at the same time with a particular identity as belonging to anywhere and everywhere; a cinema with extraordinary mobile fluency; a cross-border cinema without permanent settlement that somewhat reminds us of the motto of Argentinean directors Fernando Birri and Jorge Cedrón: 'My shoes are my country.'[41]

---

[41] Quoted in Moura, 'A Constructor of Utopias', n. p.

3

Deconstructing and Reconstructing 'Transnational Cinema'

DEBORAH SHAW

The notion of the transnational in Film Studies has developed in response to an increasing awareness of the limitations of conceptualising film in terms of national cinemas, and an acknowledgement of the changing nature of film production and distribution as a part of wider patterns of globalisation.[1] Transnational exchanges have long been central to film-making in terms of funding and the cast and crew,[2] and an increasing numbers of films in the international market cannot be identified with a single nation, with many films shooting in a number of countries, relying on a multinational cast and crew, and funded by a range of production companies. The concept of the transnational has seemed a straightforward solution for dealing with the problems inherent in the 'national cinema' label; however, what does the term actually mean? Which films can be categorised as transnational and which cannot? Does the term refer to production, distribution and exhibition, themes explored, aesthetics, nationalities of cast and crew, audience reception, or a range of these? Are mainstream Hollywood films transnational as they are distributed throughout the developed world? What about films with smaller budgets made in other national contexts that challenge Hollywood domination and

---

[1]   I would like to thank Paul McDonald for his helpful comments on a draft of this paper.
[2]   See Andrew Higson and Richard Maltby (eds), *'Film Europe' and 'Film America': Cinema, Commerce and Cultural Exchange, 1920–1939* (Exeter: University of Exeter Press, 1999).

explore the damaging effects of globalisation?[3] Is the term 'national' now entirely bankrupt, and if so what does this mean for films that engage with specifically local issues? Once we begin to ask these sorts of questions it becomes clear that 'transnational cinema' as a catch-all is inadequate to deal with the complexities of categorising both actual films and industrial practices.

This chapter seeks to bring together the work of a number of film theorists in order to consider aspects of transnational film cultures that are often taken in isolation. I then apply their findings, where possible, to my own area of expertise, Latin American cinema, and more specifically to the work of contemporary 'Mexican' directors, Alfonso Cuarón, Alejandro González Iñárritu, Guillermo del Toro, and, to a lesser degree, Carlos Reygadas.[4] They will act both as case studies for the theories developed, and illustrate new approaches needed in the theorising of 'transnational cinema'. My aim in this chapter is to deconstruct the label and identify specific categories to help prevent the vagueness and conflations that the use of the term appears to invite.

A background to the term 'transnational' in Film Studies

The need to question previous assumptions about the division of film criticism into neat national groupings has been gathering pace, as it is increasingly acknowledged that cinema is a part of the process of cultural exchange and is characterised by hybridity and its relationships with other markets.[5] This approach characterises a collection of essays contained

---

[3]   For an overview of what transnational has come to mean in other disciplines, see Steven Vertovec, 'Conceiving and Researching Transnationalism', *Ethnic and Racial Studies*, 22.2 (1999), 447–62. Vertovec usefully outlines categories to which concepts of transnationalism have been applied: these include social morphology, a type of consciousness, a mode of cultural reproduction, an avenue of capital, a site of political engagement, and a reconstruction of 'place' or locality, p. 447.

[4]   For a full analysis of the filmmaking of Iñárritu, Cuarón and Guillermo del Toro, see Deborah Shaw, *The Three Amigos: The Transnational Filmmaking of Guillermo del Toro, Alejandro González Iñárritu, and Alfonso Cuarón* (Manchester: Manchester University Press, 2013).

[5]   See, for example, among many others, Tom O'Regan, 'Cultural Exchange', in *A Companion to Film Theory*, ed. Toby Miller and Robert Stam (Oxford: Blackwell, 1999), pp. 262–94; Elizabeth Ezra and Terry Rowden, 'General Introduction: What is Transnational Cinema?', in *Transnational Cinema: The Film Reader*, ed. Elizabeth Ezra and Terry Rowden (London: Routledge, 2006), pp. 1–12 (pp. 2–3); Stephen Crofts,

within *Cinema and Nation* edited by Mette Hjort and Scott Mackenzie. One of the key essays to introduce the concept of the transnational into Film Studies was Andrew Higson's 'The Limiting Imagination of National Cinema'. In this study Higson questions the relationship between film cultures and the nation state, arguing that

> the concept of national cinema is hardly able to do justice either to the internal diversity of contemporary cultural formations or to the overlaps and interpenetrations between different formations.[6]

This problem is resolved by having 'transnational' replace 'national' as a new conceptual framework within which to examine film cultures: '"transnational" may be a subtler means of describing cultural and economic formations that are rarely contained by national boundaries'.[7]

Following Higson, it has become increasing popular to use the term 'transnational' in writings on film to show an awareness of the problems with the use of the 'national'; however, it has often been used without any definition or explanation as to what is meant.[8] Higson uses the essay to introduce the concept, and as such his essay does not attempt an exhaustive definition of what is meant by this. That said, he does explain that in the migration between 'leaky borders' 'the transnational emerges' (Higson, p. 67), and identifies production, mixed casts and crews, and distribution and reception as sites for its location (pp. 67–8). His work has

---

'Concepts of National Cinema', in *The Oxford Guide to Film Studies*, ed. John Hill and Pamela Church Gibson (Oxford: Oxford University Press, 1998), pp. 385–94.

6   Andrew Higson, 'The Limiting Imagination of National Cinema', in *Cinema and Nation*, ed. Mette Hjort and Scott Mackenzie (London: Routledge, 2000), pp. 63–74 (p. 70).

7   Higson, 'The Limiting Imagination', p. 64. Many other film and cultural critics have made similar criticisms of monolithic notions of the nation; in the same vein, Ella Shohat and Robert Stam in the introduction to their edited book argue the following: 'the global nature of the colonizing process, and the global reach of the contemporary media, virtually oblige the cultural critic to move beyond the restrictive frameworks of monoculture and the individual nation-state', Ella Shohat and Robert Stam (eds), *Multiculturalism, Postcoloniality and Transnational Media* (New Brunswick: Rutgers University Press, 2003), p. 1.

8   There has been some recent excellent work which has furthered the field of transnational film theory: this includes Will Higbee and Song Hwee Lim's, 'Concepts of Transnational Cinema: Towards a Critical Transnationalism in Film Studies', *Transnational Cinemas*, 1.1 (2010), 7–21, and Chris Berry's 'What is Transnational Cinema? Thinking from the Chinese Situation', *Transnational Cinemas*, 1.2 (2010), 111–27.

been an important stepping stone from which other writings are implicitly invited to follow, while he himself has developed his ideas elsewhere.[9]

There are, however, some difficulties inherent in the very task of attempting to provide a definition for the term 'transnational cinema'. One example of this can be found in an important chapter written by Elizabeth Ezra and Terry Rowden as an introduction to their book, *Transnational Cinema: The Film Reader* (pp. 1–12). This piece demonstrates some of the problems with meanings given to the term. While it contains many excellent points and is a useful overview of many contemporary debates, the flaw lies in an attempt to assume an essence to 'transnational cinema'. This is demonstrated in the title itself 'What is Transnational Cinema?' In their introduction to the edited book *Remapping World Cinemas: Identity, Culture and Politics in Film*, Dennison and Lim have argued that the question 'what is world cinema?' has an essentialist element built into it.[10] I would argue that the same criticism can be made of any attempt to provide a definition of transnational cinema.

While much of Ezra and Rowden's essay makes some very interesting points about the debates relating to concepts of the transnational in film, they rarely answer their own question posed in the title. When they do attempt to do this, the problems built into the question become most apparent. They first get into difficulties when providing an all-encompassing explanation of the term:

> The transnational comprises both globalization – in cinematic terms, Hollywood's domination of world film markets – and the counter-hegemonic responses of filmmakers from former colonial and Third World countries. (Ezra and Rowden, p. 1)

This seems to suggest that when we speak of transnational cinema we are talking about almost every film, both those on international release, and those which are marginalised from the global market, as long as they challenge Hollywood filmmaking approaches. Following this over-generalised definition, they make a case for a type of cinema that they see as being transnational. For the authors this is constituted by films that focus on migration and diaspora as themes (Ezra and Rowden, p. 7), and are

---

[9]   See Higson and Maltby (eds), *'Film Europe' and 'Film America'* and Andrew Higson, 'Transnational Developments in European Cinema in the 1920s', *Transnational Cinemas*, 1.1 (2010), 69–82.

[10] Stephanie Dennison and Song Hwee Lim (eds), *Remapping World Cinema: Identity, Culture and Politics in Film* (London: Wallflower Press, 2006), p. 1.

located in the 'in-between spaces of culture' (p. 4). 'More often than not ... [there is a] narrative dynamic [...] generated by a sense of loss' (p. 7), with a focus on displaced persons, seen through 'cinematic depictions of people caught in the cracks of globalization' (p. 7). The authors here demonstrate a degree of voluntarism; the politically important films informed by post-colonial fallout to which they make reference are those that they want to privilege as transnational film texts, while this voluntarism negates the earlier generalised definition provided. Perhaps what this critical reading reveals is that the term 'transnational cinema' is lacking in specific meaning in that discrete concepts have been conflated: it does not define an aesthetic approach, a movement of filmmakers, any specific national grouping, and neither does it separate out areas of study.

Categories of the transnational

In order to re-inject meaning into an emerging field that we can call transnational cinema studies, it is helpful to define key concepts, and develop meaningful categories. Such an approach has been taken by Mette Hjort in her chapter 'On the Plurality of Cinematic Transnationalism'. In this piece, Hjort also identifies a problem with the use of the term 'transnational' in that it 'does little to advance our thinking about important issues if it can mean anything and everything that the occasion would appear to demand'.[11] Her solution is to produce a 'detailed typology that links the concept of transnationalism to different models of cinematic production, each motivated by specific concerns and designed to achieve particular effects' (Hjort, p. 15).[12]

This focus on production contexts is extremely useful; I take a similar approach in this chapter, but tease out separate strands that have been conflated in the umbrella term in an attempt to distinguish between industrial practices, working practices, aesthetics, themes and approaches, audience reception, ethical questions, and critical reception. I argue that

[11] Mette Hjort, 'On the Plurality of Cinematic Transnationalism', in *World Cinemas, Transnational Perspectives*, ed. Natasa Durovicová and Kathleen Newman (Abingdon: Routledge, 2009), pp. 12–33.

[12] These categories are made up of 'epiphanic transnationalism, affinitive transnationalism, milieu building transnationalism, opportunistic transnationalism, cosmopolitan transnationalism, globalizing transnationalism, auteurist transnationalism, modernizing transnationalism, and experimental transnationalism'. See Hjort, 'On the Plurality', pp. 15–30 for further explanation of these.

if we apply a series of categories to our readings of films, we can avoid the problems detailed above. I suggest the following 15 groupings:

- transnational modes of production, distribution and exhibition
- transnational modes of narration
- cinema of globalisation
- films with multiple locations
- exilic and diasporic filmmaking
- film and cultural exchange
- transnational influences
- transnational critical approaches
- transnational viewing practices
- transregional/transcommunity films
- transnational stars
- transnational directors
- the ethics of transnationalism
- transnational collaborative networks
- national films[13]

These are clearly not self-contained categories and there is a good degree of overlap between them. Indeed, in some cases most of the above can be applied to a single film text; in others, several can be applied. Even in the case of national films there is inevitably a degree of cultural exchange in terms of influence from other filmmaking traditions. While these categories are not original in themselves, they have not, to my knowledge, been taken together in an attempt to provide a fuller understanding of transnational cinema cultures.

Transnational modes of production, distribution and exhibition
This category relates to financial questions: funding for filmmaking through co-productions; the question of niche markets; the policies of distribution and exhibition companies, and the marketing of films to global audiences. In my analysis of this category I assume hegemonic power

---

[13] Since formulating this list, one of the gaps that emerged in the writing of the book *The Three Amigos: The Transnational Filmmaking of Guillermo del Toro, Alejandro González Iñárritu, and Alfonso Cuarón* is another category, 'the politics of the transnational', needed to address the political discourses into which global films are inserted, and the relationship between these and the production and distribution companies that finance them; see Shaw, *The Three Amigos*.

structures that favour Hollywood's domination of many film markets.[14] Nevertheless, the notion of global Hollywood also rests on the fact that, 'Hollywood's links to any specific national context have become strained' (McDonald and Wasko, p. 6). This relates to international distribution and exhibition operations, co-productions and co-financing agreements with other national territories (McDonald and Wasko, p. 6), foreign ownership of many of the major studios,[15] and the employment of successful directors, crew and cast from other nations. The last point is well illustrated by the three best known Mexican directors, Alfonso Cuarón, Alejandro González Iñárritu and Guillermo del Toro, who have cultivated an auteur status to gain entry into the Hollywood film industry.

This category clearly links finance with content, as the result of transnational modes of production, distribution and exhibition are films that enter the international market. Latin America provides a wealth of examples of 'national' films entering the international market. Some of these include the Brazilian films *Cidade de Deus* (*City of God*, Fernando Meirelles and Kátia Lund, 2002), *Tropa de elite* (*Elite Squad*, José Padilha, 2007), *Central do Brasil* (*Central Station*, Walter Salles, 1998); the Mexican films, *Amores perros* (Alejandro González Iñárritu, 2000) and *Y tu mamá también* (Alfonso Cuarón, 2001); and the Argentine *Nueve reinas* (*Nine Queens*, Fabián Bielinsky, 2000), *La niña santa* (*The Holy Girl,* Lucrecia Martel, 2004), *La mujer sin cabeza* (*The Headless Woman,* Lucrecia Martel, 2008), and *XXY* (Lucía Puenzo, 2007). Central to the success of an unprecedented number of Latin American films and those from other national territories is the increased forms in which films can enter the international market. While there may be very little opportunity to buy a ticket to see non-English language films for those who do not live in big cities, world movie channels on digital television, and DVD internet rental companies have provided consumers with much greater access to foreign films.

---

[14] For an in-depth analysis of this phenomenon, see Toby Miller, Nitin Govil, John McMurria, Richard Maxwell and Ting Wang (eds), *Global Hollywood: No 2* (London: BFI Films, 2004). For a comprehensive analysis of the operations and transnational reach of Hollywood, see Paul McDonald and Janet Wasko (eds), *The Contemporary Hollywood Film Industry* (Malden, MA: Blackwell, 2007).

[15] Tom Schatz, 'The Studio System and Conglomerate Hollywood', in *The Contemporary Hollywood Film Industry*, ed. Paul McDonald and Janet Wasko (Malden, MA: Blackwell, 2007), p. 27.

Transnational modes of narration

This category relates to the content of films and the cinematic storytelling devices used that make them accessible to audiences in many parts of the world (although of course, different readings of these are produced depending on the national identities of audiences, among other factors). This category can refer to approaches used in mainstream Hollywood movies, and those used in films that combine local traditions with Hollywood influences to produce spectacular, big-budget features. These include recent highly successful Chinese language films such as *Hero* (Zimou Zang, 2002), *Crouching Tiger, Hidden Dragon* (Ang Lee, 2000) and *House of the Flying Daggers* (Zimou Zang, 2004). Mette Hjort refers to these Chinese language films as 'globalizing transnational films' in the way that they combine high production values, generic ingredients and internationally recognised stars in their bid to secure international audiences (Hjort, 'On the Plurality', pp. 21–2). Song Hwee Lim and Will Higbee, in turn, note that: 'from action thrillers to horror films, East Asian cinemas have excited critics who marvel at their ability to beat Hollywood "at its own game"' (Higbee and Lim, p. 15).

Examples of Mexican application of transnational modes of narration can be seen in films such as *Amores perros* and *Y tu mamá también*, among others. González Iñárritu and team, for instance, adopt contemporary international filmmaking trends in terms of structure, chronology, characterisation, editing and camera work in *Amores perros*, their first international hit. However, we can also apply the concept of niche markets to this category as 'transnational modes of narration' does not only refer to the most commercial films with mass appeal, but can also be used with reference to cult films or art cinema. The works of the Mexican director Carlos Reygadas provide a good example of the broader application of this category as he makes films that use an internationally recognised film language by following certain art cinema conventions and borrowing from, among others, Andrei Tarkovsky, Carl Theodor Dreyer and Abbas Kiarostami.

Cinema of globalisation

The reference here is to film texts that explicitly address questions of globalisation within their narratives, central to which are the ways in which relations of power between nations and peoples are played out on screen. This term is used by Tom Zaniello who has compiled a guide to 'films about the new economic order', as the book's subheading tells us.[16] His focus is on films from around the world 'about transnational organisations' and 'multinational corporations' and their effects on people and the environment (Zaniello, p. 17).[17] Zaniello casts his net wide and his book covers 213 films with many documentaries included. My focus here is on feature films (which is not to diminish the value of documentaries) and a few important films that can be included in this category are: *The Voyage* (Solanas, 1992), *Dirty Pretty Things* (Frears, 2002), *In This World* (Winterbottom, 2002), *The Constant Gardener* (Meirelles, 2005), *Syriana* (Gaghan, 2005), *Blood Diamond* (Zwick, 2006), *The International* (Twyker, 2009); and from Mexican directors: *Children of Men* (Cuarón, 2006) and *Babel* (González Iñárritu, 2006).

Films with multiple locations
Most examples of the 'cinema of globalisation' are also 'films with multiple locations'; however, the use of a number of geographical sites does not necessarily equate with cinema of globalisation. Borders crossings are frequently instrumental in terms of plot and aesthetics, and depend for commercial success on harnessing a tourist gaze; nevertheless, they are often not used predominantly to make social and political points about the nature of globalisation. Such films include, among many others, the James Bond films, and the Bourne franchise: *The Bourne Identity* (Liman, 2002); *The Bourne Supremacy* (Greengrass, 2004); *The Bourne Ultimatum* (Greengrass, 2007) and *The Bourne Legacy* (Gilroy, 2012). While the latter critique rogue elements within the CIA, they do not take on multinational corporations in the way that the above-mentioned films do, and they are first and foremost action-adventure films that use locations to provide exotic backdrops, while the practices of the CIA are used for their narrative potential rather than to make serious social commentary.

---

[16] Tom Zaniello, *The Cinema of Globalization: A Guide to Films about the New Economic Order* (Ithaca: Cornell University Press, 2007).

[17] His specific categories are: 'films about global labor and labor unions affected by globalization; films about global capital and multinational corporations; films about the transnational organizations (WB, IMF, WTO) most closely identified with globalization and global capital; films about labor history and the daily life of working-class people as they relate to the development of globalization; films about the environment directly related to changes in labor or capital; and films about changes in both the workplace and the corporate office in the era of multinational corporations' (Zaniello, p. 17).

Exilic and diasporic filmmaking
This kind of filmmaking has been foregrounded in the work of Hamid
Naficy (2001), who has labelled it 'Accented Cinema'. He uses the term
to refer to the products of displaced filmmakers: those who explore their
experiences of exile and emigration in their work.[18] For Naficy, these
filmmakers 'work in the interstices of social formations and cinematic
practices',[19] and are generally outside of the dominant modes of production
(Naficy, 'Situating Accented Cinema', p. 111). In his book he considers
the strategies used by such filmmakers to produce a form of personal
counter cinema (Naficy, *An Accented Cinema*, pp. 6–7). Those whose
films he studies and analyses include Atom Egoyan, Mira Nair, Trinh T.
Minh-ha, Ghasem Ebrahimian, Fernando Solanas, Chantal Akerman and
Emir Kusturica, to name a few.[20]

In the case of Latin America, this category is useful when considering a
previous generation of filmmakers from Southern cone countries during the
years of dictatorship. Directors include the Argentine Fernando Solanas,
who made films in France; and the Chileans Raúl Ruiz, who also went
into exile in France, and Miguel Littín, who went to Mexico. However,
the main type of exile that can be applied to the current generation of filmmakers is economic exile, with bigger budgets luring the Brazilian directors Walter Salles and Fernando Meirelles, and the Mexicans Cuarón,
Iñárritu and del Toro to other national territories, predominantly the USA,
to further their careers. It should be noted, nonetheless, that Iñárritu and
del Toro have spoken of their fears of kidnap and partially attributed their
'exile' to this; indeed, del Toro's father was kidnapped.[21]

Cultural exchange
This clearly connects with ideas associated with 'cultural exchange',
which frequently characterise such interactions. The term is taken here
from Tom O'Regan who uses it to refer to a wide range of systems and

[18] Hamid Naficy, *An Accented Cinema: Exilic and Diasporic Filmmaking* (Princeton:
Princeton University Press, 2001).

[19] Hamid Naficy 'Situating Accented Cinema', in *Transnational Cinema: The Film
Reader*, ed. Elizabeth Ezra and Terry Rowden (London: Routledge, 2006), p. 111.

[20] In a related vein, Tim Bergfelder has made a strong case for the centrality of exile
and immigration in European cinema: see Tim Bergfelder, 'National, Transnational, Or
Supranational Cinema? Rethinking European Film Studies', *Media, Culture and Society*,
27.3 (2005), 315–31.

[21] Jason Wood, 'A Life in Pictures: Guillermo del Toro' (8 July 2008). Available
at: http://www.bafta.org/access-all-areas/videos/a-life-in-pictures-guillermo-del-toro,466,
BA.html (Last accessed 6 July 2010).

processes that underpin the transnational nature of cinema.[22] For O'Regan 'cultural exchange can be found in filmmaking and film criticism, film reception, and film marketing' (O'Regan, p. 262), and involves the circulation of 'cultural materials from one filmmaking and cultural tradition to another' (p. 262), with materials in his formulation including texts (p. 262), concepts (p. 263), filmmaking practices (p. 264), reception, critical approaches, personnel, (p. 265), 'technologies of exhibition, production and marketing' (p. 265), and exhibition venues (p. 266).

While there are, then, many examples of cultural exchange, one of the most obvious can be found in film texts that do not clearly fit into a single geographical grouping due to an array of national identities of cast, crew, writers, production companies, shooting locations and settings. There are multiple examples of films that fit within this category; some of the best known include Lars von Trier's *Breaking the Waves* (1996), and *Dancer in the Dark* (2000); *The Others* (2001) by the Spanish director Alejandro Aménabar, *In This World* directed by Michael Winterbottom (2002), Michael Haneke's *Hidden* (2005), and *Slumdog Millionaire* (2009) directed by Danny Boyle.[23]

The work of Cuarón, González Iñárritu and del Toro also involves many levels of cultural exchange. Their films have been shot by their own cinematographers, even when employed on Hollywood projects (Cuarón's regular cinematographer is Emmanuel Lubezki; Iñárritu has always worked with Rodrigo Prieto, and del Toro's cinematographer is Guillermo Navarro). They have all benefitted from working in a number of locations, with multinational casts and crew, and they have made films in Spanish and English, while securing funding from a range of Hollywood, US independent, Mexican and Spanish companies. One of the best examples of cultural exchange is seen in *Babel*, directed by González Iñárritu. The cast and crew included Mexicans, Italians, French, North Americans and Moroccans, and it was shot in the USA, Japan, Morocco and Mexico, and features five languages (English, Spanish, Japanese, Arabic and Berber).

[22] O'Regan, 'Cultural Exchange'.

[23] Despite the fact that *Hidden* was considered one of the best 'foreign' language films of 2006, it did not make the Oscar nominations as the rules for the academy awards stipulate that the director, cast and language used should be from the same country. Haneke is an Austrian director, and the film is in French and stars Juliette Binoche and Daniel Auteuil. This illustrates the fact that Hollywood has not yet successfully dealt with the complexities of how to categorise films with a multinational cast and crew.

Transnational critical approaches and Transnational influences
Another form of cultural exchange can be found in 'Transnational critical
approaches' and 'Transnational influences' which I examine together here
as the methodology developed in the former allows a heightened awareness of the latter. These categories assume intertextuality in that every
film made has been consciously or unconsciously shaped by pre-existing
cultural products from all over the world. This, in turn, also infers that
national cinema cannot exist in isolation, and here we can apply Dudley
Andrew's notion of a world systems approach. In his words:

> You can't study a single film, nor even a national cinema, without under-
> standing the interdependence of images, entertainment, and people all
> of which move with increasing regularity around the world. The movies
> are a model for 'the glocal'.[24]

Andrew applies the analogy of genealogical trees to traditional studies of
national cinema in the ways that scholars have examined each nation's
cinema as a discrete object of study, arguing that 'their elaborate root and
branch structures seldom interfere with one another' (Andrew, p. 21). He
critiques this methodology and advocates the use of the concept of waves
to replace that of trees. A world systems approach is characterised, then,
by waves of influence between national cinemas and from film to film in
terms of approach, narrative and visual style. [25]
    His insights necessitate a new approach to any study of 'national'
cinemas and directors. To turn once again to Mexican examples, this way
of thinking ensures that more sophisticated answers are given to the questions relating to degrees of 'Mexicanness' of leading directors born in that
country. Some may argue that Carlos Reygadas is more Mexican in his
filmmaking than Guillermo del Toro. On the surface, this may appear to
be the case because the former has shot his films exclusively in Mexico,
and works within specific national locations, while the latter has not made
a film in Mexico since *Cronos* (1993). Yet, this is made more complex by
the fact that Reygadas' influences are unapologetically from international

----

[24] Dudley Andrew, 'An Atlas of World Cinema', in Stephanie Dennison and Song
Hwee Lim, *Remapping World Cinema: Identity, Culture and Politics in Film* (London:
Wallflower Press, 2006), pp. 19–29 (p. 22).
[25] For another influential essay discussing relationships between cinemas from across
the world, see Lúcia Nagib, 'Towards a Positive Definition of World Cinema', in Stephanie
Dennison and Song Hwee Lim, *Remapping World Cinema* (London: Wallflower, 2006),
pp. 30–7.

masters of cinema, as has been seen (as are del Toro's), while the latter is working hard to promote filmmaking opportunities in Mexico.

Transnational viewing practices
These are central to any discussion of influences and critical approaches, as well as to all of the other categories. They can be sub-divided into three key concepts. The most obvious refers to the viewing of any film made and/or set in a different national context from that of the audience, and the divergent readings that may arise from the national/regional identities of audiences.[26] The second relates to 'structures of cinematic experience', to use Charles Acland's term. [27] Acland argues that megaplexes create a form of popular cosmopolitanism that has its own structures of feeling (Acland, p. 237) and 'arrange a localized encounter with a transnational commercial film culture' (p. 239), which creates a cosmopolitan spectator within a specific atmosphere of social life (p. 240). Shared practices of cinema-going unite cinema spectators around the world and seek emotional responses encouraged through the marketing of films according to generic markers. Nevertheless, as the first concept makes clear, local factors will ensure tensions between specific local responses and 'felt internationalism'.[28]

The third concept refers to the fact that different sectors of the community will seek out films from cultures with which they identify. To give a few examples, Latino communities in the USA are more likely to see Latin American films than Anglo communities. They will also seek out films made by Hispanic directors or starring Hispanic actors.[29] Bollywood films are extremely popular with Indian immigrant communities (among

---

[26] See Ulf Hedetoft, 'Contemporary Cinema: Between Cultural Globalisation and National Interpretation', in *Cinema and Nation*, ed. Mette Hjort and Scott Mackenzie (London: Routledge, 2000), pp. 278–97; and Andrew Higson, 'The Limiting Imagination', pp. 68–9.

[27] Charles R. Acland, *Screen Traffic: Movies, Multiplexes, and Global Culture* (Durham NC: Duke University Press, 2003).

[28] Acland's thesis is rather weakened by the fact that he concentrates on cinema institutions and ignores textual matters, and his fascinating idea about felt internationalism does not fully consider how national audiences may read a text differently, regardless of the shared cinematic experience provided by the megaplexes.

[29] For more on Latino audience trends, see Diana I. Rios, 'Chicana/o and Latina/o Gazing: Audiences of the Mass Media', in *Chicano Renaissance: Contemporary Cultural Trends*, ed. David R. Maciel, Isidro D. Ortiz and Maria Herrera-Sobek (Tucson: University of Arizona Press, 2000), pp. 169–90.

others) in a range of national locations.[30] Likewise, mass-produced
Nigerian films are popular with Nigerian immigrant communities around
the world (Andrew, p. 26). These phenomena have led to alternative modes
of distribution with the circulation of videos and DVDs in specialist shops
often bypassing the cinema distribution circuits. Transnational viewing
practices draw our attention to the fact that there are many forms in which
films cross borders, with film a central part of an informal economy.

Transregional/transcommunity films
There is some overlap here as these categories refer to the films themselves that are distributed and well known to those within a region or
diasporic populations, but not globally. Thus, there are films that are
known by Chinese-language communities, Hindi speakers, or Hispanics
to give three examples, but not to other members of the international
cinema-going public. Likewise, gay and lesbian audiences may form a
community of viewers and are likely to be aware of films from around
the world that straight audiences may be ignorant of.

Transnational stars
These can also be broken down into transregional, transcommunity
or global stars. While Brad Pitt and George Clooney may be known
throughout most of the developed world and beyond, Shah Rukh Khan and
Amitabh Bachan are transregional and transcommunity Bollywood stars;
household names in India and Pakistan, but known to few outside of the
South Asian community in the United States and Europe. Transnational
stars from the Hispanic community include the Spaniards Penelope Cruz,
Antonio Banderas, Javier Bardem, and the Mexicans Gael García Bernal
and Diego Luna. While they have appeared in a number of 'national' films
that have been internationally distributed, they have reached the heights
of global fame via their appearance in Hollywood feature films.

Transnational directors
This is clearly a category that overlaps with many of the above in that, for
instance, the filmmakers need to be fluent in transnational modes of narration, and are physical embodiments of cultural exchange. In broad terms,
it refers to directors who work and seek funding in a range of national

---

[30] See Brian Larkin, 'Itineraries of Indian Cinema: African Videos, Bollywood, and
Global Media', in *Multiculturalism, Postcoloniality, and Transnational Media*, ed. Ella
Shohat and Robert Stam (New Brunswick: Rutgers University Press, 2003), pp. 170–92.

contexts, while they have their films distributed in the global market. An early example of such a director is Luis Buñuel; other more contemporary examples include Lars von Trier, Michael Haneke, Alejandro Amenábar, Ang Lee, Fernando Meirelles, Walter Salles and Baz Lurhmann.

Cuarón, Iñárritu and del Toro clearly belong in this category, as a brief glance at their trajectories reveal. Following Cuarón's first Mexican feature, *Solo con tu pareja/Love in the Time of Hysteria* (1991), he made *A Little Princess* (1995) and *Great Expectations* (1998), both of which are entirely US funded. After returning to Mexico to make *Y tu mamá también,* released in 2001, Cuarón moved to English territory with *Harry Potter and the Prisoner of Azkaban* (USA, UK, 2004) and *Children of Men* (USA, UK, 2006), with the majority of the funding coming from US production companies. Del Toro relocated to Spain to make *The Devil's Backbone* (2001), thanks to the promise of money from the Almodóvar brothers' production company, El Deseo, although the Mexican company Anhelo Producciones and del Toro's production company the Tequila Gang co-produced the film. There was a similarly complex funding arrangement between Spanish and Mexican companies for *Pan's Labyrinth* (2006), also rooted deeply within a Spanish historical context, with a predominantly Spanish cast. Del Toro is equally well-known for his Hollywood commercial productions, *Mimic* (1997), *Blade II* (2002), *Hellboy* (2004), and *Hellboy II The Golden Army* (2008). Like his compatriots, Iñárritu has also moved out of Mexico following his first successful 'national' film. Following *Amores Perros* he made an independent US feature *21 Grams* (2003), set and filmed in Memphis, before relocating to the multinational spaces of *Babel* (2006) and on to the migrant spaces of Barcelona in *Biutiful* (2010).

Cuarón, del Toro and Iñárritu make us question traditional ideas about the 'auteur' as representative and bearer of national and/or ethnic identity' (Ezra and Rowden, p. 3) in their movements across geographical borders. The fact that the three directors, between them, have set their films in the USA, the UK, Morocco, Japan, and Spain has meant that the Mexican auteurist director is no longer perceived as an allegorical voice of the nation, as was previously the case.

The ethics of transnationalism

This area of study has been the focus of recent work by Mette Hjort, who has added a much needed ethical dimension to writings on transnational film. In her article, 'On the Plurality of Cinematic Transnationalism', she notes:

> There is nothing inherently virtuous about transnationalism and there
> may even be reason to object to some forms of transnationalism [...].
> My own view is that the more valuable forms of cinematic transna-
> tionalism feature at least two qualities: a resistance to globalization as
> cultural homogenization; and a commitment to ensuring that certain
> economic realities associated with filmmaking do not eclipse the pursuit
> of aesthetic, artistic, social, and political values.
>
> (Hjort, 'On the Plurality', p. 15)

Her focus is on a form of 'milieu-building transnationalism' which
involves collaborations between filmmakers of small nations as the best
way to achieve this.[31] A clear example of this would be the way Cuarón,
Iñárritu and del Toro have forged links and worked together in order to
be able to foster a Mexican filmmaking culture, and to balance artistic
and moral integrity with the realities of Hollywood domination. They
have played a strategic game and have succeeded in making personal
projects alongside or even as a part of Hollywood productions. Questions
of artistic integrity are more complex than at first they appear, and a decision to make a 'Hollywood' film does not mean a loss of quality.

Rather than accuse the filmmakers of betraying their Mexican identity
through their recent work, it is more fruitful to frame the debate around
questions of power. As Tom O'Regan has noted in his essay on cultural
exchange, cinema generates institutions built on unequal power relations:

> The international industry is both dominant and predatory. It is preda-
> tory in that it is naturally expansive. It seeks new personnel for its
> productions with the result that many talented directors are lost from
> the national context in which they began. (O'Regan, p. 269)

Transnational modes of production, distribution and exhibition open up
the field for many individual directors, and a few films from non-English
speaking national contexts, but they do not threaten US hegemony.
Despite its transnational reach, the US dominated global system will
only ever accommodate a handful of non-English language films at any
one time, and individual Mexican directors have chosen to travel in and
out of its systems to varying degrees as they want to make films that
will consistently secure international releases and consolidate their status

---

[31] Hjort is referring specifically to *Advance Party*, von Trier's project in which his
plans to shoot three films in Scotland create opportunities for Scottish filmmaking.

as star directors. In ethical terms, then, what needs to be addressed is not whether individual directors feel compelled to work in the USA or Europe, but how can nationally produced films survive in a Hollywood dominated market.

Transnational collaborative networks
As we have seen, these can take the form of partnerships between small nations to enable a resistance to (US dominated) globalisation in film-making. The category can apply more broadly to any form of cross-border collaborations among filmmakers to generate the production of films. Another effective technique is demonstrated in a strategy used by our three directors, along with Carlos Cuarón and Rodrigo García.[32] The five have formed a production partnership company, Cha cha chá, and touted for business among major Hollywood Studios to guarantee funding for future projects. The company has cannily employed media generated notions of the three star directors, 'the three amigos', to generate interest. They were taken up by Universal Pictures and its specialty branch Focus Features in a deal which provides a collective budget of $100 million for a five film package, guaranteeing the filmmakers creative control.[33]

Thus, national identity has been used to help further Mexican film culture, sustained by a mixture of US and Mexican funding. What is most noteworthy is that arrangements like this one entirely disrupt traditional debates about cultural imperialism as in this case, it is US money that is helping to create independent and financially viable films by Mexican directors, with, of course, the promise of healthy returns at the box office. This is not to say that the power imbalances and ideological controls theo-rised by critics of cultural imperialism are not as relevant today as they

[32] García is a successful television and film director and son of the well known novelist Gabriel García Márquez.
[33] Peter Knegt, 'CANNES '07 | Cuaron, Del Toro, and Inarritu Form 'cha cha cha'; Trio Ink 5 Film Pact With Universal/Focus' (18 May 2007). Available at: http://www.indiewire.com/article/cannes_07_cuaron_del_toro_and_inarritu_form_cha_cha_cha_trio_ink_5_film_pac/. (Last accessed 1 July 2010). See also Adam Dawtrey, 'Universal pacts with Mexican trio Cuaron, del Toro, Inarritu to make five pics' (18 May 2007). Available at: http://www.variety.com/index.asp?layout=cannes2007&jump=story&articleid=VR1117965227. (Last accessed 5 July 2010). One film, *Rudo y cursi* (*Rough and Corny*) was released in 2008 in Mexico. It is directed by Carlos Cuarón, and stars Gael García Bernal and Diego Luna. It has been described as a comedy that shares similar characteristics with *Y tu mamá también*, and it tells the adventures of two half brothers who escape from their life working on a banana plantation through their success as footballers.

always have been, but there are new power configurations, and individual filmmakers are learning to play systems to their advantage.

National films
I would like to end with this category as it is important to remember that much film production is made for domestic markets, focuses on specifically local issues, and relies on modes of narration that may not appeal to international audiences. Academics and international audiences often have little awareness of large sectors of the world's film production, precisely because it is not transnational. At a recent talk at the University of Portsmouth the Oscar-winning young South African director and writer Tristan Holmes observed that some of most successful films in his country among the white population are conservative and patriarchal cinematic texts made for Afrikaaner audiences, with these films unknown in international film circles.[34] Likewise, specific political circumstances may ensure that films are not distributed overseas; for instance, North Korean propagandist films are also only made for a national population, and due both to the isolated and closed nature of the regime and the nature of the films themselves, are not part of any international distribution networks.[35]

In the case of Mexico, despite much talk of a New Wave of filmmaking and the emergence of high-profile filmmakers, much of the national cinematic culture does not reach foreign audiences. Few non-Mexicans beyond a minority of aficionados will be aware of the 200 movies featuring masked wrestlers (*luchadores*) popular from the late 1950s until the mid-1970s.[36] They are also probably unaware of the number of domestically successful romantic comedies, the critically acclaimed work of a generation of women directors, and the rise in films dealing with the historical roots of Mexican national identity. [37] These are examples of national films,

---

[34] Tristan Holmes' film *Elalini* won the award for the Best Foreign Film in the 2006 Student Academy Awards. His talk at the University of Portsmouth took place on 25 February 2009.

[35] For more information on North Korean film culture, see Hyangjin Lee, *Contemporary Korean Cinema* (Manchester: Manchester University Press, 2000). I am grateful to Ruth Doughty for this source.

[36] Robert Michael "Bobb" Cotter, *The Mexican Masked Wrestler and Monster Filmography* (Jefferson, NC: McFarland & Company, 2005); see also Evan Lieberman, 'Mask and Masculinity: Culture, Modernity, and Gender Identity in the Mexican *Lucha Libre* films of El Santo', *Studies in Hispanic Cinemas*, 6.1 (2009), 3–17.

[37] For an overview of these trends, see Miriam Haddu, 'The Power of Looking: Politics and The Gaze in Salvador Carrasco's *La otra conquista/The Other Conquest*', in

that do have some transregional and transcommunity reach, but have very limited international distribution.

All films are to a degree national, and there does not have to be conflict between the terms 'national and 'transnational'; that is, there is a link between national identities and storytelling at the heart of cinema, even when we take on board all the nuances and questioning of the national that transnational critical approaches have brought. Film may not be able to provide access to the truth of a nation, yet there is no film that does not have something to say about the discursive and mythical construction of national identities. As Shohat and Stam write, 'contemporary theory sees nations as narrated, in the sense that beliefs about the origins and evolution of nations crystallize in the forms of stories' ('Introduction', p. 9). What can perhaps be added is that there is a transnational element built into the national, as 'origins and evolutions' are characterised by intertextual influences and border crossings on many levels, as the above categories have demonstrated.

The above categories alert us to the importance of specificity in any discussion of 'transnational cinema'. It has proven easy to conflate the terms 'international', 'global', 'transregional' and 'transnational', while rejecting 'national' cinema as somehow no longer relevant. In addition, writers all too often do not indicate whether their use of 'transnational' refers to viewing practices, financing strategies, themes, modes of narration, influences or critical approaches, among other factors. I will give one final example from a Mexican context to demonstrate how breaking down the term can help in film analysis. *Y tu mamá también* is made by a predominantly Mexican cast and crew for the domestic and foreign markets and was mostly funded by private Mexican production companies. However, it was taken up by US and international distribution company 20th Century Fox, and thus entered global distribution and exhibition networks. It has transnational filmic influences ranging from Jean-Luc Godard to US teen sex comedies and the road movie, but subverts the generic conventions of the latter two in order to comment on aspects specific to Mexican culture. By utilising the categories in this way we do not have to decide whether it is a national or transnational film as it is both in industrial and textual terms. We can thus rescue the concept of 'transnational cinema' if we break it down into specific categories and apply them carefully in any analysis of film cultures.

Contemporary Latin American Cinema: Breaking into the Global Market, ed. Deborah Shaw (Lanham: Rowman and Littlefield, 2007), pp. 153–72.

4

Ibero-Latin American Co-productions: Transnational Cinema, Spain's Public Relations Venture or Both?*

TAMARA L. FALICOV

The definitive Ibero-American co-production model: Programa Ibermedia

Programa Ibermedia (hereafter, Ibermedia) is a co-production film fund sponsored by Spain, Portugal and 18 member countries in Latin America. Its purpose is to promote the development of projects directed towards the Ibero-American market. Funded primarily by and based in Spain, this film-funding pool receives funds from each member country to comprise an Ibero-American audiovisual fund. As of 2011 the Ibermedia member countries are Argentina, Bolivia, Brazil, Chile, Colombia, Costa Rica, Cuba, Dominican Republic, Ecuador, Guatemala, Mexico, Panamá, Peru, Portugal, Puerto Rico, Spain, Uruguay and Venezuela, with Guatemala entering as the newest member in 2009. Each country makes an annual commitment (minimum $100,000) to the collective fund. The countries then compete via production companies for backing in various programmes, such as a script development fund, a co-production fund, a training grant, funds for exhibition and distribution, and an international sales loan introduced in 2006 known as 'delivery'.

Ibermedia is a funding mechanism supervised by an Ibero-American organisation called CAACI (La Conferencia de Autoridades Audiovisuales y Cinematográficas de Iberoamerica, or Conference of Ibero-American

* This essay is a modified and expanded version of 'Programa Ibermedia: Co-Production and the Cultural Politics of Constructing an Ibero-American Audiovisual Space', *Spectator*, 27, no. 2 (2007): 21–30.

Audiovisual and Film Institutes). The heads of national film institutes established this fund in 1997 during a meeting on Margarita Island, Venezuela, creating a pool of funds for filmmakers and production houses to collaborate and compete for a chance to make a film, along with the help of one or more countries. Ultimately, the objective of Ibermedia is to promote the interchange of audiovisual professionals of member countries (see www.programaibermedia.com).

Ibermedia's function was described in a document produced during the Summit of the Americas in 1996:

> The question is how one could contribute to the development of an Ibero-American film and television industry that is competitive in the world market, that is oriented towards the technological future, that is capable of projecting its own culture, and in addition, will contribute to creating employment and reducing the commercial deficit.[1]

Ibermedia is modelled after the success of the European Union film programme, Eurimages, in which each country (Western, Central, and Eastern European) contributes to a fund in accordance with what the nation can afford. Ibermedia has also looked to the European Union's film production initiative, MEDIA Plus Programme, as a model. The idea of a pan-Ibero-American fund translates into an audiovisual market that is approximately 450 million strong. This helps overcome the inability of some countries to amortise production costs, especially in smaller Latin American countries.[2] Although Spanish is the second most common native language in the world, with approximately 330 million speakers, as a group they are sixth in terms of purchasing power.[3] As a result, people simply do not go to the cinema as often.[4]

In Ibermedia's case, Spain pays the highest sum per year—in 2008 this translated into roughly 3.3 million dollars, currently comprising over 50 per cent of the fund. Other countries each pay according to what they can afford. Argentina, for example, used to contribute $200,000 in 1998,

---

[1] Ibermedia, Summit of the Americas (Chile: November 10–11, 1996): p. x.

[2] Federación de Asociaciones de Productores Audiovisuales Españoles (FAPAE), 'Ibermedia' (Madrid: April 1997), p. 5.

[3] See Colin Hoskins, Stuart McFadyen and Adam Finn, *Global Television and Film: An Introduction to the Economics of the Business* (New York: Oxford University Press, 1997), p. 40.

[4] Lauren Kogan, 'The Spanish Film Industry: New Technologies, New Opportunities', *Film Historia*, XVI.1–2 (2006). Available at: http://www.publicacions. ub.es/bibliotecaDigital/cinema/filmhistoria/2006/Ensayo_TheSpanishFilmIndustry_ NewTechnologies_5.htm (Last accessed 28 January, 2011)

but after the post-2001 financial crisis, its contribution was reduced to $100,000. In fact, it was unable to pay the contribution in 2002, but by 2008, it was contributing $400,000.[5] Venezuela puts in $400,000 (2006 figures), and Brazil, which used to contribute $300,000 in 1998 is now the second-largest contributor, at $629,000. In 2006, Portugal contributed $300,000, and Mexico used to contribute $500,000, but since 2008 has fallen to $250,000. Since 2007, Chile contributes $150,000, and Colombia, Cuba and Uruguay each put in $100,000.[6]

All member countries are eligible to compete for the large sums of money that are awarded to film projects in various stages of completion. Ibermedia prides itself on the fact that all member countries have a chance of reaping large benefits (Fermin, personal interview). Development grants are awarded most typically to first-time filmmakers, as they provide workshop training funds to help the director improve upon and polish the script. The co-production fund is not as likely to be awarded to first-time projects, as only up to 50 per cent of the funding may be awarded by Ibermedia; the rest must come from additional financing sources. To meet the eligibility requirements for the co-production fund: films must be in Spanish or Portuguese; competition is for a loan, not a grant; and the director, actors, and technical crew must be from an Ibero-American country. Competitions were held annually until 2006 and are now held twice a year, until they revert back to once a year in 2012.

Since Ibermedia's inception, the majority of selected films have been completed and released, and many have gone on to win international prizes. From its inaugural year to 2003, 530 projects were selected; out of those, 104 were co-production projects, 137 were awarded distribution and promotional credits, 121 were awarded script-development grants, and 168 were given training grants for film professionals.[7] For the year 2000, $2.3 million was allotted to 23 projects, all of which cobbled together other forms of private and state funding.[8] In 2004, 32

[5]   Zuri Fermín, Ibermedia administrator, personal interview, 30 May 2003. Statistics about Argentina's payment history from the Secretaría General Iberoamericana (SEGIB) study, 'Programa Ibermedia, 1998–2008, Evaluacion'. Available at: http://www.segib.org/documentos/esp/IBERMEDIA_PDF.pdf (Last accessed 1 February, 2011).

[6]   Teresa Hoefert de Turégano, 'The International Politics of Cinematic Coproduction: Spanish Policy in Latin America', *Film and History*, 34.2 (2004) 19, with newer statistics by SEGIB: 22, see note 5 above.

[7]   'Ibermedia inicia una nueva etapa con la intención de dar mayor protagonismo a la distribución', *CINEinforme*, 43 (October 2003), 24.

[8]   '23 coproducciónes: Acuerdo para promover el cine iberoamericano', *La Nación* (Espéctaculos/Entertainment section), 23 October 2000, n.p.

co-production projects were funded, representing production companies from thirteen countries. A total of 4.2 million dollars was awarded. Out of the 32 projects, five were given to Spanish companies and eight involved Spain as a co-producer.[9] In 2008, a total of 6.5 million dollars were allotted during the two competitions during the year. In the first ten years of its existence (1998–2008), 250 Ibero-American films have had financial assistance from this film finance pool. Films that have benefited from Ibermedia funding include Emilio Mallé's *Rosario Tijeras* (Colombia/ Mexico/Spain/Brazil, 2005), Andres Wood's *Machuca* (Chile/Spain/UK/ France, 2004) and Lucrecia Martel's *La ciénaga* (*The Swamp*, Argentina/ France/Spain, 1999). Since 2003, a major emphasis for funding has been on the perennially weak distribution link Latin American film producers typically confront, due to the practical monopoly status that the US majors hold in Latin America. In order to confront this problem, Ibermedia offers a fund that assists distributors in subsidising the distribution of Latin American films throughout Ibero-America. For example, in 2004 Macondo Cine Video was given a subsidy to distribute the Uruguayan– Argentine co-production *Whisky* (Juan Pablo Rebella and Pablo Stoll) in Mexico. Similarly, Atlanta Films from Portugal was funded to distribute Lucrecia Martel's Argentine–Spanish film *La niña santa* (*The Holy Girl,* 2004).

Despite the focus on various grant competitions, the most popular fund and competition is the co-production competition, and this article will focus on that competition, which in 2003 accounted for 80 per cent of Ibermedia funding. ('Ibermedia inicia', 24) I will examine how this form of film finance has been utilised in the past decade. Specific co-productions will be analysed in terms of their themes and content to understand more fully how co-production funding might impinge upon a film's narrative. This essay will discuss the strengths and pitfalls of the case of Ibermedia.

What is a co-production?

Co-production is a funding model used as early as the 1920s.[10] European cinema has utilised this measure as a strategy to ensure distribution throughout the continent, and as a means of accruing production funding

---

9   'Ibermedia aprueba ayudas a la coproducción para 32 títulos, 13 de ellos con participación Española', *CINEinforme*, 45 (February 2005), 34.

10   Sharon Strover, 'Coproductions International' 1995: http://www.archives.museum. tv/eotvsection.php?entrycode=coproductions (Last accessed 26 February 2013).

through various state and private-sector funding outfits. As Baer and Long point out, the 1990s and 2000s have seen an outpouring of international co-productions due to their emblematic status as globalised products. They are 'financed by global capital, featuring international casts, shot in several countries and often several languages, and foregrounding the hybrid status of their production contexts in both their formal construction and narrative content'.[11]

In the case of Ibermedia, co-production is categorised as either "technical–artistic" or as a purely financial arrangement. The former implies that the amount a country invests determines the percentage of actors and/ or technicians that will work on a film. The latter category is a strictly financial arrangement that has no bearing on the artistic or technical aspects of production.

For example, Argentine director Fabián Bielinsky's film *El aura* (*The Aura,* 2005) was a financial co-production: Spain's Tornasol Films and France's Metropolitan Films had minority financial investments alongside Argentina's majority investment.[12] An artistic-technical co-production attempts to integrate actors from the co-producing countries into the narrative. Aristarain's *Martín* (*Hache*) (Argentina/Spain, 1997), typifies this arrangement. The story follows an Argentine teenager sent after a near drug overdose to spend time with his Argentine father, who is living in Madrid. The cast comprises an Argentine actor (Cecilia Roth), two Argentine–Spanish actors (Federico Luppi, who lives in Spain with dual citizenship, and Juan Diego Botto, born in Argentina, but who has lived in Spain since he was a child), and a Spanish actor (Eusebio Poncela). The bi-national narrative works as a natural bridge between the two countries and thus results as a credible co-production plot. These productions are considered 'natural' co-productions in the sense that their narratives lend themselves to this form of production.[13] This chapter will focus on the merits of and mistakes made in the use of the technical–artistic subcategory of co-production.

[11] Hester Baer and Ryan Long, 'Transnational Cinema and the Mexican State in Alfonso Cuaron's *Y tu mama tambien*', *South Central Review*, 21.3 (Fall 2004), 150–68 (p. 150).

[12] Alberto Signetto, Video Interview with Pablo Bossi, producer of *El Aura* (2004). Available at: http://www.makingofeuropa.net/makingclip.asp?documentID=924 (last accessed 20 January 2011).

[13] Doris Baltruschat, 'International TV and Film Co-Production: A Canadian Case Study,' in *Media Organization and Production*, ed. Simon Cottle (Thousand Oaks, CA: Sage Publications, 2003), p. 189.

There has been much debate regarding how co-produced films can have potentially damaging effects on the narrative content of films. In the European context, the term 'Europudding' describes the detrimental effect that occurs with attempts at constructing a pan-European culture, which may result in a polyglot mess. In Ibero-America, more than the issue of language (mainly Spanish and Portuguese), is the issue of economic differentials between Spain and the rest of Spanish-speaking Latin America. Rather than a Europudding, co-production might be seen as something akin to a 'Latin American' *molé* with a sprinkling of Spanish *manchego* cheese. In other words, some technical–artistic films have an 'added-on' or 'supplementary' feel to them when the Spanish actors present do not integrate well into the script. This differs from Spanish–Latin American co-productions of the 1930s and 1940s that included actors from many countries in a hybrid, 'tutti-frutti' configuration that incorporated the songs and dances of the respective countries.[14] Paul Julian Smith rightly observes that this choice of including cast and crew from both countries has been done in order to qualify a film as a 'national' picture in both countries and thus meet the criteria for state subsidies.[15]

A recent film that successfully integrates both nations into the narrative also illustrates these power dynamics between Spain and Latin America in the Spanish–French–Cuban co-production *Habana blues*, directed by Benito Zembrano (2005). This film not only won the Ibermedia co-production award, but it was also granted a MEDIA programme grant for €168,000 for its submission as a Spanish film, and support from Eurimages.[16] The plot revolves around two Cuban musicians who secure a recording contract from Spanish record producers. The film self-consciously raises issues of producing cultural products for the Spanish market in a scene where there is heated discussion between the Cubans and the Spaniards. A musician balks when he is told that the record is for the Spanish market and he must change a stanza in his song because it is 'too local'. One of the record producers explains that 'We have to think of our [Spanish and Latino] audience.... Business is business.' The filmmaker is ironically commenting on the contradictions that arise when

---

[14] Gerard Dapena, 'In Search of Gardel's Guitar: Representing the Transhispanic Musical Nation', paper delivered at the Second International Conference on Latin(o) American and Iberian Cinemas, University of Hawaii-Manoa, November 2005.

[15] Paul Julian Smith, 'Transatlantic Traffic in Recent Mexican Films', *Journal of Latin American Cultural Studies*, 12.3 (2003), 389–400.

[16] 'El programa MEDIA apoya 12 títulos presentes en las deferentes secciones del Festival de Cannes,' *CINEinforme*, 45 (April 2005), 46.

countries with more power, resources and influence 'collaborate' with smaller ones.

The film, refreshingly enough, does not result in a disjointed mix of Cuban and Spanish, due to its realistic rendering of life for Cubans during the 'Special Period' (following the fall of the Soviet Union). This film continues in the tradition of co-productions that Laura Podalsky notes register 'how nations define themselves against other nations'.[17] In *Habana blues*, in a later plot twist, the Spanish producers become beholden to their US parent company, which has stipulated that the Cuban band members must market themselves as dissidents for the US market. The tension revolves around a disingenuous and mercenary transnational record company and 'authentic' Cuban musicians with integrity.

How co-productions impinge on film narratives: the case of Spaniards in Latin America

A large percentage of co-productions are the 'technical–artistic' type, and many Latin American producers prefer to co-produce with Spain (in the case of Brazil, there is a common affinity to Portugal – a topic that exceeds the scope of this chapter). In addition to the financial incentive is a geographic one: co-producing with Spain gives these countries a gateway to Europe. The result? One finds the over-representation of Spanish actors in Latin American co-productions.

For the purposes of this study, it is possible to categorise, albeit unscientifically, various tropes of Spaniards typically found in contemporary co-productions. By delineating the various ways in which Spaniards enter into specific Latin American narratives, we find how it is that economic imperatives of funding can shape film narratives in specific ways. While I have tried to provide examples from Ibermedia-funded films, I have also included co-productions funded privately or through means other than Ibermedia. This list is by no means exhaustive. The following are examples of four common tropes: the sympathetic Spaniard, the Spanish anarchist, the evil or racist Spaniard and the Spanish tourist.[18]

[17] Laura Podalsky, 'Negotiating Differences: National Cinemas and Co-productions in Prerevolutionary Cuba', *The Velvet Light Trap*, 34 (Fall 1994), 68.

[18] Libia Villazana also explores typologies of the Spaniard in Spanish–Latin American co-productions in her article, 'Hegemony Conditions in the Coproduction Cinema of Latin America: The Role of Spain', *Framework*, 49.2 (2008), 73–7.

The sympathetic Spaniard

In Solveig Hoogesteijn's Ibermedia-funded Venezuelan–Spanish film *Maroa* (2005), Tristán Ulloa plays Joaquín, a youth orchestra teacher from Spain, who works in a reform school in Caracas. He notices the talent of street urchin Maroa (Yorlis Domínguez), and mentors her as she learns to play the clarinet. He is sympathetic to her plight and chided by Maroa about the fact that his foreigner status makes him 'clueless' about life on the streets in Venezuela. The presence of his character is somewhat unusual, as one does not often see foreigners helping truly disadvantaged children, but the director manages to turn him into an outsider character, and one that can relate to Maroa's marginal status as a street child. He then becomes a sacrificial lamb in that he gets deported back to Spain for his good intentions.

In an earlier film, Adolfo Aristarain's *Un lugar en el mundo* (*A Place in the World,* Argentina/Spain/Uruguay, 1992) the protagonist Hans (José Sacristán) is a good if disillusioned Spaniard who assists the Argentines Mario (Federico Luppi) and his wife, Ana (Cecilia Roth), who have decided to move to the rural province of San Juan, Argentina, after living in exile in Spain. The three work together to fight a ruthless landlord who tries to crush their newly formed wool cooperative.

The Spanish anarchist

The stereotypical Spanish anarchist can provide a left-leaning filmmaker with a character to act as a foil against other characters. Tzvi Tal discusses the image of the idealistic Spanish anarchist figures in both Puenzo's *La historia oficial* (*The Official Story,* Argentina, 1985) and Larrain's *La frontera* (*The Frontier,* Chile/Spain, 1991) as a way for the scriptwriter to discuss democratic ideals while simultaneously 'eliding the contradiction between the past revolutionary idealist and the present day pragmatism that the Left was facing at the time the film came out post-dictatorship'.[19] In other words, the ideals of the Left were safely embodied by the Spanish anarchist and the scriptwriter avoided having to invoke the recent leftist guerrilla legacies in Argentina and Chile. Neither film was funded by Ibermedia, but both films were assisted financially by Spanish national television, Television Española (TVE).

---

[19] Tzvi Tal, 'Viejos republicanos españoles y joven democratización latinoamericana: imagen de exilado en películas de Argentina y Chile: *La historia oficial* y *La frontera*', *Espéculo: Revista de estudios literarios,* 15 (2000), 7. Available at: http://www.ucm.es/info/especulo/numero15/tzvi_tal.html. (Last accessed 30 January 2011).

In Marcelo Piñeyro's *Caballos salvajes* (*Wild Horses,* Spain/Argentina, 1995) the character José, played by Héctor Alterio, is a self-proclaimed anarchist who lost family and retirement funds during the Argentine military dictatorship. He is characterised as Argentine, but his accent slips into Spanish throughout the film. When he calls himself an anarchist, the viewer may associate him with a Spanish émigré to Argentina, although this is never mentioned. In actuality, the actor Héctor Alterio was in exile in Spain for many years after 1974, when he received death threats from the Argentine paramilitary group the Triple A (Argentine Anticommunist Alliance), which had ties to the military government. He resided in Spain until the triumph of democracy in 1983, when he returned to Argentina. His grown children, both of them actors, live in Madrid. Marvin D'Lugo has noted how both Héctor Alterio and Argentine actress Cecilia Roth's 'star persona[s] have crossed over to both markets, which leads to the blurring of the national.'[20]

The evil/racist Spaniard

In Carlos Carrera's *El crimen del Padre Amaro* (*The Crime of Father Amaro,* Mexico/Spain/Argentina/France, 2002), Spanish actor Sancho Gracia plays the role of Father Benito Díaz, a priest in Mexico. Although he is painted as a corrupt individual, he is not framed any more culpably than any other questionably suspect character in the film, such as Padre Amaro himself, the local narco-traffickers, or the bishop. However, it is telling that the Spaniards are part of the decadent, morally suspect Catholic establishment. Although I have placed them in the 'evil Spaniard' category, others have commented that the presence of Spanish priests in Latin America has become 'naturalised' and that they symbolise neutral figures who are not out of the ordinary. Libia Villazana has commented on the fact that the Spanish priests in this film were a natural component of this co-production, as Spanish priests are commonplace throughout Latin America ('Hegemony', 77). The film received both a development grant and a co-production grant from Ibermedia.

Critics have noted that Maribel Verdú's character Luisa Cortés, in Cuarón's *Y tu mamá también* (Mexico, 2001) manipulates best friends by being a love interest to both of them and spurring them to jealousy. She is considered an allegory for the vampiric Spanish coloniser, sucking dry

---

[20] Marvin D'Lugo, 'The Geopolitical Aesthetic in Recent Spanish Films', *Post Script*, 21.2 (Winter–Spring 2002), 5. See also Juan Carlos González Acevedo, *Che, qué bueno que vinisteis: El cine argentino que cruzó el charco* (Barcelona: Editorial Dieresis, 2005).

the youth of Mexico (Baer and Long, 'Transnational Cinema', p. 162). This film was funded with private funds from Mexican companies, as was *Amores perros* (2000); both utilise lead Spanish female actors who are rising stars in their country. Interestingly enough, both characters embody tragic figures in the end – Luisa dies, and Valeria (the lead female character in *Amores perros*), who is a former supermodel, has a leg amputated, precipitating the end of her career. One might speculate that the directors were astute in hiring European actresses for a film that was to be marketed in Spain as well as Mexico. Emily Hind has suggested that perhaps there could be the category of the 'doomed Spaniard' as other Spanish characters have died in contemporary Mexican film.[21] One might consider that the directors/writers were wreaking a subtle but symbolic form of "Moctezuma's Revenge" on the (former) coloniser.

In Jeffrey Middents' work on Ibermedia co-productions, he finds that in some films such as Marcelo Piñeyro's *Plata Quemada* (*Burnt Money*, 2002), the presence of the Spaniard is represented in a harsh light (as in the case of Eduardo Noriega's character, Angel who plays a heroin-addicted assassin), but additionally, he is portrayed in a very feminised way. Middents notes that this 'feminisation' of the Spaniard both in terms of male and female characters serves to make them vulnerable in narratives of overarching *machista* themes. For example, in Peruvian director Francisco Lombardi's films, Spanish actresses often play roles that are 'coded as Spanish, and this serves to further marginalise her character within each narrative, thus highlighting the male homosocial relationships that dominate his [Lombardi's] work'.[22] Therefore, this feminised/vulnerable representation might also be conceptualised in the same vein as the trope of the 'doomed' Spaniard, which on some level could be seen as a form of resistance in a post-colonial interpretation by Latin American filmmakers (to be discussed in a later section).

An ugly side of Spaniards comes out in Adolfo Aristarain's *Lugares communes* (*Common Ground*, Spain/Argentina, 2002). Fernando and his wife Liliana (Federico Luppi and Spanish actor Mercedes Sanpietro) have flown to Madrid to visit their son and family, and Liliana, herself a Spaniard in exile in Argentina, has a conversation with her daughter-in-law, Fabiana (Yael Barnatán). During their discussion, Fabiana tells her

---

[21] Emily Hind, 'Provincia in Recent Mexican Cinema, 1989–2004', *Discourse*, 26.1–2 (2004), 26–45 (p. 43).

[22] Jeffrey Middents, 'Ibermediating National Cinemas', paper delivered at the Society for Cinema and Media Studies (SCMS), Philadelphia, March 2008.

mother-in-law how much she would like her to come to Madrid and help take care of the children, rather than an 'illiterate Ecuadorian maid, or an African immigrant'. She then exclaims, 'We are being invaded.'

The Spanish tourist

In Cuban films of the Special Period, there has been a sure fire means to incorporate Spanish actors (and other co-producers) in the image of the omnipresent tourist in Havana or Varedero Beach. There are many examples of this in contemporary Cuban cinema.[23] In the case of Alexis Valdés's *Un rey en la Habana* (*A King in Havana*, Cuba/Spain, 2005), the Spanish tourist who has arrived into town to marry the protagonist's sweetheart, is depicted as arrogant, spoiled, and ultimately, a buffoon.

Un rey en la Habana is told from the point of view of Papito (Alexis Valdés), who has forever loved Yoli (Yoleima Valdés), the girl next door. When she mistrusts him, she then meets Mr Arturo, an older Spanish tourist who comes to Havana bearing gifts for the whole family. True to the comedic genre, many family members discuss the way they will sell his gifts on the black market, and they aim to see how they can take him for all the money they can obtain from his clutches. The Spaniard is depicted in one scene bellowing that 'Spain is a superior country'. Clearly, the family is withstanding his obnoxious behaviour out of economic necessity. Moments later, when he tries to have a sexual encounter with Yoli, he has an overdose of Viagra, prompting a heart attack, and a frozen erection after death. His corpse is found that way, thus making his death a comical and undignified situation. This film, which parodies the unequal relationship between Cubans and tourists also reveals in a playful manner the urge Cubans might have to make the Spaniards look clownish and tactless. This form of parody signals a resentment of the economic and social power that tourists such as Spaniards might hold over their Cuban brethren's heads. As in the Cuban–German co-production *Hacerse el sueco* (Playing the Swede, Cuba/Spain/Germany, 2001), in which a German tourist disguised as a Swedish scholar pulls off a complicated robbery and thus is considered an unsavoury character, these depictions could be seen as a subtle form of challenge and resistance to the foreigner-Cuban power dynamic.

---

[23] A few examples are the Cuban co-productions *La vida es silbar* (*Life is to Whistle*, 1998), *Viva Cuba* (2005) and *Havana Blues* (2005).

Directors' strategies to confront these limitations

While some scriptwriters and directors are able to incorporate actors into storylines that are credible and natural, there are those who find ways around the restrictions or else poke fun at them. In one case, a director hired actors with dual citizenship to help meet technical–artistic investment requirements. For the Ibermedia-funded Chilean–Spanish–UK–French co-production *Machuca*, director Andrés Wood hired Federico Luppi, who has dual Spanish and Argentine citizenship, to play the part of an Argentine businessman who frequently has trysts in Santiago, Chile, with the main character's mother. It was a way to resolve the Spanish actor requirement while maintaining an appearance of verisimilitude to 1970s Chile.[24] Colombian director Víctor Gaviria plays a joke on his audience in *Sumas y restas* (*Addictions and Subtractions,* Colombia/Spain, 2004) when out of nowhere a random Spanish waiter appears in a scene in a Medellín restaurant. This was the director's ironic nod to some of the narrative awkwardness that has played out in the technical–artistic co-production realm. Thus, the trope of the 'random' Spaniard is now immortalised by Gaviria's film. Despite these occasional narrative flaws, many co-productions achieve credibility and box-office success with Ibermedia support.

Critical responses to Programa Ibermedia

Since the founding of this programme, academics and journalists have responded both favourably and critically to this programme's existence. For instance, José Moreno Domínguez describes how this initiative has worked to foster an Ibero-American integration which is sorely needed, given how few films from Latin American nations cross borders and are seen by their neighbours. By fostering co-productions, Domínguez argues that this gives countries an opportunity to interact artistically, professionally and economically. Nonetheless, he argues that during the fund's initial period from 1998–2005, there was much support for co-production funding and initiatives such as professional training. However, what was lacking was an emphasis on circumventing the hegemonic power that the US majors have on distribution.[25] He points out a glaring fact that

---

24 Victor Sánchez, Interview with the author, 6 July 2005.
25 José Manuel Moreno Domínguez, 'Diversidad audiovisual e integración cultural:

US film distributors account for 95 per cent of Colombia's sector. The second stage of Ibermedia's history runs from 2005 to 2008 (ending the year the article was written). During this period, Domínguez finds that funding decisions have more emphasis on assisting companies to circulate completed films (called 'delivery') in an effort to provide avenues for these films into global circuits such as film festivals, and in emerging markets such as helping Ibero-American production companies interface with Asian companies ('Diversidad', p. 113). For Domínguez, the larger hegemonic player is not Spain, but rather the US corporate system of film studios, exhibition and distribution, most commonly thought of as Hollywood. Lluís Bonet would concur with this argument in that he points out a major criticism waged at Ibermedia is their weak effort at confronting the monopoly that the US majors hold on distribution in Ibero-America in addition to the strong alliances that domestic exhibitors have with them.[26]

Ibermedia collaborations

In 2007, Programa Ibermedia teamed up with some of the most important Ibero-American film festivals, namely San Sebastian and the Guadalajara film festival to assist in funding post production initiatives such as San Sebastian's 'Cine en Construcción' programme. This competition provides post-production funds to a small number of Ibero-American films. By teaming up with prestigious film festivals such as these, Ibermedia then gains entry into important launching pads for film directors/ producers to gain distribution deals and garner important awards.

A 2010 initiative called 'Ibermedia TV' may have been created as a response to criticisms raised by scholars such as Néstor García Canclini and others who have observed that Ibermedia, in order that it truly be seen and recognised as a known cultural form in Ibero-America needed to reach a wider audience via broadcast (versus cable) television channels. In addition, in forging ties with television and other media that could also serve as a form of distribution and dissemination, Ibermedia would help gain Ibero-American cinema visibility. [27] Ibermedia TV began its first season

analizando el Programa Ibermedia', *Comunicación y sociedad, nueva época*, 9, (January–June 2008), 95–118.

[26] Lluís Bonet, 'Industrias culturales y desarrollo en Iberoamérica: Antecedentes para un debate', in Néstor García Canclini (ed.), *Iberoamérica 2002. Diagnóstico y propuestas para el desarrollo cultural* (México, Santillana, OEI, 2002).

[27] Néstor García Canclini, 'Cooperación, Diálogo: ¿Son las palabras más apropiadas?'

broadcasting a weekly selection of 52 films from the region on various public television channels throughout Latin America, Spain and Portugal. Selected by a panel of Latin American film experts, including Orlando Senna from Brazil, they include both Ibermedia-funded and non-funded productions. For example, the Bolivian film *Cuestión de fe* (*Question of Faith*, Marcos Loayza, 2001), *Taxi para tres* (*Taxi for Three*, Orlando Lubbert, Chile, 2001) and a film from the Dominican Republic, *Sanky Panky* (Enrique Pintor, 2007) were chosen to air for the first season. The programme's title, 'Nuestra TV/Nossa TV' is slated to continue running during the 2011–12 and 2012–13 seasons (see 'Ibermedia TV' on website for more information on films selected for all three seasons).[28]

Positive attributes of Programa Ibermedia

State-government funds allocated via film institutes often propagate cycles of veritable feasts or famine, depending on the economic situation and the cultural policies in place. This volatility stands in contrast to Programa Ibermedia, which has proven to be a stable and consistent model. For example, Uruguay has had problems paying the $100,000 member contribution, which has resulted in petitions, protests, and even threats of hunger strikes by filmmakers and members of the film sector. It is clear that Uruguay would not have as much success arranging funding without its involvement in a co-production fund of this sort. As Uruguayan producer Jorge Sánchez Varela points out:

> Undoubtedly, the Ibero-American producers realised that it is much more viable to work together on a project than each individually. And, in the case of Uruguay, it is even more notorious: a project solely funded by Uruguay is pretty difficult in trying to accumulate the resources, and then try to sell the project in the international market – this is because the internal market is not large enough to recoup the costs of even a pretty good film.[29]

V Campus Euroamericano de cooperacão cultural, Almada, Portugal (2007), p. 9. Available at http://www.redculturalmercosur.org/docs/Garcia-Canclini.pdf (Last accessed 30 January 2011).

    28 www.programaibermedia.com. This website is the most comprehensive way to access general information about the fund and its various competitions.

    29 Diego Barnabé, 'Uruguay puede quedar fuera del fondo Ibermedia para la producción audiovisual si no paga sus deudas' (Interview with José Sanchez Varela, Taxi Films, with participation by Elena Villardel, head of Programa Ibermedia), *Radio El Espectador*,

After resolving fiscal problems, Uruguay was reinstated into the programme in 2005. That year five projects were funded (two co-productions and three script development projects) totalling $260,000.[30] In 2003, in an effort to demonstrate how useful Uruguay's inclusion into Programa Ibermedia was on an economic level, filmmaker Walter Tournier explained that 'for every 100,000 dollars Uruguay contributes to the fund, it receives almost three times more from Ibermedia'. This, Tournier emphasised, is useful because it helps them gain more funding through co-production with other countries. Thus, he continued, 'if we get at least 150,000 dollars to make a film, with additional co-production funding, we should be able to locate 500,000 or 600,000 dollars total in funding, and these monies stay in the country'.[31]

Any country that wins a competition may select any other member country or countries with whom they would like to collaborate on a co-production. Therefore, one could conceivably only have the wealthiest countries on board consistently being chosen to collaborate. However, an economic advantage in turning to smaller, relatively poorer countries like Bolivia is their lower production costs. This helps their local film sector financially with the money spent during on-location production.

Ibermedia-funded projects have been remarkably successful in terms of winning awards and recognition. Some recent award-winning films include Javier Fuentes-Leon's *Contracorriente* (*Undertow*, Peru/Colombia/France/Spain, 2010), Pablo Trapero's *Carancho* (Argentina/Chile/France/South Korea, 2010) and Gerardo Chijona's *Boleto al paraíso* (*Ticket to Paradise*, Cuba/Spain/Venezuela, 2010). Actors working on Ibermedia films felt it helped them gain insights in interacting with professionals from other countries. Pablo Echarri, an Argentine actor who starred in a Spanish–Argentine–French co-production, *No debes estar aquí* (*You Shouldn't Be Here*, 2002), felt that working on co-productions was useful to his craft:

Uruguay, 17 May 2000. Available at http://www.espectador.com/text/clt05171.htm (Last accessed 30 January 2011).

30 'Ibermedia financiará cinco películas uruguayas,' *La República*, 25 November 2005. Available at: http://asoprod.org.uy/Ibermedia_financiara_cinco_peliculas_uruguayas.php. (Last accessed 28 January, 2011).

31 'Forma en que Uruguay cumplirá con Ibermedia no satisface a cineastas', *El Espectador*, 11 August 2003. Available at: http://www.espectador.com/principal/noticias/ind0311182.htm. (Last accessed 1 February, 2011).

You have to understand that an actor is not owned by his country. As part of your personal growth there is the possibility of widening your horizons. Spaniards like Argentine actors a lot. There are actors such as Héctor Alterio, Federico Luppi, that continue to be important in Spain. I cannot know what destiny lies ahead of me. I am not going to be hypocritical as to say: no, I will always stay here.[32]

Clearly, despite the narrative awkwardness that can arise as the result of including Spaniards in a Latin American storyline, it is still true that having a star vehicle from Spain, such as Immanol Arias or Tristán Ulloa, may translate into bigger box office numbers for a relatively wealthy market such as Spain.

Negative attributes of Programa Ibermedia

There have been some veiled criticisms of Programa Ibermedia in terms of transparency and power dynamics. For example, the literature on the judging procedure states that the representatives of each member country (generally film institute officials) who form part of the Ibermedia Intergovernmental Committee (Comité Intergubernamental Ibermedia, or CII) are responsible for judging projects on an annual basis. They also approve the budget and allocate it to the various competitions after they are reviewed by the Ibermedia staff (Unidad Técnica Ibermedia, or UTI). The staff is credited for checking the irregularities in the proposals, and are seen as the ones who make technical decisions.[33] There have been criticisms that the judging does not vary year to year, but the reality is that the judging is done by the heads of film institutes, who do vary every few years with shifts in government administrations. The CII not only evaluates which proposals will get funded, but also determines what amount of money each project will be awarded.

Another problem has surfaced with regard to Ibermedia's funding structure. On the one hand, it is considered to be democratic due to the

---

[32] Jon Apaolaza, 'Latin American Actors in Spain: The Vanguard in the Artistic Exchange', *The Thinking Eye: Latin American and Spanish Cinema Online* (August 2003). Available at: http://www.elojoquepiensa.udg.mx/ingles/revis_06/index.html (Last accessed 30 January 2011).

[33] Agustina Salvador, 'Varias banderas unidas para un mismo fin,' *La Nación* (Espectáculos/Entertainment section), 27 January 2005. Available at: http://www.lanacion.com.ar/674328-varias-banderas-unidas-para-un-mismo-fin (Last accessed 31 August 2012).

fact that each country pays what it can afford. On the other hand, the largest donor in the group is Spain, and the operation is housed in Madrid. While this expense might be seen as a donation to the fund and a clear benefit to the organisation, Spain is not simply acting altruistically. A member of the Spanish Agency for International Cooperation, Alberto García Ferrer, presented the results of a study conducted about Programa Ibermedia, claiming that Spain did not enter films into the competition, and that it merely gave funds to benevolently assist Latin American film workers accrue hours of labour through Ibero-American film projects.[34] This assertion was patently false, as Spain does participate and win in Ibermedia competitions.

In fact, Ibermedia administrators do not think it is problematic that Spain has more decision-making power due to its monetary contribution to the fund. Victor Sánchez felt that Spain's position was justified, stating that 'because Spain bankrolls one-half of the fund, there is nothing wrong with allowing it to have a bigger voice so as to oversee a lot of these projects'.[35] Moreover, the majority, that is 73 per cent (€1,863,137 – 2008 figures) of Spanish funds originate from the Agency for International Development Cooperation (AECID; Agencia Española de Cooperación Internacional para el Desarrollo) a development agency dependent on the Ministry of External Relations, whose sole purpose is to maintain positive relations with other countries, including former colonies. Making up the remainder of the funds, approximately 16 per cent of the funding (€400,000) came from the Spanish Film Institute (ICAA), while the remaining 12 per cent (€300,000) came from the agency 'Cultural Cooperation' (Cooperación Cultural), which forms part of the Spanish Ministry of Culture (SEGIB study, 'Programa Ibermedia, 1998–2008, Evaluación, pp. 21–2). In essence, Programa Ibermedia is seen by the Spanish as an avenue to gain prestige through its cultural collaboration with Latin America. As a point of comparison, the European co-production fund Eurimages has also been criticised in much the same way, except that critics allege that Eurimages is an extension of the French system, which has given French producers an unfair advantage.[36]

34 Alberto Garcia Ferrer, 'Cine, televisión y cooperación iberoamericanos', lecture given at the Universidad 3 de Febrero on 30 August, 2006.

35 Victor Sánchez, Interview with the author, 30 May 2003.

36 Angus Finney, The State of European Cinema: A New Dose of Reality (London: Cassell, 1996).

Although Latin Americans may feel that Spain's involvement reeks of
a past paternalistic relationship and a present attempt at neocolonialism,
this is partially – but not completely – without merit. For one, Spain
does, in the end, lose money in this endeavour (to be explained below),
but it gains in terms of gaining prestige for assisting in the production
of quality, award-winning films. Ibermedia administrator Victor Sánchez
opined, given the past colonial relationship between Spain and Spanish-
speaking Latin America, the following sentiment:

> I am a Spaniard. I am not going to completely trash my culture, but it
> is true, perhaps we are trying to redeem ourselves for historical debts
> we owe to the region. But when countries in Latin America do well
> via stable economies and healthy film industries; that helps Spain too.
>   (Interview with Author, 2003)

In his view Spain has been trying to redeem itself in the eyes of Latin
America for the five hundred years since it first colonised the region.
Although it is probable that Spain has set up collaborations in the realm
of culture in an attempt to rectify past wrongs, this must be situated in the
global economic context: Spain maintains a distinct monetary advantage
when it co-produces with poor Latin American nations such as Cuba or
Bolivia. Clearly, the cost of making a film in those locales is far more
economical for Spanish producers. Nonetheless, Spain's involvement with
Ibermedia is said to be a 'loss leader' in this proposition. The organisation
formulated statistics in 2005 that demonstrated that in fact, to that point in
time, Spain had lost money in this film fund proposition. It found that the
countries that put in a smaller annual contribution had a greater benefit in
the long run. According to the organisation, Spain gets less money than it
puts in: Peru and Bolivia get $1.70 for every $1.00 that Spain contributes,
Brazil gets $1.18 for every $1.00 that Portugal contributes, and the rest
of the member nations gain $1.60 for every $1.00 contributed by Spain
(Victor Sánchez, Interview, 6 July 2005).

The bottom line is that Spain still maintains the largest film industry
in Ibero-America, and Latin America as a whole is the largest market.
Thus, while Spain has an obvious agenda for their heavy involvement
with Ibermedia, it has proven to be the most beneficial and successful
film finance pool the region has currently. In Brazil's case, there are often
Brazil–Portugal co-productions due to the language affinity, but Portugal
serves more as a gateway country than an economic resource.

Libia Villazana argues that there is a major loophole in the regulations stating who may have access to Ibermedia film funding. Despite clear rules stating only *independent* film production companies are eligible to apply, Villazana points out that multimedia conglomerates such as Argentina's Patagonik (a company that is 30% owned by Buena Vista International, or Disney, partially owned (30%) by Spain's Telefonica Media (one of the largest telecom companies worldwide), and 30% by Artear Argentina, the television branch of the multimedia conglomerate Grupo Clarín, and owners of channel 13, Artear) has managed to secure Ibermedia loans (and prestige) when technically they were not eligible to do so. Films such as Marcelo Piñeyro's *Kamchatka* (Argentina/Spain, 2002) and Julia Solomonoff's *Hermanas* (*Sisters*, Argentina/Brazil/Spain, 2005) were produced by Patagonik. According to Villazana, when she asked Elena Villardel, the head of the Ibermedia film office about this discrepancy, Villardel blamed the INCAA, the Argentine National Film Institute, for not realising that Patagonik was creating smaller production company names under which to apply for funding (Villazana, 'Hegemony', pp. 69–70). Therefore, in terms of transparency, there have been reports that funding has been misappropriated.

Ibermedia can be considered a victim of its own success. Countries such as France, Italy, and even the US studio cartel, the Motion Picture Association of America (MPAA), have requested membership in Ibermedia, but Spain felt that it would compromise the spirit of the Iberian and Latin American aspect of the fund.[37] They feel threatened by these other countries' participation, even if it would mean an increase in the funding pool.

Outgrowths of Ibermedia

Other Latin American nations from Central America have been excluded from the fund due to fiscal constraints. In 1998 Costa Rica pledged $50,000 to Ibermedia, but had to withdraw the next year. When it became clear that the annual membership cost of $50,000 was prohibitive for Central American countries, the CAACI allowed these countries to pool $50,000 to enter the fund collectively, but stipulated that they had access to every competition except for the co-production fund. At that point in

[37] Norma Vidal-Villegas, 'La salida natural para el cine español es Iberoamérica', *El Economista* (2000). Available at http://www.americaeconomica.com/repor/ncine.htm (Last accessed 23 January 2011).

time, none of the countries agreed to this proposal, however, in 2006, Panamá joined, followed by Costa Rica in 2008. These countries, along with Guatemala (joined in 2009), comprise the Central American countries that have joined Ibermedia to date. Costa Rica, in its second year of funding was already able to reap the benefits of membership. In 2009, five film projects, one by veteran filmmaker Oscar Castillo, and others from first-time directors were selected for co-production funding amounting to $215,000 dollars. Laura Pacheco, the vice-minister of Culture in Costa Rica stated that 'being a member of Ibermedia is essential for the development of cinema in Costa Rica'.[38]

For those countries who are not members of Ibermedia, and for those who are, there emerged an excellent alternative film funding mechanism called CINERGIA, an organisation created in 2004 by the head of a private film school in Costa Rica, María Lourdes Cortés. Cortés pooled together funds from her university, Veritas; the Hivos Fund, a Dutch foundation; the Foundation for New Latin American Cinema (founded by Colombian Nobel Prize laureate Gabriel García Márquez) and the Gothenburg Film Festival Fund. Based in Costa Rica, it has the purpose of creating a Central American version of Ibermedia. Member countries include Belize, Costa Rica, El Salvador, Guatemala, Honduras, Nicaragua, Panamá, and Cuba.

This fund grew out of the realisation that Central American countries needed a smaller regional fund to help producers professionalise more before competing against larger industries such as Argentina and Brazil.[39] Cortés observed that the smaller member countries of Ibermedia had a harder time competing against the more developed ones. For instance, Puerto Rico, which became a member in 2002, was not awarded a co-production credit until 2004 due to logistical and monetary problems.[40] CINERGIA has helped Central American filmmakers not only financially, but also by inviting directors to participate in screenwriting workshops, where they meet well-known distributors and producers from other parts of Latin America and Europe. CINERGIA hopes to encourage the creation of a regional pan-American source of collaboration.

[38] Natalia Rodríguez y Prensa MCJ, 'Cinco proyectos de cineastas nacionales escogidos por Ibermedia', 21 July, 2009, *Red cultura*. Available at: http://www.redcultura.com/php/Articulos293.htm) (Last accessed 13 January, 2011)

[39] María Lourdes Cortés, Interview, 24 November 2005.

[40] Velda Gonzáles, Sub-Director of Programming, Puerto Rico Film Commission, email correspondence, 30 October 2006.

Cortés notes that CINERGIA has been recently strengthened by having some countries join Ibermedia; it is ensuring that some of these film projects will be funded and completed.[41]

New changes in Ibermedia's operations

In late 2011 Ibermedia announced some changes to its procedures. As mentioned previously, beginning in 2012, the call for competition will no longer be twice yearly, but annually. Moreover, the fund categories of film exhibition and 'delivery' will be terminated. The distribution competition will be reformulated, and a minimum and maximum grant amount will be established for fiction and documentary film projects. For feature fiction films, the maximum to be awarded is $150,000 and the minimum is US$80,000. There is no minimum for the documentary category, but the maximum allowable amount is $100,000. Finally, the rules were modified in terms of adjudicating the film projects. For 2012, each member country will nominate two projects for funding consideration, which will be automatically awarded. The Ibermedia staff (UTI) will ensure that all applications conform to the regulations, and for the preselected co-production competition, an expert panel composed of representatives of each member country will evaluate the co-production submissions and proffer advice about strengthening the projects and determining funding awards.[42]

Conclusion

Programa Ibermedia remains the most successful film finance pool in Latin America. Nonetheless, it is a state-administered film fund like those in Europe that do not transcend problems of paternalism and the inherent power dynamics that surface when there are inequalities of power and resources. Still, the fund has tried to be democratic, and to date there have been films initiated or produced from every member country, no matter how small. Ibermedia's support of technical–artistic productions has made it complicit in the problem of how economics can have a hand in shaping

41 María Lourdes Cortés, email correspondence, 31 January 2011.
42 'El Programa Ibermedia anuncia cambios para 2012' LatAmCinema.com, 7 December, 2011. Available at: http://www.latamcinema.com/noticia.php?id=3862, Last accessed 31 August 2012.

culture to meet its directives: the brief overview of Spanish character tropes in Ibero-American film is the beginning of a more comprehensive study of how these narratives of cultural collaboration can work seamlessly or lack credibility.

5

Building Latin American Cinema in Europe: Cine en Construcción/ Cinéma en Construction

NURIA TRIANA TORIBIO

On 26 and 27 of March of 2009, the famous Latin American Film Festival in Toulouse, France (Rencontres Cinémas d'Amérique Latine de Toulouse (ARCALT)) celebrated its yearly edition. Within it, a series of independent Latin American film industry professionals presented their films-in-progress to a very special and influential audience. This audience was made up of a group of industry professionals, festival programmers, distributors and members of cultural institutions in France who had the power to award enough funds to bring these film projects to a post-production stage or ensure that films would be seen widely in France and, therefore, by a much larger audience than most filmmakers outside the main Hollywood-dominated distribution channels might realistically expect.

Meanwhile, between 22 and 23 September, in the Basque city of Donostia/San Sebastián (Spain), as part of the 57th 'Festival International de Cine de Donostia–San Sebastián/ Donostiako Nazioarteo Zinemaldia' (18–26 September 2009; hereafter, Zinemaldia), different independent filmmakers had the opportunity to undergo the same process of being selected by a jury of film professionals and representatives of Spanish cultural institutions, including in this case, the Instituto Cervantes and Casa de América. There were also scouts for films from major festivals such as the Cannes International Film Festival.[1]

---

[1] See http://www.cinelatino.com.fr/fr/cineconst/cc13.htm. (Last accessed 23 May 2010).

Cine en Construcción is an initiative of the 'Recontres Cinémas d' Amérique Latine', which was later adopted by Zinemaldia in 2002 and subsequently forged by these two festivals into what it is today: a competition for development funds that makes possible the financing and completion of independent Latin American projects including those of Brazilian filmmakers.[2] Its main objective is to bring them to the stage of post-production and, in some cases, to help them be distributed in Europe – to this effect, the French CICAE (Conféderation Internationale des Cinémas d'Art & Essai), offers a prize which enables a film to be shown in the thousand cinemas of the AFCAE (Association française des Cinémas d'Art & Essai) network in France and then abroad, and the Spanish *Instituto Cervantes* takes prize-winning films to its sites worldwide.

This project launches two annual 'convocatorias' or calls for projects (one in March/April at Toulouse, and one in September at San Sebastián). The success of this contest for post-production funds and help with distribution and exhibition is palpable. Their achievements so far are summarised at http://www.cinelatino.com.fr:

> From the start of Cine en Construcción in 2002 and in 16 sessions (8 in Toulouse and 8 in San Sebastian): 88 projects at the stage of post-production have been shown to professional audiences. 77 were brought to the final stages, 4 were not, 1 is still in the postproduction process. 6 from the latest meeting (September 2009) are in the last stages. 13 films were selected for Cannes Film Festival. 23 films have found distribution in France and 12 in Spain. 8 of the selected new directors have attended the 'Résidence de Cannes' (Cinéfondation) after taking part in Cine en Construcción.[3]

Among the films that have been finished with the funds provided and have been selected subsequently by other prestigious festivals such as Cannes,

---

[2]   As well as the information obtained from official websites of both festivals and Cine en Construcción itself and the additional pages for Cine en Construcción in Clubcultura and Facebook, my research has benefited enormously from the generous help provided by Marina Díaz López, from the Instituto Cervantes in Madrid (November 2007) and from an email interview with José María Riba, who was involved in the creation of Cine en Construcción and worked for the initiative at Zinemaldia until March 2008. Linda Pariser (director of ¡Viva! Spanish and Latin American Film Festival at Cornerhouse, Manchester (UK) from 1994 to 2008) offered her insights into the project. My deepest thanks to them.
[3]   http://www.cinelatino.com.fr/dossiers/dossiers.php?val=103_cine+construccion +17 (Last accessed 23 May 2010).

are *Una novia errante* (*A Stray Girlfriend*, Ana Katz, 2007, Argentina/ Spain) and *El baño del Papa* (*The Pope's Toilet*, Enrique Fernández and César Charlone, 2005, Uruguay/Brazil/France) which in 2007 were shown in Cannes' official section 'Un Certain Regard'. Moreover, *El baño del Papa* was chosen to be Uruguay's submission to the 2008 Academy Awards or Oscars.[4] Other great successes which also started as Cine en Construcción projects are *Historias mínimas* (*Minimal Stories*, Carlos Sorín, 2002, Argentina) and *Iluminados por el fuego* (*Blessed by Fire*, Tristan Bauer, 2005, Argentina), which won the Spanish Goya for the best non-Spanish film in the Spanish Language in 2004 and 2006 respectively. Consequently, Cine en Construcción has now secured an entry as an important date in the calendar of independent filmmakers in Latin America and this has meant that more partners have been attracted to the venture.[5]

This support for Latin American cinema is far from merely symbolic, even if it is not very substantial, given the expensive nature of filmmaking. There is a range of available grants and prizes that vary from year to year. For instance, the winner in Toulouse in 2008 received a €4,000 grant from the National Film Centre (Le Centre National de la Cinématographie (CNC)) in order to carry out post-production in France. In the same year, the company Mac Guff Ligne offered montage and special effects, and the creation of soundtrack and the company Médiavision offered a publicity campaign valued at €20,000.[6] Zinemaldia provided even more prizes than Toulouse up to 2009, the main one being bringing a film project to completion, including post-production, whatever the cost. Prizes such as these can make a substantial difference to projects and are most welcomed by filmmakers themselves.

Mikel Olaciregui, Zinemaldia Festival director from 2001 to 2010, argues from his experience that new technologies offer new possibilities for filmmakers in the region:

> [There] are a lot of interesting movies being made in Latin America thanks to the use of digital cameras, and now through the Films in

4   http://www.clubcultura.com/noticias/leer.php?not_id=5046 (Last accessed 23 May 2010).
5   For a full list of partners see: http://www.clubcultura.com/cineenconstruccion/ historia.html. (Last accessed 23 May 2010). See also http://www.sansebastianfestival. com/es/cineenco.php?id=169 (Last accessed 24 May 2010).
6   See http://www.cinelatino.com.fr/fr/cineconst/cc13.htm (Last accessed 18 March 2008).

Progress (*Screen International*'s translation for Cine en Construcción) awards, and with the help of Spanish post-production companies, we can assist these film-makers in completing and showing their films.[7]

It is not negligible for these Latin American filmmakers that in many cases their films would return to the festival after winning the respect of these first gatekeepers, the jury of Cine en Construcción, as well as being selected for other even more prestigious festivals. Evans reports:

> Last year's Films in Progress award winners are also screening in the *Horizontes [Latinos]* section. They include Ana Katz's Argentinean film *A Stray Girlfriend/Una novia errante*, Luis Vera's Chilean political drama *Fiestapatria* and the taut relationship movie *The Milky Way/A via láctea* by Brazilian Filmmaker Lina Chamie.
>
> (Evans, 'Latin Lovers', p. 19)

This kind of exposure in a FIAPF Category A International Festival such as Zinemaldia can generate an interest in the media and can prove to be vital for the future of an independent film. Finding a place in the alternative distribution system that international film festivals constitute and perhaps the only other channel for distribution outside the Hollywood and exhibition systems, cannot be underestimated.[8] As Evans states, 'San Sebastian attracted more than 1,700 delegates plus a further 1,500 press' (p. 19) in 2007 alone.

The fact that any prize awarded through Cine en Construcción will allow a film to circulate and be marketed as 'a San Sebastian award winner' is

---

[7] Chris Evans, 'Latin Lovers', *Screen International*, 1612, 21–27 September 2007, pp. 19–21.

[8] La Fédération Internationale des Associations des Producteurs de Film or FIAPF is an association of television and film producers that grew out of an earlier group of the same name in the 1950s. Its current incarnation started in 1977. FIAPF has, among other roles, that of sorting out the dates of film festivals so that overlap does not occur and participating in the process of jury selection, screening facilities and upholding quality level. This organisation has awarded 'A category' to a group of festivals and this allows them to be international and award prizes in competition. It is their concern that the dates of these A festivals do not coincide. These are, in chronological order, Berlin, Mar del Plata, Cannes, Shanghai, Moscow, Karlovy-Vary, Locarno, Montreal, Venice, San Sebastian, Tokyo and Cairo. From May 2003 Andrés Vicente Gómez has been its president. See http://www.fiapf.org/. Many film critics do not consider this group of festivals as the most significant. For instance, filmmaker and former festival director Mark Cousins qualifies FIAPF's list as 'pointless'. See Mark Cousins, 'Widescreen on Film Festivals', in *Film Festival Yearbook 1: The Festival Circuit*, ed. Dina Iordanova and Ragan Rhyne (London: Wallflower Press, 2009), pp. 155–8.

not without significance. As Thomas Elsaesser notes, 'No poster of an independent film can do without the logo of one of the world's prime festivals, as prominently displayed as Hollywood productions carry their studio logo'.[9] These 'badges of honour' in the form of festival logos are part of what Liz Czach has named 'critical capital' (adapting the concept of 'cultural capital' coined by Pierre Bourdieu), and which she defines as 'the value that a film accrues through its success in the festival circuit'.[10] The logo of Cine en Construcción itself has become a coveted emblem, which is included in the participant films' publicity and the credits.

Finally but no less importantly, are the networking opportunities that attending Zinemaldia and being in San Sebastian to take part in Cine en Construcción provide filmmakers and which are also highly valued by independent directors. Lina Chamie tells Evans that 'Films in Progress is proving vital for films like mine looking for completion funding and advice from the industry about gaining international recognition' (Evans, 'Latin Lovers', p. 19).

Many paths to follow

> Despite the omnipresence of film festivals, there has been very little published on film festivals that is based on a systematic, academic study. The most common type of festival publication recounts the history of one selected film festival. These publications are often realized in coop-eration with the festival organization (...) or are dedicated to influential directors and/or tend to focus on glamour, scandals and stars.[11]

We must bear in mind that Cine en Construcción is a competition created and based within film festivals. As such, it shares much with these events and our understanding of its workings has to be guided by the possi-bilities for development that these events allow. In order to view Cine en Construcción within this context, we need perhaps to step back and consider the festival phenomenon in itself and where the work of cultural

---

9 Thomas Elsaesser, *European Cinema Face to Face with Hollywood* (Amsterdam: Amsterdam University Press, 2005), p. 87.

10 Liz Czach, 'Film Festivals, Programming, and the Building of a National Cinema', *The Moving Image*, 4.1 (2004), 74–88 (p. 82).

11 Marijke de Valck, *Film Festivals: From European Geopolitics to Global Cinephilia* (Amsterdam: University of Amsterdam Press, 2007), p. 16.

and cinema researchers is taking us in order to understand fully the value
and role of initiatives such as the one analysed in this chapter.

Studying film festivals has evolved from the situation described by
de Valck in her monograph *Film Festivals: From European Geopolitics
to Global Cinephilia*. The epigraph at the start of this section quotes
her describing the type of publication that used to be common before
researchers such as her started to transform the field. Nowadays, the
'burgeoning field' [12] of film festival studies has become a central part of
the transnational and cosmopolitan current in Film and Screen Studies.
If this trend keeps its momentum and this phenomenon continues to be
matched by a continuing interest in research related to the organisational
and economic factors involved in the cinema industry, it is going to
be increasingly usual to find research focusing on the artistic, cultural,
economic and political roles that film festivals have played and are likely
to play in the future as some of the oldest and most enduring institutions
for transnational strategies.

Since festivals embody the idea of a confluence of nations, thinkers
who reflect on the changing uses of culture in the era of globalisation,
for instance George Yúdice, are attracted to the concept of the festival to
illustrate the extent to which the transnationalisation of cultural industries
mirrors the evolution of other industries affected by transnationalisation:

> Nowadays, a film or artistic festival is to a large extent as international
> as the clothes we wear or the cars we drive, whose parts are made of
> steel manufactured in one country, electronic parts from another, with
> leather or plastic from a third and all of them assembled in countries
> different from the ones above. [13]

As well as such an increase in number, the possible theoretical avenues
that underpin the study of film festivals are many. Another pioneer in
this field of research, Elsaesser, points out a few 'strategies of access' in
his own work on the subject and suggests that 'the film festival circuit
presents both a theoretical challenge and a historical missing link in our
understanding of European cinema, not just since 1945, but since the
demise of the historical avant-garde in the 1930s' (Elsaesser, *European*

---

[12] Marijke de Valck and Skadi Loist, 'Film Festival Studies: An Overview of a
Burgeoning Field', in *Film Festival Yearbook 1: The Festival Circuit*, ed. Dina Iordanova
with Ragan Rhyne (London: Wallflower Press, 2009), pp. 179–215.

[13] George Yúdice, *El recurso de la cultura: usos de la cultura en la era global*
(Barcelona: Gedisa, 2002) p. 32 (my translation).

Cinema, p. 83). Although he insists on the Europeanness of the original phenomenon, it is important to point out here that most of the scholars who have been showing an interest in the different possibilities that the study of film festivals offer are not based in Europe: for instance, Clara Kriger in Argentina, Kay Armatage and Liz Czach in Canada, Vanessa Schwartz, Jeffrey Ruork, J. David Slocum, Toby Lee and Tamara Falicov in the USA. Moreover, there are many journalists and film researchers based in Asia or working on Asian cinemas who have trained the spotlight on crucial festivals such as the Pusan International Film Festival or Hong Kong International Film Festival (for instance, Ruby Cheung).

Many of these writers and scholars combine scholarly work and involvement in festivals themselves, for instance Armatage and Czach have worked for Toronto International Film Festival and this insider knowledge of the festival's organisation is transferred into their research. In Europe, Marijke de Valck and Skadi Loist in Amsterdam host and disseminate research on festivals through the *Film Festival Research Network*. In the UK, Felicia Chan, Janet Harbord, Lucy Mazdon and Julian Stringer have been looking at the festival phenomenon from different angles since the 1990s.

As these scholars' work indicates, we can expect a multitude of different paths and theoretical frameworks to be applied to these events/phenomena, because film festivals are, as Harbord proposes, 'mixed spaces crossed by commercial interests, specialized knowledge and tourists trajectories'.[14] But also because festivals themselves are of different kinds: some are competitive and international, some of them include events to attract producers and distributors of film, some are simply showcases without prizes and some are, as Elsaesser puts it, 'festivals of festivals' (*European Cinema*, p. 87) and show a selection of what other festivals have shown.

The activities or initiatives attached to them are multifarious and over-determined too. It is in such a context that Cine en Construcción must be understood, as we will see later. In order to explain the multiple roles that these talent contests or funding initiatives have and the many masters whom they serve, we need to uncover a few details about the history of these initiatives.

As de Valck explains, the path that led to the creation of talent contests such as Cine en Construcción started at the end of the 1960s, when festivals were affected by the events of 1968. The ripples of the cultural, social

---

[14] Janet Harbord, *Film Cultures* (London: Sage, 2002), p. 60.

and political upheavals that took place in Paris in May that year reached the Cannes Film Festival with the effect of both disrupting the festival's functioning and jolting its participants and organisers into discarding their past role as contributors to showcases of national cinemas 'too focused on stars and prizes' (de Valck, *Film Festivals*, p. 62).

As a result of these transformations, at the end of the 1960s, festivals became sites of political discussion and adopted the discourse of the cinephile directors and critics, who expected film festivals to become the vehicle of transit of the New Cinemas movement and effect 'a global reconsideration of the role of film festivals now that the status of cinema and film directors had grown' (de Valck, p. 62). The consequence of these new priorities was long-lasting, as de Valck explains:

> After the upheavals of 1968 and 1971, the festival programs were opened up to world cinema. Festival programmers started scouting for quality productions around the globe, looking for discoveries and new waves. They did not have to feel restricted by the borders that had previously been set by channels of diplomacy or nationalist biases and the festival programs became more diverse as a result.
>
> (*Film Festivals*, p. 94)

This transformation, connected with a new political agenda, was adopted by the local cinephiles of the 1960s generation as eagerly as the context in which each particular festival took place allowed for.[15] For example, it has to be pointed out at this stage that the two A-class Spanish-speaking festivals could not pursue this political agenda for long or showcase New Cinemas unfettered. Tamara Falicov observes how the Festival Internacional Cinematográfico de Mar del Plata 'ceased under the succeeding military dictatorships with the attendant censorship and economic disasters' (Falicov, *Cinematic Tango*, p.110) between 1970 and 1995. Zinemaldia (then Festival Internacional de San Sebastián) was also affected by censorship and state control as the freedom of speech was curtailed in Spain under Francisco Franco's dictatorship (1939–1975).

Within those festivals which took place in democratic societies, the new political and world-cinema priorities in festival organising meant that soon they were all competing with each other for that undiscovered gem

---

[15] See Tamara Falicov, *The Cinematic Tango: Contemporary Argentine Film*, (London: Wallflower, 2007). See also Nuria Triana Toribio, 'El festival de los cinéfilos transnacionales: Festival Cinematográfico Internacional de la República Argentina en Mar del Plata, 1959–1970', *Secuencias: Revista de historia del cine*, 25 (2007), 25–45.

of Iranian cinema or that new Taiwanese director. The fact that so many festivals were after new, original world films led to a new development that de Valck summarises thus:

> Festivals, in their turn, realized that they could distinguish themselves from other festivals not only by means of discovering of talents from established film countries, but also via new cinemas from developing film countries. Because financial resources for producing such films were limited in many of these new countries (sic), international film markets like the one in Cannes were used to find interested investors, close (co-) production deals and secure other types of funding.
>
> (de Valck, *Film Festivals,* p. 94)

The next stage, as de Valck further explains, was to support talent that was curtailed not simply by economic constraints but also by political ones.[16]

> The anti-government nature or anti-authoritarian inclination of most cinematic movements created the demand for independent platforms to accommodate the young, critical voices without censorship. Film festivals satisfied this demand and also developed the ambition to deploy careful programming to intervene directly in the international political debates and participate in film culture. (…) Western film festivals took over the task of supporting (the visibility) of political cinemas from other parts of the globe. (de Valck, *Film Festivals,* p. 178)

These two factors, seeking funding and seeking political freedom, combined themselves when one of the festivals which undertook the mission in its programming, International Film Festival Rotterdam, created the Hubert Bals Fund in memory of its charismatic and influential director. This initiative signalled the 'emergence of specialized festival funds in the contemporary international film festival circuit' (de Valck, *Film Festivals,* p. 180). The Hubert Bals Fund, as de Valck points out, supports young talent from economically weak film industries whose films 'are formally innovative' (p. 180) and in doing this, aids filmmakers who in their own countries would run the risk of encountering censorship problems, alongside economic ones.

---

[16] Many international film festivals continue to see their role as political platforms. For a discussion on how this engagement with politics takes place in the present see Screen Staff, 'Festivals Feel the Political Heat,' *Screen International*, 1704, 2–8 October 2009, pp. 10–11.

Cine en Construcción shares many traits with initiatives such as the Hubert Bals Fund but it also explores the potential that the film markets offer. José María Riba, one of the founders of Cine en Construcción, declared in 2008 that:

> Rotterdam para mí fue un ejemplo en general. No tanto el fondo Hubert Bals, que se enfoca en el desarrollo de proyectos que serán películas futuras, como el CineMart que organizan.

> Rotterdam was an inspiration for me. Not so much for the Hubert Bals Fund, because it focuses on developing projects that will one day become films, but more for the CineMart they organize.[17]

While acknowledging the inspiration that other specialised festival funding initiatives provided, Riba clarified that:

> [E]l terreno de las ayudas a escritura y a desarrollo de proyectos está muy cubierto en festivales y foros de todo el mundo, en cambio Cine en Construcción sigue siendo el único lugar donde compiten películas ya rodadas. (Riba, email interview, n.p.)

> The business of enabling scriptwriting workshops and developing projects is well catered for by many festivals and fora throughout the world, however, Cine en Construcción is still the only place where movies that have been filmed [but not completed] can compete.

The remit of the activities of Cine en Construcción has expanded over the years to enable access to information about their award winners as well as on the situation and trends of cinemas in Latin America via their different websites and web-networks in France and Spain, such as their site in the Rencontres Cinémas d'Amérique Latine de Toulouse (ARCALT) , their site in Zinemaldia, as well as the site dedicated to showcasing the participant films and which is housed by the cultural on-line magazine *ClubCultura*, owned by FNAC Spain.[18]

Another form in which Cine en Construcción disseminates information and tracks the success of those involved in the initiative is through the

---

[17] José María Riba, email interview with the author (23 and 27 March 2008).

[18] FNAC is a French multinational company founded in 1954 which sells cultural goods and services throughout Europe. For more information on the group and its *ClubCultura* activities see Nuria Triana Toribio, 'Auteurism and Commerce in Contemporary Spanish Cinema: *Directores Mediáticos*', *Screen*, 49 (2008), 256–76.

Facebook page 'Cinéma-en-Construction-Cine-en-Construccion' which is accessible to anyone using the network. That Cine en Construcción and the Film Festivals that created it should be taking full advantage of the networking opportunities provided by Internet sites is a logical consequence of the primary role that festivals have, in the eyes of many researchers and critics: the function of providing an alternative distribution network to Hollywood, as suggested earlier. Festivals have had that function for some time now, as Piers Handling, head of Toronto Film Festival explained in Kenneth Turan's pioneering monograph on Film Festivals *Sundance to Sarajevo: Film Festivals and the World They Made*.[19]

The belief that film festivals' principal function is to showcase films that would not otherwise be seen is still popular in more recent assessments. Leonard Klady continues to defend this view in 2007 from the pages of *Screen International*, in an article arguing that this important role is still performed by Film Festivals.[20] However, before we get too excited we have to heed the warning of Piers Handling that 'a lot of work only gets shown now at festivals' (cited in Turan, *Sundance*, p. 8).

Be that as it may, along this other highway that non-Hollywood cinema travels, as we are often reminded by scholars in the area, festivals may be, among other things, the only place where the two separate worlds may meet:

> [T]he festival circuit is also a crucial interface with Hollywood itself, because taken together, festivals constitute (like Hollywood) a global platform but one which unlike Hollywood is at one and the same time a 'marketplace' (though perhaps more like a bazaar than a stock exchange), cultural showcase (comparable to music or theatre festivals) a 'competitive venue' (like the Olympic Games), and a world-body (an ad-hoc United Nations, a parliament of national cinemas, or cinematic NGOs, considering some of the various festivals' political agendas).
>
> (Elsaesser, *European Cinema*, p. 88)

Therefore it is very tempting to consider Cine en Construcción's primary role as providing this access to the exposure, distribution and exhibition possibilities that festivals provide for world cinema. Whilst this is an important aspect of Cine en Construcción the focus of the remaining part

---

[19] Kenneth Turan, *Sundance to Sarajevo: Film Festivals and the World They Made* (Berkeley: University of California Press, 2002), p. 8.

[20] Leonard Klady, 'Not the Whole Picture', *Screen International*, 1614, 5–11 October 2007, p. 28.

of this chapter will be to explore the relation between Latin American filmmakers who participate in Cine en Construcción and the festivals themselves. More precisely, what these filmmakers and their films can do and have done for Zinemaldia. For the moment I will concentrate on the Spanish-language component of this event but without forgetting that its roots lay firmly in France.

Symbiotic relationship: maintaining *Zinemaldia*'s brand

> [One] reason why film festivals turned to specialized programming [in the late 1960s], was the need for distinction. The number of film festivals increased and all of them instructed their programmers to go and scout out 'good' films for the festival. Because everybody was fishing in the same pond and established filmmakers preferred the major film festivals, newcomers on the festival circuit needed something else to be competitive. A specialization would allow them to unify their programs for the festival audience at home, while at the same time carving a niche into the global cultural agendas. (de Valck, *Film Festivals*, p. 179)

There is such a proliferation of international film festivals in the world that the cover of a 2007 issue of *Screen International* in September (the festivals' busiest month) showed a man dressed in suit and tie, flat on his back on what looked like a pristinely made hotel bed, clutching his briefcase and with the bedroom key still in the other hand. In the foreground, there were bags bearing distinguishable logos and names of famous festivals. The headline reads 'Festival Frenzy: Exhausted Executives Are Starting to Question which Autumn Festivals to Attend, Forcing Events to Define Their Role'.[21]

The need for festivals to make themselves unavoidable entries in the calendar of film sales agents, producers and national cinema institutions delegates has a history as long as that of most of the festivals themselves, as de Valck indicates in the above quote. Making themselves unavoidable has been achieved by several means. One of the main strategies has been that of finding a specialisation and within it a distinctiveness, a role at which to excel and which will be indelibly matched to the event in the festival-goers' minds. As one critic suggests, 'the key thing that these multiple festivals share is a need to differentiate themselves from each

---

21 *Screen International*, 1612, 21–27 September 2007, p. 1.

other' (Turan, *Sundance*, p. 5). The Sundance Film Festival, for instance, is synonymous with supporting American Independent Cinema, although Sundance has supported Latin American projects).[22] Pusan International Film Festival is the first port of call for Asian cinema, and so on.

Cine en Construcción is the result of a long-standing strategy of specialisation in independent cinema and cinema in Spanish on the part of Zinemaldia as the only category A Festival in Europe in a Spanish-speaking country.[23] The Spanish press often remarks on Zinemaldia's independent streak. In 2004 David Sequera made this point in his festival report for *Cineinforme* qualifying Zinemaldia as an 'altar for independent cinema' and arguing that 'if Venice and Cannes increasingly give centre-stage to Hollywood-made glamour, San Sebastian seeks to position itself as the great festival for independent cinema category A' (Sequera, pp.7–8).[24] The bad news for Zinemaldia is that this is hardly an original area of specialisation: discovering new independent talent *is* the task at which most international festivals want to excel, particularly since the developments of the late 1960s which were alluded to earlier (de Valck, pp. 93–4).

Zinemaldia's specialisation in Spanish-language cinema has also been established for a long time. As Evans puts it: 'San Sebastian is a champion for Spanish and Latin American talent (...). There is also a wide range of Spanish-language titles competing in the long-standing *Horizontes Latinos* section and the competition funding initiative Films in Progress [from 2002]' (Evans, p. 19).

It may seem natural and logical that a film festival which takes place in Spain would choose a Spanish-language specialisation. Zinemaldia may be known as a champion for Spanish and Latin American talent but the cause is not without fellow champions, even within Spain itself such as Festival de Cine Iberoamericano de Huelva, and evidently in Latin America. Huelva's Festival was created in 1975 and has become one of the main events for the showcasing of Latin American filmmakers and their films in Europe. But unlike Zinemaldia, Huelva is not recognised as an international festival by FIAPF, and, therefore, is not in its list of main

[22] James Mottram, *The Sundance Kids: How The Mavericks Took Back Hollywood* (London: Faber and Faber, 2006), pp. 37–48

[23] The other A category festival taking place in a Spanish-speaking country is The Festival Internacional de Cine de Mar del Plata in Argentina (Mar del Plata International Film Festival) with a chequered history, including a 25-year interruption.

[24] David Sequera, '52 Festival Internacional de Cine de San Sebastián: un altar para el cine independiente', *Cineinforme*, 43 (2004), 7–16.

festivals. And, we cannot underestimate that funding contests such as the one discussed in this chapter have the crucial effect of creating a sense of loyalty and a bond between filmmakers and certain festivals.

> It is no wonder that the most prestigious world festivals increasingly offer competitive production funds, development money as prizes, or organize a talent campus (Berlin) in order to bind new creative potential to a particular festival's brand image. It means that now certain films are being made to measure and made to order, i.e. their completion date, their opening venue, their financing is closely tied in with a particular festival (or festival circuit) and many filmmakers internalize and target such a possibility for their work. (Elsaesser, p. 88)

Zinemaldia's specialisation and the loyalty to the brand that this can generate are made possible by the shared language and culture among Spanish-speaking nations. It is often expressed in Spanish industrial cinema and critical circles that the right strategy to adopt in the face of the inequalities caused by globalisation in the audiovisual field is to play the language and culture card. This means that the industries of Spanish-speaking countries should join forces and capitalise on the language they share. To this end, Spanish-speaking nations are urged, from Spain, to 'launch a common cinema space'.[25] An increasing number of researchers are questioning the crucial role that co-production agreements and strategies for transnational production such as the Ibermedia project have in the creation of this supposedly shared space. There are dissenting voices, particularly from outside Spain, which call into question a process which is neo-colonialist in the eyes of many. Collaborations such as these have winners and losers and more importantly cannot be exempt from ideology and history.[26]

It is illustrative to quote at length Isabel Santaolalla's analysis of the language in which these collaborations between Spain and Latin America

[25] Antonio Chavarrías, 'La coproducción con Latinoamérica: cambiar es posible', *Academia: revista del cine español*, 24 (2004), 12–14.

[26] It is necessary to note that there has been a long tradition of study and analysis of co-productions in Spanish cinema (within and outside the Spanish academy). One outstanding example is the Spanish *Asociación de Historiadores del Cine* which dedicated its 7th Conference in 1997 to the Study of Co-productions: 'Las coproducciones en el cine español: Problemas estéticos e industriales y de definición nacional'. In 2008, the Centre for Media and Screen Studies annual conference in Philadelphia included a panel dedicated to the discussion of the project of collaboration between Spain and Latin American cinema industries, Ibermedia.

is sometimes expressed, because it will help to direct our gaze to the myths of the shared *comunidad transatlántica* (transatlantic community), *mercado natural* (natural market) or 'historical connection'. She argues:

> Sometimes comments on types of coproductions are extremely revealing. For instance, when producer Pedro Zaratoegui remarked that '[...] film co-productions [with Spanish-America] should be compulsory in Spain, as they are a cultural duty and a moral obligation' (Sánchez & Martialay 1995, p. 93) or director Pedro Carvajal defended the view that 'we have an obligation in Spain to open up our cinema to Latin America' (Muñoz 1997, p. 53) they were in curious ways unlocking a sense of imperial guilt, thereby inscribing the dynamics of colonial relations in today's film industry. In fact, one can almost hear the echoes of the –unquestionably much more monolithic- rhetoric circulating in Spain in the 1940s and 1950s, as illustrated, for instance, by this comment published in 1944 in the official film magazine *Primer Plano*: 'Nobody can – or to be more precise, nobody should – try to deny us the American market. And out of loyalty, when the moment comes, it will be our duty to accept and prioritise whatever comes from there.' (Garay 1944, n.p.)[27]

Santaolalla has unearthed here a series of issues that have to be addressed in view of what Zinemaldia and Cine en Construcción aim to do: to bring to completion and enable the distribution projects from Latin American filmmakers in Europe.

Néstor García Canclini highlights the persistence of the *legados coloniales* (colonial legacies)[28] i.e. the narrations forged during the colonial epoch and which government officials, journalists and writers still use. Expressions such as *comunidad atlántica, mercado natural, encuentro intercultural* (intercultural encounter) or phrases such as cultural duty and moral obligation are examples of these colonial legacies.[29] García Canclini further argues that there was a type of rhetoric prevalent around 1992 when the default mode of expression coming from European cultural institutions was to brush the conquest under the carpet. When addressing the reason why Latin America and Spain share a language, something that

---

[27] Isabel Santaolalla, 'A Case of Split Identity? Europe and Spanish America in Recent Spanish Cinema', *Journal of Contemporary European Studies*, 15.1 (2007), 67–78 (p. 70).

[28] Néstor García Canclini, *La globalización imaginada* (Buenos Aires: Paidós, 2005 [1999]), p. 83.

[29] The imperialist mindset in which Spanish cinema has developed since its inception is addressed in Nuria Triana Toribio, *Spanish National Cinema* (London: Routledge, 2003), particularly at pp. 28–31.

has arguably generated a shared culture, the predominant discourse was
that of *encuentro intercultural*. García Canclini suggests:

> No fue un encuentro, como si dos sociedades se hubieran reunido en
> medio del Atlántico para una amable feria de intercambios, sino una
> historia de combates e imposiciones.
>   La crítica desconstructiva sigue siendo necesaria en tanto las imágenes
> destinadas a enmascarar la violencia y la dominación persisten en ferias
> internacionales, en libros escolares y en discursos de reuniones guberna-
> mentales iberoamericanas donde el entusiasmo por negocios 'comunes'
> despoja de conflicto a los imaginarios de la memoria.
>
> (García Canclini, *Globalización*, p. 88)

> It was not an encounter, as if two societies got together in the middle
> of the Atlantic for a pleasant exchange, but a history of battles and
> impositions.
>   Deconstructive criticism is still necessary whilst the images destined
> to mask violence and domination persist in international cultural fairs,
> school books and the discourse of the *Iberoamerican* governmental
> meetings where the enthusiasm for business in common eschews the
> conflict from the memory's imaginaries.

This quotation is taken from García Canclini's chapter entitled 'Mercado
e interculturalidad' (Interculturality and the Market) and in this chapter he
addresses events such as international cultural fairs, a type of showcase
of culture that can be very similar to a film festival. It is at events such as
these where the temptation to let bygones be bygones becomes the main
guiding light in the rhetoric, for the sake of economic gain.

   In full knowledge of these traps in which the discourse of ventures that
link Spain and Latin American can be snared, it is illustrative to examine
the language in which the creation of Cine en Construcción is articulated. The first manifesto of Cine en Construcción included in the Festival
Programme of 2002 decreed: 'For the first time, two European festivals
are working together to provide new opportunities for Latin American
cinema, currently facing an unprecedented financial crisis, making it
particularly difficult to finish projects.'[30] It is quite significant that these
early documents do not speak of *encuentro intercultural* or of *historic
debt* or even of a shared cultural space or *mercado natural* (Chavarrías,

---

[30] 'Zinema Eraikitzen/ Cine en Construcción', in *Catálogo del 50 festival Internacional
de San Sebastián/Zinemaldia* (San Sebastián: Festival Internacional de *San Sebastián/
Zinemaldia*, 2002), pp. 291–5.

p. 12) in the manner much literature on co-productions written in Spain still does, long after 1992. Cine en Construcción's early descriptions of their own strategies concentrate instead on economic need and a crisis that has to be addressed in Europe.

The establishing documents of Cine en Construcción do not indulge in an overtly imperialistic form of expression, nor have any of those I have interviewed during my research used that language tainted with the rhetoric of the past. However, and in the spirit of a continuing deconstructive vigilance that García Canclini advises, we cannot fail to notice that these European festivals, whilst providing new opportunities to independent Latin American talent, put themselves in a position of midwives of the resultant films. This role in which they cast themselves is far from innocent.

Janet Wolff warns that there is inevitably an influence that emanates from mediating agents through the choices they make and the work they enable:

> Although one would not expect any direct intervention by the respective 'patron' into what the artist actually produces, it is clear that founding bodies are no more neutral than any social organization, and that the success of some artists at gaining sponsorship and the failure of others is likely to be related to the type of work they do.[31]

This reflection has led those of us who research transnational strategies to consider that perhaps there are grounds to discuss more this mediation as the two festival juries act as gatekeepers of independent Latin American Cinema in Europe. As was mentioned at the start of this chapter, a sample of the winners of Cine en Construcción is chosen to be circulated via the websites of the Instituto Cervantes throughout the world, which means that some films will have access to a distribution circuit and some will not. These gatekeepers may indeed be very politically and socially responsible and very attuned to the cultural diversity of the Latin American national cinemas, but they are gatekeepers nonetheless.

One could argue that Zinemaldia's history has always included Latin American cinema in its projects. The 'founding fathers' of Zinemaldia in 1953 were Basque small-business men and shopkeepers who created San Sebastian's film festival partly to revive the city's past as an aristo-

---

[31] Janet Wolff, *The Social Production of Art* (London: Macmillan, 1993 [1981]), p. 45.

cratic holiday resort at a time when Franco's Spain had been given the cold shoulder by democratic Europe. One of the founders of the festival, Dionisio P. Villar, provides a candid and unfettered view of the kind of relationship that the 'fathers of the festival' wanted with Latin American distributors:

> Ah!, y no olvidarse que debe mirar a HISPANOAMERICA (sic). El centro de contratación de películas europeas para esos países hermanos debe hacerse en España. Aquí se les entiende y comprende. Los distribuidores de películas y propietarios de cines podrían pasar unos días de vacaciones en España y además hacer sus negocios.

> Ah! And don't forget that [the festival] must look to HISPANOAMERICA. The centre for the acquisition of the distribution and exhibition rights for European films to those fraternal countries must be Spain. Here we understand them and empathise with them. Film distributors and cinema owners could spend their holidays here and do business.[32]

This sentiment could not be further from what seems ostensibly to be the present-day strategy in relation to Latin American cinema industries: Cine en Construcción is an initiative intended to help finance Latin American Independent projects. However, Cine en Construcción also doubles up as a reminder of the fact that the relationship between the old metropolis and its former colonies may well continue to provide a sound investment for Zinemaldia.

As discussed above, festivals specialise as the channel through which independent cinema travels, and it is a very good idea, from the perspective of film festivals, to ensure a healthy and continuous supply of independent talent, even when the strategies to do so have a neo-colonialist taint to them. Herein lies the mutual dependence that Cine en Construcción generates. Zinemaldia needs to promote Latin American talent since this:

(a) Ensures a supply for the festivals themselves and the festivals in its circuit, but also, for example, showcases festivals that have fed from Zinemaldia in the past, such as ¡Viva! Spanish and Latin American Film Festival at Cornerhouse/Instituto Cervantes, Manchester, UK.

---

[32] Dioniso P. Villar, 'Cómo, por qué y para qué se creó la Primera Semana Internacional del Cine', in *Historia de 12 Festivales*, ed. José M. Ferrer and Luis Gasca (San Sebastián: Festival Internacional del Cine, 1965), pp. 3–7.

(b) Keeps Zinemaldia's profile as a supporter of independent Latin American talent high, whilst ensuring that such talent will think of Zinemaldia (rather than the Festival de Cine Iberoamericano de Huelva, for instance) as their gateway to Europe.

These colonial legacies and the neo-colonialist special relationship between Spain and Latin America can give Zinemaldia a certain advantage when in competition with other initiatives for the support of Latin American cinemas (and other world cinemas). The Hubert Bals Fund, mentioned above, or Berlin International Film Festival have been providing for two decades funding for Independent World Cinema and many grants have gone to Latin American projects.[33] But arguably, the Netherlands lacks the special relationship and shared language factor.

Making a small dent in the forces of globalisation

The consensus around those who observe and analyse the phenomenon of film festivals in detail is to declare that their proclaimed mandate is to provide an alternative to Hollywood in distributing films of quality that would not otherwise be seen.[34] Festival directors and programmers, including Mikel Olaciregui declare this to be Zinemaldia's main aim.[35]

Harbord (pp. 59–75) and others have suggested this role is only a part of the remit of festivals. In order to get the other aspects of their remit we have to read symptomatically into the writings of business-minded industry journalists. Leonard Klady, regular contributor to *Screen International*, wrote a piece in 2007 to remind the industry sceptics that 'film festivals may often seem to be venues for photo opportunities rather than screenings of new films' (Klady, p. 27). In short, that which festivals

---

[33] The winner of the World Cinema Audience Award in 2009 and the Sebastian Award within Zinemaldia, *Contracorriente* (*Undertow*, Fuentes-León, 2008, Peru/Colombia/France/Germany) was partially funded by German co-producers which the director contacted at BIFF.

[34] See, for instance, Elsaesser, *European Cinema*, pp. 88–9; Bill Nichols, 'Discovering Form, Inferring Meaning: New Cinemas and Film Festivals Circuit', *Film Quarterly*, XLVII.31 (1994), 16–30 (pp. 16–18).

[35] Bijan Tehrani, 'Mikel Olaciregui talks about San Sebastian International Film Festival', *Cinema without Borders*, 24 September 2007. Available at http://www.cinemawithoutborders.com/news/130/article/ 1357/2007-09-24.html (Last accessed 23 May 2010).

purport to be their main objective is, in fact, a sidebar. Klady reminds his colleagues that festivals are, among other things, still providing that alternative avenue for independent or small budget cinema to travel. He writes 'unlike the realities of the marketplace, the ability of a movie to travel the festival circuit is, if not unfettered, considerably more democratic' (p. 27). What for an external observer is perhaps the raison d'être, the industry sees as something that happens between photo opportunities and star presence.

Kay Armatage, who combines having been a programmer of Toronto International Film Festival from 1983 to 2004, with a career in film studies academic research, argues that we must not be too taken in by altruistic declarations of programmers and festival directors:

> Even people who should know better believe that the role of film festivals is to show worthwhile films to a committed audience, to provide an alternative distribution system to films that otherwise would not be shown (…). However, film festivals, especially the largest and most prestigious ones, are events in which the primary industry is the festival itself. (Armatage, 'The Festival in the City', n.p.)

In the first section of this chapter, I discussed that whilst ostensibly fulfilling this higher calling of enabling a type of cinema to exist that otherwise would not, a significant amount of energy, resources and initiatives such as Cine en Construcción ensure Zinemaldia's own sustainability. Cine en Construcción has been discussed, up to this point, as one tool put to use to look after the future of the festival, and I have not focused in my study on the other functions and purposes this initiative has.

In the final section of my study I suggest that, even at the risk of being seen as wearing the rose-tinted glasses that researchers such as Armatage recommend we discard, it is illustrative also to look at those functions and objectives of Cine en Construcción. For instance in its liaison with cultural institutions such as Casa de América but particularly with the Instituto Cervantes, Cine en Construcción provides a genuine alternative distribution system to films that will not reach the mainstream distribution circuits. This alternative channel departs from Zinemaldia but goes beyond the festival.

More importantly, this cultural traffic between Latin American cinemas and Europe counteracts the more hegemonic cultural highway as far as audiovisual cultures in the American continent is concerned. As García Canclini observes:

> La cuestión de cómo está reconfigurándose el espacio latinoamericano en un espacio euroamericano o interamericano se plantea de distintas maneras en la economía en los medios, la cultura de élite y la cultura política. (García Canclini, *Globalización*, p. 104)

> The question of how Latin American space is reconfiguring itself either as a euro American or as inter American space has different answers depending on whether we are considering the economy, the media, elite culture or political culture. USA is nowadays the dominant reference point in political culture and audiovisual media.

Cine en Construcción is fostering cinema projects and as cinema these products would, in theory, come under the domination of the USA in their movements. However, as García Canclini and others have suggested, what is central to the concerns of the USA – i.e. Hollywood – is not enabling the transit of other cinemas but is having the highest share of the market in all territories.

A Euro-Latin American space is being configured, for instance, in élite cultural production and distribution. García Canclini points out how literary publishing houses in Spain and Italy are pivotal in the Latin American market (*Globalización*, pp. 150–4). A sector of independent Latin American cinema is showing signs of travelling on that same transatlantic axis, rather than through the dominant one controlled by the USA. The European initiative, Cine en Construcción with its links with the Instituto Cervantes enables this alternative. Even in the smallest way, this reconfiguring is an attempt to shift the axis of audiovisual distribution and exhibition and challenge the dominant axis of the 'USA as dominant reference point in communication' as García Canclini indicates (p. 104).

In 2006, Zinemaldia's director Mikel Olaciregui and the then director of the Instituto Cervantes, César Antonio Molina, came to an agreement to institutionalise the travel of a selection of films from Cine en Construcción to sites of cultural organisation throughout the world. As the Basque daily newspaper, *Deia* explained:

> El acuerdo estipula que cada ciclo de Cine en Construcción que se exhiba estará formado por cinco películas que se enviarán a cinco centros del Instituto (…) que cuenta actualmente con un total de 56 centros en 37 países.

> The agreement stipulates that each season of Cine en Construcción to be shown will be made up of five films which will be sent, in the first

instance, to five centres of the Instituto Cervantes, which at the moment has a total of 56 sites in 37 countries.[36]

Marina Díaz López, who coordinates these seasons in her capacity as Técnica de Cine y Audiovisual (Cinema and Audiovisual Media Officer), points out that:

> We started with one season, then another up to four seasons of five films each and each programme would be sent to a series of *Instituto* sites. Each of these screenings is accompanied by an introduction to the film made by the director or producer or another film professional involved. This talk also includes a section on the work and role of *Cine en Construcción*. The professionals involved know that they are going to spend four years travelling with their films to different sites throughout the world: Amman, Athens, Beirut, Bucarest, Cairo, Dublin, Manchester, Moscow, Roma, Salvador da Bahia, Sao Paulo, Tunisia and Warsaw, (and a mini tour of Poland including Torun, Lodz, Krakow). The *Instituto Cervantes* pays for the travel expenses of the accompanying professional and a symbolic amount for exhibition rights.
>
> (Díaz López, n.p.)

She further explains that the work that the Instituto Cervantes does for Cine en Construcción falls within the remit of the cultural institution, as an important part of their commitment is to support film culture in Spanish. Their work with the initiative, which goes beyond the mere provision of an alternative showcase for films, in fact becomes an opportunity for networking for the film professionals involved:

> The idea that was conjured up between them and us was that of establishing an alternative route for the films. Many of these are small budget films, made by young directors, although sometimes we have had projects from experienced and relatively well-known ones such as the Argentine Edgardo Cozarinski.[37] This route takes films to places less within reach of film festivals presenting cinema in Spanish. The incentive we can offer to filmmakers is that the Instituto Cervantes has a network of sites in Arab countries, Asia, Brazil, and in Central Europe. We also offer the incentive of, wherever possible, putting the

[36] EFE, 'El Festival de Cine de Donostia exhibirá sus filmes en el Instituto Cervantes', *Deia*, 3 February 2006, p. 68

[37] Edgardo Cozarinski took part in Cine en Construcción with his film of 2004, *Ronda nocturna* (*Night Watch*).

director or film professional accompanying the film –say, an actor– in touch with a local director or actor working in comparable conditions on site. Both would then present the film together. Getting in touch with local novice independent directors enables us to reach local audiences more easily but also helps the Latin American directors to have a person with whom they can dialogue. (Díaz López, n.p.)

César Antonio Molina declared in 2006 that '[e]l cine es la actividad de mayor éxito de cuantas lleva a cabo el Instituto Cervantes' (Cinema is the most successful of all the activities that the Instituto Cervantes carries out) (EFE, p. 60) and therefore it is arguable that through this collaboration both Cine en Construcción and the Instituto Cervantes benefit reciprocally and as Díaz López confirms 'this is the most important activity we perform [in the cinema and audiovisual section]' (Díaz López, n.p.).

Five Cine en Construcción films are selected to tour and the cycle starts in October and finishes in the spring. In order to illustrate this alternative distribution and exhibition, it is perhaps illustrative to see how Cine en Construcción arrives at one of the nodes of the net: Manchester and Leeds (as well as screenings organised at Liverpool, where the Instituto has no site).

In the case of Manchester (as in other cases) this liaison involves Instituto Cervantes' partners, such as art-house cinemas and universities in the vicinity, thus increasing the audience of the five films in the season. The local art-cinema venue, Cornerhouse, collaborates with the Instituto Cervantes and showcases some of the films in cinema conditions, which the Instituto venue lacks. They show the five films in the yearly sample between the two sites. Cine en Construcción during 2007 brought filmmakers accompanying the season of five films and taking part in Q&A sessions with the audience. For instance, Fernán Rudnik presented his film *Pueblo chico* (*Little Village*, 2003) on 19 September 2007 and he and the head of programming, Linda Pariser, explained the purpose of Cine en Construcción. The previous year, *El juego de la silla* (Musical Chairs) by Ana Katz (Argentina) was brought to Mancunian audiences in the same context as part of the sample of 5 films shown in Manchester between the Instituto Cervantes and Cornerhouse. On 12 November 2008, Cornerhouse screened *La demolición* (*The Demolition*, Marcelo Mangone 2007, Agentina), following the screening with a Q&A session with Assistant Director Matías Scartascini, whilst the rest of the sample was shown at the Instituto Cervantes sites in Manchester and Leeds and a few further screenings were organised at Liverpool's art cinema.

Taking into account the fact that these films are shown in cultural institutions that are perhaps only frequented by the type of audiences already interested in world cinema, it would be easy to dismiss this exercise as irrelevant in the grand scheme of things. However, I would like to consider it as proof of the reconfiguration of the cultural space which is taking place with cultures in Spanish, even if its underpinnings are neo-colonialist.

Film Festivals, whilst ensuring their own survival, provide an alternative to the unequal manner in which globalisation operates in the film arena. Activities such as workshops, funding contests and scriptwriting residencies are becoming pivotal elements in ensuring a healthy supply of world cinema to the many festivals that take place in the world but at the same time, filmmakers are looking at these festival-created initiatives as a form of ensuring their own survival in filmmaking. The fact remains that film festivals may be considered as film showcasing sites but they are in equal measure the sites where films are generated. Whether these strategies are to the detriment or benefit of the film industries in Latin America will have to be decided by the audiences and the filmmakers themselves.

6

Pedro Almodóvar's Latin American 'Business'

MARVIN D'LUGO

Remapping Latin America onto Spain

Almodóvar's 2006 film *Volver* (2006) is the product of an intense period in which the Spanish filmmaker's production company, El Deseo, actively engaged in a series of strategic co-productions with Latin American producers. These were more than simply efforts at commercial opportunism, and rather reflected Almodóvar's long-standing connections to Latin America that date back to his early career when he regularly included actors and songs from the region in his films. What had once seemed like random motifs, now retrospectively come into focus in this film as part of a more ambitious transterritorial aesthetic that seeks to engage audiences in both Spain and Latin America in what the cultural critic Néstor García Canclini describes as the co-production of a transnational Hispanic identity.[1] As I will argue in this chapter, *Volver* is a pivotal work both within Almodóvar's filmography and in bringing to light the cultural dynamic that informs El Deseo's larger Latin American project.

That process is given self-referential prominence in the film when Penélope Cruz sings the title song, an Argentine tango, at a party she has been hired to cater for a film crew shooting in her gritty Madrid neighbourhood. On one level the musical performance seems misplaced in what has been up to this point a grim melodrama of domestic violence and the struggles of the urban poor. Yet, her performance is motivated as the Cruz character, Raimunda, hears guitar chords and recalls events from

---

[1] Néstor García Canclini, Consumidores y ciudadanos: conflictos multiculturales de la globalización (Mexico City: Grijalbo, 1995), p. 130.

her childhood associated with her mother, thus prompting her to sing the tango. Only later do we realise that the plot of *Volver* is a dramatisation of the song's lyrics of return to an emotion-charged past.

Tango music and lyrics have long been a musical refrain in Almodóvar's films going back 20 years to *La ley del deseo* (*Law of Desire*, 1987).[2] But until *Volver*, the use of such melodies had been largely background to the principal action. Here, however, the tango assumes a strategic position at the centre of narrative and emotional gravity, condensing into lyrical form the film's story of return and reencounter, and engaging the audience in the recognition of a shared trans-Hispanic cultural heritage.

Reflecting the tango's nomadic musical tradition,[3] the version Cruz sings[4] is a flamenco hybrid of the Argentine song that comes to embody Almodóvar's vision of a deterritorialised Hispanic community taking shape in Madrid. The particular transnational origin of 'Volver' the tango, first performed by the legendary Argentine *tanguero* Carlos Gardel in John Rheinhardt's, *El día que me quieras* (*The Day You Love Me*, 1935), provides an example of an earlier age's version of that same transnationalism.[5] In the earlier film, as in Almodóvar's, the lyrics are intended to evoke memories of exile and return to the places of one's past.

If the song suggests a certain transnational itinerary, the singer, Penélope Cruz, does as well. A Spaniard by birth, in the last decade Cruz

---

2   Pedro Ochoa, *Tango y cine mundial* (Buenos Aires: Ediciones del Jilguero, 2003), p. 99. Ochoa specifically notes the inclusion of tango melodies in *La ley del deseo* (1987), ¡*Átame!* (*Tie Me Up, Tie Me Down!*, 1989); *Kika* (1993) and *Todo sobre mi Madre* (*All About My Mother*, 1999).

3   See Ramón Pelinski, *El tango nómade: ensayos sobre la diáspora del tango* (Buenos Aires: Corregido, 2000).

4   The song is actually a dubbing of Cruz's voice by that of Flamenco star Estrella Morente.

5   With the advent of sound motion pictures in the late 1920s, various Hollywood studios sought ways to maintain their overseas markets through multilingual films; that is, versions of English-language Hollywood productions reshot in various European languages. Given the size and importance of the Spanish-language market, Spanish-language films, sometimes called 'Films Hispanos', were developed, but with relatively little success. One notable exception were the nine features produced by Paramount starring Carlos Gardel and shot either in their Paris or New York Studios. Unlike many Films Hispanos, these were not re-makes of English-language films, but based on original scripts to capitalise on Gardel's star status. For a detailed account of the multi-lingual productions see Natasa Durovicová, 'The Hollywood Multilinguals 1929–1933', in *Sound Theory Sound Practice*, ed. Rick Altman (New York and London: Routledge: 1992), pp. 38–53; for a discussion of Gardel's Films Hispanos, see Simon Collier, *Carlos Gardel: su vida, su música, su época*, translated by Carlos Gardini (Buenos Aires: Plaza & Janés, 2003).

has become an international icon of *Latina* sexiness. In striking ways, her roles in Spanish, Hollywood, and other international co-productions, and important performances in two previous Almodóvar films *Carne trémula* (*Live Flesh*, 1997); *Todo sobre mi madre* (*All About My Mother,* 1999), combined with her high-profile appearances in cosmetics commercials, have transformed her into the ubiquitous face of Hispanic female beauty on three continents. By showcasing the song and the singer in this manner, Cruz is seen as embodying the essence of Almodóvar's broader conception of the film and its complex cultural politics in which the old nation-specific cultural marks of identity are placed under textual erasure, giving way to a new transnational cultural mode.

From a conceptual perspective, the musical sequence demonstrates García Canclini's assertion of the 'transnationalisation of economy and of symbols, revealing that individuals are simultaneously members of national populations but also of transnational and intercultural communities as well' (García Canclini, *Consumidores*, p. 184).[6] In this way, the back story of *Volver* involves the contingent histories of the transfer and transformation of 'traditional', collective creative forms that imply an essential dissolution of the binary conception Spain–Latin America.

Affirming an aesthetic multi-perspectivism built around the intertextual and intermedial blending of various cultural elements, Almodóvar has aligned Spanish viewers with Latin American audiences in terms of a borderless 'Hispanic Atlantic' community sustained by centuries of transnational cultural exchange.[7] To add further complexity to this intertextual dynamic, we note that *Volver* effectively updates social themes, characters and situations Almodóvar has developed over the last 25 years, since his first cross-over international success, *¿Qué he hecho yo para merecer esto?* (*What Have I Done to Deserve This?* 1985). In much the same way that this earlier film had focused on Spanish internal migration to the city, *Volver* now pairs that theme with the contemporary Spanish audience's awareness of the polemical topic of foreign immigration as it has altered the ethnic face of peninsular society since the 1990s. We in fact see that emerging demographic at certain key moments when Raimunda is shown on crowded city streets amidst a diverse ethnic array of urban

---

6   Unless otherwise indicated, translations here and elsewhere in the text are my own.

7   For further discussion of the 'Hispanic Atlantic' see Joseba Gabilondo, 'Introduction' to the Special Section: The Hispanic Atlantic, *Arizona Journal of Hispanic Cultural Studies*, 5 (2001), 91–113; Marvin D'Lugo, 'Across the Hispanic Atlantic: Cinema and its Symbolic Relocations', *Studies in Hispanic Cinemas*, 5.1–2 (2008), 3–7.

dwellers. These recent immigration patterns, glimpsed at as the back-drop to the action of *Volver*, have placed Spain in a new network of cultural contacts with Eastern Europe and Africa, but more importantly with Latin America.[8] Yet, the film is less involved with the sociology of a refigured Spain than with its aesthetic dimension, specifically the way popular mass-media help to construct powerful memory-making fictions that enable audiences to appreciate and identify with the transnational Hispanic cultural narrative. Importantly, the Madrid presented in the film is almost entirely devoid of the imagery associated with the Spanish capital. Rather, as García Canclini notes more generally, the notion of the particular urban milieu as the 'capital of the nation,' has, through migration, become the point of intersection of multiple cultural traditions (García Canclini, *Consumidores*, p. 47). So, for as much as a Spanish viewer may follow the film in its national cultural specificity, Almodóvar has left *Volver*'s mise-en-scène suggestively porous for its potential Latin American audience.

To more fully appreciate these textual gestures toward an integrated pan-Hispanic cultural paradigm, we need to see *Volver* as an extension of the broader cultural project of Almodóvar's own production company, El Deseo, founded in 1986 by the director and his brother Agustín Almodóvar. Since its 2000 production of Mexican director Guillermo de Toro's *El espinazo del diablo* (*The Devil's Backbone*), El Deseo has engaged in a series of co-productions with Latin American producers that has supported works by Chilean, Mexican and Argentine filmmakers. Agustín Almodóvar describes the company's international collaborations as constituting 'un encuentro maravilloso de sensibilidades distantes pero muy cercanas' (a marvellous encounter of distant but very closely aligned sensibilities).[9]

We may get a sense of those sensibilities in a particularly crucial inter-text, Almodóvar's 1995 film, *La flor de mi secreto* (*The Flower of My Secret*). Like *Volver*, it is a film that looks back to *What Have I Done?* but it also contains the seeds of the principal plotline that will take shape a decade later in *Volver*. One scene in *La flor* crystallises this geopolitical

[8] For a discussion of the subgenre of immigration films which introduces essays on the extensive history of the migratory theme in Spanish cinema since 1930, see my essay, 'El cine de la inmigración: Crónicas de un género anunciado', Introduction to *Fotogramas para la multiculturalidad: Migraciones y alteridad en el cine español contemporáneo*, ed. Móncia Cantero-Exojo, María Van Liew and José Carlos Suárez (Valencia: Tirant lo Blanch, 2011), pp. 9–21.

[9] Paché Meyero, 'Agustín Almodóvar, productor de cine', *La voz de Avilés*, 21 November 2001 (n.p.).

question on the level of individual consciousness. The scene in question is built around a single brief shot of the bedroom of the film's heroine, Leocadia Macías (Marisa Paredes) and might otherwise go completely ignored by audiences if it were not for Almodóvar's notes about this particular mise-en-scène appended to the published film script.[10] In that commentary, which Almodóvar titles 'El mapa' (The Map) and 'La cama y sus alrededores' (The Bed and its Surroundings) he retrospectively lays out the underlying design for the film in which, as he notes, geography replaces religion (Almodóvar, *La flor de mi secreto*, pp. 169–74).The map embodies a particular conception of Spain as a geopolitical entity that weighs heavily on Almodóvar's thinking about individual and cultural identity. The scene is introduced through an initial high-angle shot of the bedroom with the image of a map framed on the wall hanging over Leo and estranged husband Paco's bed. It is an over-sized version of one of those classroom maps of Spain showing all the rivers, provinces and their capital cities. More appropriate for a classroom wall than as an adornment in a bedroom, the map is curiously positioned over the bed where the protagonists sleep, giving it a prominence in key sequences as though pointing Almodóvar's audience toward the psychic force of the geopolitical Spain that hovers over the minds and the imagination of his protagonists, Leo and Paco.[11] He says of the map, 'vigila nuestros sueños, hace guardia en las puertas de nuestra intimidad, simboliza algo en lo que uno cree, algo que nos infunde confianza, nos cobija y nos protege' ('It keeps watch over our dreams and stands guard at the doors of our intimate being, symbolising something in which we believe, something that instils confidence in us and which covers and protects us'; Almodóvar, *La flor de mi secreto*, p. 173).

Almodóvar has, in effect, reduced the nation to a finite object while also imbuing it with unconscious power over people's minds; this is the symbolic meaning of its position 'over the bed'. At the same time, its location, so prominently underscored in Almodóvar's own writing, suggests that this concept of the nation is under a certain mark of scrutiny, a hypothesis that will be borne out by the subsequent narrative development. The plot of *La flor de mi secreto* focuses on the marital discord

[10] Pedro Almodóvar, *La flor de mi secreto* (Barcelona: Plaza y Janés Ave Fénix/Serie Mayor: 1995).

[11] That same map appears only one other time in Almodóvar's films, hanging on the wall of another bedroom, this time, of Mateo Blanco a.k.a. Harry Caine in *Los abrazos rotos* (*Broken Embraces*, 2009). The repetition of the map is, of course, one of those little auteurist touches in Almodóvar's films that scholars love to deconstruct.

between the philandering Paco and emotionally fraught Leo, each meticu-
lously characterised through geography: Paco is engaged with the European peace-keeping operations in Bosnia and Leo is self-absorbed with
her husband's indifference to her and her family's troubled adjustment
to contemporary urban life. In this way, the sexual scenario that so often
dominates Almodóvar's films is transformed into a geopolitical allegory
of Spain's past and future, with Leo, the heroine, caught between those
two versions of cultural identity.

Almodóvar disrupts this framing of individual consciousness by the
weight of national geography by inserting three critical textual fissures
that collectively shatter the sense of Spain as a psychic imaginary binding
together the traditional Iberian community. These are all auditory intertexts, all the more emotionally powerful and profound for the audience in
that they transcend the limits of the fiction and suggest a sonic authority
outside the frame of the visible. The first is the voice and image of Costa
Rican–Mexican Chavela Vargas entoning the lyrics of 'El último trago'
('The Last Drink'), a classic Mexican ballad. The combination of the
singer's voice and her dispassionate rendering of the song lyrics shake
Leo out of her emotional stupor. Emanating from a television monitor
in a bar, Chavela's words appear to function as the sage advice of one
jilted lover to another as they help Leo to distance herself from her melodramatic role as the betrayed wife. The technological insertion of the
singer's voice on the television screen underscores the ways in which the
urban mise-en-scène of modern Spain has become a mediascape in which
musical sounds in particular have brought diverse members of Spanish
and Spanish-American communities together in emotionally supportive
ways. The brief musical interpolation anticipates the next Latin American
sonic insertion, the voice of Cuban singer Bola de Nieve singing 'Amor y
vida' (Love and Life), a Cuban *son*, a popular musical form, that is heard
from an off-screen source as Leo, thrown into a crowd of anti-government
student protesters, is thrust into the arms of the man who will provide her
an intellectual, cultural and emotional salvation, Ángel (Juan Echanove).

The two sentimental ballads remind us of spaces of identification within
the cultural imaginary that lie beyond the borders of the finite geopolitics
of an old Spain. Notably, they serve as efforts to call the heroine back to
life. Even though 'Amor y vida' is first heard only as background music
to Leo's reencounter with Ángel, it later becomes the topic of discussion
of their shared interest in Latin American music.

A third Latin American voice, that of Caetano Veloso, singing 'Tonada
de luna llena' ('Song of the Full Moon'), is also extra-diegetic, serving

as a point of closure to the film, as it accompanies the final credit scroll; but it may be seen as an opening as well, providing a further link for the characters beyond the confining city visualised in the cinematic narrative. The *tonada* is the product of Venezuelan composer Simón Díaz, whose music has been identified with the effort to resurrect a Latin American folkloric tradition in the face of the growing menace of American music.[12]

As Kathleen Vernon notes, Almodóvar's musical punctuation with these three renditions of Latin American music emphasises the androgynous nature of the singers' voices.[13] Chavela Vargas's is a rough bass voice, while those of Bola de Nieve's and Caetano Veloso's are higher pitched, suggesting a blurring of simplistic gender identifications through voice. These are 'uncanny voices', as Vernon argues (p. 59), as they suggest a moving away from the fixed places of gender identity to new positions in culture, an auditory parallel to Almodóvar's progressive refiguring of the fixed and static spaces of traditional culture as new and expansive transcultural Hispanic spaces come into focus.

The map and its counterforce, the three songs, immediately suggest on a meta-level the larger processes at work in Almodóvar's transnational aesthetics. In this auditory framing of the visual narrative the physical borders of the old geopolitical Spain are penetrated by sounds that also carry their own cultural weight. It is not simply the representation of an alternative vision, but a deeply rooted sense of a community unbound by spatial or even temporal limits. Their disruption of the closed world embodied by the map offers alternate ways of seeing (and hearing) oneself in the world and connecting with others that is being reordered by the intricate weave of story and song. That depiction of Latin American popular cultural materials as a counterforce to the insularity that has trapped Leo is only vaguely suggested in *La flor de mi secreto*. In time, however, it will gain a more decisive prominence in Almodóvar's films, principally through the aesthetic revisions of plotlines, images and sounds aimed at undercutting the old geopolitics of fixed individual and national identities. This process, in fact, will come into focus more pointedly in *Volver.*

[12] Simón Díaz is well known for his recovery of the songs of the Venezuelan plains, turning this genre of folkloric composition into an authentic musical genre performed by singers from across Latin America.

[13] Kathleen Vernon, 'Queer Sound: Musical Otherness in Three Films by Pedro Almodóvar', in *All about Almodóvar: A Passion for Cinema,* ed. Brad Epps and Despina Kakoudaki (Minneapolis and London: University of Minnesota Press, 2009), pp. 51–70 (p. 59).

Narratives of reencounter

Though less explicitly marked as a cross-cultural element in the film, the plot of *Volver* provides an important bridge to Latin American popular narratives, further contributing to the film's transnational appeal. García Canclini's insistence on the mass-mediatised concept of identity: 'la identidad es una construcción que se relata' (Identity is a construction that is narrated) (García Canclini, *Consumidores*, p. 123), enables us to appreciate the special status of melodrama as a key axis of narrative meaning in *Volver*. Of the various audiovisual strains of melodrama, Jesús Martín-Barbero identifies one in particular, what he calls 'the melodrama of reencounter' that occupies a central place in the film's plot. He describes this genre-within-a-genre as providing the formula for a prodigious number of Latin American telenovelas: 'Del hijo por el padre o del padre por el hijo, lo que mueve la trama es siempre el desconocimiento de una identidad y la lucha contra los maleficios, las apariencias, contra todo lo que oculta y difraza una lucha por hacerse reconocer' ('the reencounter of the son by the father or the father by the son, what moves the plot forward is always the non-recognition of identity of one's family members and the struggle against evil, false appearances, against everything that hides or disguises the struggle for self-identity').[14]

The particular melodrama of reencounter that gives formal direction to *Volver* deals with the unravelling of events years before the film opens when Irene (Carmen Maura) discovered her husband's infidelity and in revenge, burnt down the hut where he and another woman from their Manchegan village were bedded down. The contemporary action begins after Irene's presumed death, with the return to the village of her daughter, Raimunda, Raimunda's sister Sole (Lola Dueñas) and her daughter Paula (Yohana Cobo), now a young woman. They have come ostensibly to clean their parents' gravesite but the visit rekindles emotional memories that still connect these characters from the city to their rural past. Days after her return to Madrid, Raimunda's husband, Paco, tries to rape his step-daughter Paula. To defend herself, the young girl stabs him with a kitchen knife resulting in his death. While attempting to dispose of the body, Raimunda receives a phone call from Sole that her mother's sister, Aunt Paula has died. When Sole returns to Madrid after the funeral, she

---

[14] Jesús Martín-Barbero, 'La telenovela en Colombia: antecedentes y situación actual', in *El espectáculo e la pasión: las telenovelas latinoamericanas*, ed. Nora Mazziotto (Buenos Aires: Ediciones Colihue, 1995), pp. 43–62 (p. 59).

discovers that Irene, whom everyone presumed had died in the forest fire years earlier, and whom she now takes to be a ghost, has hidden in the trunk of her car. Sole takes her mother in and, to avoid questions about her mysterious reappearance after her presumed death, has her pose as an undocumented Russian working in her clandestine beauty salon. The rest of the film involves the reencounter/ reconciliation of mother with daughters, the final disposal of Paco's body and the parallel narrative of Agustina, Raimunda's friend from the village whose mother had been the other woman burned to death by Irene.

Almodóvar's version of the narrative of reencounter emphasises the continuity between rural and urban scenarios, framing these around the traumatic memories of the past that still haunt the characters after they have abandoned the village for the city. Beneath this plotline, which is laden with Spanish cultural specificity, we find a familiar trope of Latin American melodramatic cinema that dates back to the early sound period, as recalled in numerous Mexican brothel melodramas like Antonio Moreno's *Santa* (1931) and Arcady Boytler's *La mujer del puerto* (*The Woman of the Port*, 1933). The pivot of this hybrid plotting, as suggested earlier, is the rebranded Gardelian tango which reinforces the linkage between village and city along the temporal axis that suggests that there are shared experiences that transcend national borders. To naturalise these connections within the plot, 'Volver' is described in the film's dialogue as the song which, years earlier, Irene had taught Raimunda in preparation for tryouts for child singers for a television programme. Further underscoring the leitmotif of return, her musical performance at the party is also the narrative juncture when Paula becomes aware of aspects of her mother's past (up to this point, Raimunda had only given her mother sketchy references to her own past life). For that spectator-auditor of *Volver*, the particular resurrection/ return of Irene at the precise moment when Raimunda sings 'Volver' works metaphorically to prompt a series of associations of voices, sounds and rhythms to express what historians of popular culture describe as 'the people's hunger to see and hear themselves'.[15] The tango and the melodramatic formulation of reencounter thus become mutually reinforcing structures which, as they are inflected in a contemporary Spanish world, blur the boundaries that otherwise politically separate Spain from Latin America.

---

[15] Jesús Martín-Barbero, *De los medios a las mediaciones: comunicación, cultura y hegemonía* (Mexico City: GG, 1987), p. 182.

We need to recognise that this is not simply the casual interpolation of an arbitrarily chosen Latin American song into a Spanish film; it is, first and foremost, a showcasing of both a shared musical heritage – marked by the refiguring of an Argentine source into a Spanish flamenco form – and the underscoring of the cultural leitmotif of exile and return. The striking staging of the number halts the actions and thus involves a sustained engagement of the film's presumed audiences in reinvesting personal and historical elements into a new aesthetic and narrative continuum. In this way, the song becomes a synecdoche for collective memory in the same way that in the diegesis it is the synecdoche for the heroine's personal past. By contrast to the intermedial 'fissures' noted in *La flor de mi secreto*, *Volver* proposes a coherent historicised vision of a communal culture that had previously only been glimpsed at as fragmented images and sounds in Almodóvar's work.

Within the narrative design of *Volver*, indeed, the staging of Raimunda's performance opens up a form of historical perspectivism, reminding audiences of the auditory migration of Latin American musical sounds that recur throughout all periods of Almodóvar's career. Centuries of cultural exchange and transfer between Spain and Latin America[16] have defied the imposed logic of a colonial culture and normalised, certainly for Almodóvar's generation, through the series of transnational absorptions of Latin American cultural materials – musical forms, narratives, language itself – by Spanish audiences. 'Transnational' in the context within which it operates progressively in Almodóvar's cinema comes to mean both a narrative formulation and, extra-textually, those cultural flows that defy or simply ignore the constructed cultural practices sanctioned by nation states. Within this model, as Walter Mignolo notes more generally, the Spanish language is not simply the imagined patrimony of the national state, but, on the contrary, the agency through which common, transnational outlooks are achieved.[17]

In that reinforcement of the linguistic connections, the film further exploits a range of other patterns of verbal expression – dialogues, diction – that evoke the verbal style of radio soap operas of an earlier era as part of a shared cultural heritage. Reynaldo González has observed the

[16] Lluis Bonet and Alberto de Gregorio, 'La industria cultural española en América Latina', in *Las industrias culturales en la integración latinoamericana*, ed. Néstor García Canclini and Carlos Moncloa (Mexico City: Grijalbo, 1999), pp. 87–128 (p. 87).

[17] Walter Mignolo, *Local Histories/ Global Designs: Coloniality, Subaltern Knowledges and Border Thinking* (Princeton NJ: Princeton University Press, 2000), p. 219.

powerful transnational circulation of radio soap operas within the Spanish-speaking world, even prior to the contemporary *telenovela* craze. These 'auditory spectacles',[18] as he explains, have seldom respected national borders (González, p. 41) and have involved complex chains of cross-fertilisation between Spanish scripts and rebranded Latin American texts within which local referentiality was largely played down (p. 69). Thus the *radionovela* and the telenovela historically found their appeal in the voice dramas of depoliticised borderless melodramas.

Though we never see a radio set in the film, nor the dramatisation of the act of listening to the radio programme, radio effectively becomes the implicit mediation of the female voice in the film. We hear a fairly continuous flow of voices of actresses shaped by the style and substance of dialogues from radio soap operas and similar genre programmes, especially at those moments in the action when the women confess family secrets that require detailed plot descriptions. The origin of this hybridised construction of dialogue dates back to the filmmaker's childhood when it was radio not film that captured the imagination of his mother and sisters. In the 1950s, Almodóvar tells interviewers, he devoured radio serial melodramas that his mother and sisters were listening to: 'The environment of the period was rigid and severe. In my town there was not a lot of opportunity to see many movies'.[19]

Notably, the serialised nature of radio melodrama provided a time-structure that could easily fit into and supplement rather than disrupt the experiences of everyday life. The porous nature of the auditory experience, as cultural theorists have noted, became embedded in the recollection of personal experiences,[20] thereby integrating a mass-mediated verbal style into interpersonal social discourse. We observe this during the scene of Aunt Paula's wake in the village when the neighbour, Agustina (Blanca Portillo), recounts to the local women assembled in the house how the supposed ghost of Irene spoke to her to announce Paula's death, inviting Agustina to enter the house to find the deceased's body. This scene pointedly evokes the tradition of the radio transmission of gothic ghost stories

---

[18] González, Reynaldo, *Llorar es un placer* (La Habana: Editorial Letras Cubanas, 1988), p. 13.

[19] Quoted in Boquerini, Francisco Blanco, *Pedro Almodóvar* (Madrid: Ediciones JC, 1989), p. 14.

[20] William Rowe and Vivian Schelling, *Memory and Modernity: Popular Culture in Latin America* (London and New York: Verso, 1991), p. 98.

with an emphasis on the power of Agustina's voice to manipulate the emotions of the assembled audience of village women.[21]

The wake scene dramatises the impact of the auditory experience of mass-mediated programming on the everyday rituals of the closed community in which imagination takes precedence over any lived or observed experience. In this way, the film underscores certain connections between the audience, literally the 'listeners,' and the radio story. From the perspective of popular auditory culture, it coincides perfectly with the belief system of the village in which the women take more stock in what they hear than in what they see. Tellingly, it was the deceased Aunt Paula who, owing to her blindness, best embodied the belief in the superiority of the auditory over the visible world. In this, she is something of an allegorical figure representing the traditional community, be it Spanish or Spanish-American, or both, for whom the acoustic reality and the voices of the past have more force than the world that these people may see with their own eyes.

Feminised oral culture structures the narrative enunciation of *Volver*, often through rhetorical gestures that recall *radio-teatro* techniques involving the exposition of plot complexity and, the pillars of serialised fiction, 'the dialectic between repetition and innovation'.[22] We find the most extreme version of this near the end of the film, when Irene and Raimunda are seated on a Madrid park bench as the mother recounts to her daughter how she discovered Raimunda's father's infidelity with Agustina's mother years earlier and burnt down the thatched hut where the adulterous couple slept, killing them. Though the scene is shot with a series of extreme close-ups of the faces of the two women, it still involves excessive exposition of soap opera plot details expressed through Irene's speech. What is significant about this and other recyclyings of radio voices and rhetoric is that, like the mass-mediated musical sounds, they become the technologies of memory, constructing and circulating versions of personal past experience as parcels of a larger communal memory culture.

[21] Pedro Almodóvar, *Volver: Guión* (Madrid: Ochoymedio/Libros de Cine, 2006), p. 71.

[22] Nora Mazziotti, 'Intertextualidades en la telenovela argentina: melodrama y costumbrismo', in *El espectáculo de la pasión: las telenovelas latinoamericanas*, ed. Nora Mazziotti (Buenos Aires: Colihue, 1995), pp. 153–64 (p. 156).

Building collective memories

The cumulative effect of these multiple auditory intertexts in *Volver* is to confirm for Almodóvar's transnational audience a profound sense of community through a pluralisation of personal histories. This is what Birgit Neumann, speaking of the literary representation of memory, notes as one of the fundamental privileges of fictional texts: their power 'to integrate culturally separate memory versions by means of mutual perspectivisation'.[23] By proposing multiple and hybrid renderings of the past that cut across time and space, as Neumann argues, the text 'conjures up 'echoes and undertones of a community's past' (Neumann, p. 339). This strategy enables Almodóvar to destabilise the presumed national specificities related to his individual characters so he may realign them within a common Hispanic transnational discourse.

The credit sequence and opening scenes of *Volver* provide a demonstration of the complexity of this process. Even before the film begins, the panels and logos indicating the film's multiple co-producers (the regional government of Castilla-La Mancha, Televisión Española), we hear monaural sounds of an old Spanish recording: Conchita Panadés, accompanied by a female chorus singing 'Las espigadoras' (the poppy gatherers) from the *zarzuela*, or light opera, *La rosa del azafrán* (Jacinto Guerrero, 1931). The image then cuts to the curious folkloric ritual of the women of the village of Alcanfor de las Infantes cleaning the tombs of their departed family members as the fierce southern wind blows against their faces and scatters leaves. Superimposed over these images, the camera tracks laterally from right to left announcing the principal producer, El Deseo, and the authorial rubric: 'Un film de Almodóvar', finally tracking to the back of a tombstone which bears the title letters: *Volver*. This visual design recalls in more modest form the credit sequence of Victor Fleming's *Gone with the Wind* (1939).[24] As in that Hollywood epic, which Almodóvar once jokingly described as his cinematic autobiography, the visual impression is of the wind sweeping the film titles across the screen.

This seemingly simple prologue to the story reveals layers of intertextual allusions, underscoring for audience as well as characters the mise-en-scène of the graveyard as allegorical *lieux de mémoire* (sites of

---

[23] Birgit Neumann, 'The Literary Representation of Memory', in *Cultural Memory Studies: An International and Interdisciplinary Handbook*, ed. Astrid Erll and Ansgar Nünning (Berlin: Walter de Gruyter, 2008), pp. 301–10 (p. 309).

[24] It may also be a parody of the opening scene of Douglas Sirk's tearjerker, *Written on the Wind* (1956).

memory), to use Pierre Nora's formulation.[25] Not only are the music and credit titles suggestive of times past, but the *zarzuela* chorus, with its euphoric paean to country life offers a culturally specific memory of the immediate Spanish post-Civil War period which promoted zarzuela music on Spanish radio as an autochthonous form of 'música con *enjundia*' (music with substance).[26]

The women's ritual cleaning of the graves of family recalls a society in which mnemonic practices (repeating the ritual in an effort to remember the deceased) are attached to oral performances that negate both print and even image culture.[27] The connection between this communal way of remembering the deceased and the sound of the wind and the cemetery metonymically defines the village as the place of the dead. The milieu in effect permits these characters, rooted in traditional culture, to disengage from the material world that surrounds them so as to reposition themselves in a closed auditory world in which the past is not distinguished from the present.[28] Consonant with that complex intertextual cluster of meanings, Juan José Millás provides a prefatory letter to Almodóvar in the Spanish published version of the film script of *Volver,* making note of the similarity of the spectral rural world of Almodóvar's film and the folkloric rural space of Juan Rulfo's Mexican masterpiece, *Pedro Páramo.*[29] The association with the Rulfo novel is especially significant in that it combines the telling identification of oral culture in his films with a deepening sense of a transcendent narrative cluster involving canonical literature that relates to the rural–urban intra-history that is shared by Hispanic audiences.[30]

[25] Pierre Nora, 'Between Memory and History: *Les Lieux de mémoire*', *Representations*, 26 (1989), 7–25.

[26] Manuel Vásquez Montalbán, *Crónica sentimental de España* (Barcelona: De bolsillo, 2003), p. 45.

[27] Aleida Assmann, 'Canon and Archive', in *Cultural Memory Studies: An International and Interdisciplinary Handbook*, ed. Astrid Erll and Ansgar Nünning.Berlin and New York: Walter de Gruyter: 2008), pp. 97–107 (pp. 104–5).

[28] Steven Marsh, 'Missing a Beat: Syncopated Rhythms and Subterranean Subjects in the Spectral Economy of *Volver*', in *All about Almodóvar: A Passion for Cinema*, ed. Brad Epps and Despina Kakoudaki (Minneapolis and London: University of Minnesota Press, 2009), pp. 339–56 (p. 342).

[29] Of special note here is Julio Estrada's extraordinary study of the acoustic dimension of Juan Rulfo's brief corpus of fictions, *El sonido en Rulfo: 'el ruido ese'* (Mexico City: Universidad Nacional de México, 2009).

[30] Almodóvar, Pedro, 'Colocar la cámara, llenar la pantalla de sonidos', in *La propia voz: el cine sonoro de Lucrecia Martel* (Gijón: Festival Internacional de Cine de Gijón, 2008), p. 8.

The community of the dead, now cast in a 'voice drama,' is important here precisely as it replaces the specificity of political geography with Almodóvar's 'sentimental geography'. As disembodied from its source, the acoustic force of the wind, as subsequent action will indicate, further intensifies the free flow of the characters' imagination, as well as the audience. Beatriz Sarlo tells us that early radio transmissions in Latin America functioned as a bridge between traditional society and modernisation; its appeal was its fantastic condition as wireless, suggesting something of the marvellous, as one is able 'to communicate with what you cannot see, to transcend the limits of the material world, something therefore connected in the popular imagination with the para-normal'.[31] The opening sequence of *Volver*, with its preponderance of disembodied sounds and 'echoes' of the past, alludes precisely to the auditory culture which, as the film insists, was an integral part of pre-modern, rural culture. Spanish as well as Latin American audiences are often separated from their provincial roots by no more than one or two generations, further buttressing the sense of a pluralised perspective rooted in a shared sense of the past.

In particular, Almodóvar's melodramatic heroine, Raimunda, embodies that double consciousness of living in the present but emotionally tied to the past. She exemplifies what Sarlo terms 'una modernidad periférica' (peripheral modernity).[32] Writing about the historical context of Argentine urban space of the early decades of the twentieth century, Sarlo describes a space in which 'han llegado las herramientas de la modernidad pero donde todavía persisten los hábitos mentales y perspectivas de la cultura tradicional. Es una "cultura de mezcla"' (where the tools of modernisation have arrived but where there still exist the mental habits and outlooks of traditional culture still persist. It is a 'hybrid culture' (Sarlo, *Una modernidad periférica*, p. 28).[33]

Various images in *Volver* crystallise Raimunda's interstitial positioning between her past in the tradition-laden village of her birth and the modernity of the city. She is seen, for instance, in a brief scene as a cleaning attendant at the Santiago Calatrava-designed futuristic passenger terminal

---

[31] Beatriz Sarlo, *La imaginación técnica: sueños modernos de la cultura argentina* (Buenos Aires: Ediciones Nueva Visión, 1992), p. 115.

[32] Beatriz Sarlo, *Una modernidad periférica: Buenos Aires 1920–1930* (Buenos Aires: Ediciones Nueva Visión, 1988), p. 28.

[33] Martín-Barbero speaks of the same phenomenon, calling it 'una modernidad contemporánea' (a contemporary modernity); see *De los medios a las mediaciones*, p. 165, in which the individual suffers cultural discontinuities. Although they may possess all the outward dressing of modernity, he or she remains trapped in the past.

at Barajas Airport. Having secured the job of preparing a midday meal for the members of a film crew shooting in the neighbourhood, she needs to make the appropriate purchases of food. A shot of her in a public market buying vegetables for the meal is accompanied by the refrain of Alberto Iglesia's musical leitmotif used earlier in the film with shots of the rural landscape of La Mancha. The scene then cuts to an exterior shot showing Raimunda, now laden with grocery bags, trudging up a dusty street. For a moment, the image, in combination with the preceding musical cue, suggests Raimunda's return to the space of the village. Only as the scene progresses do we recognise that she is in the same Madrid working-class barrio of the preceding action. As this image of the urban periphery reflects, she is, in fact, suspended between the rural world she has left and the urban world in which she tries to survive.[34]

There is a particular intertextual density to Raimunda's character, not easily reducible to a simple historical or demographic formula. Actualised through the figure of Penélope Cruz, Raimunda suggests both a human trajectory and the redrawing of cultural and national boundaries. Updating the displaced Gloria from *¿Qué he hecho yo?* with whom she shares many of the same melodramatic features, she even repeats Gloria's patricidal role when she takes responsibility for Paco's murder.[35] To dispose of the body, Raimunda, with Paula's help, drags the corpse to the freezer case of her friend's restaurant. Raimunda's actions effectively mirror a crucial link with *La flor de mi secreto* and the character Leo, a woman who also had her roots in a Manchegan village. But unlike Gloria, Leo has apparently moved beyond the working-class immigrant community and is a successful author of harlequin romances. One of her commissioned novels is *La cámara frigorífica* (*The Refrigerator Murder*), not the escapist harlequin romance her editors want, but a bizarre love story involving hiding a corpse in a freezer. Leo explains that her fiction is based on a true story, taken from a news report from Puerto Rico. In this way, Raimunda's melodramatic itinerary mirrors a grim detail of Latin American social reality. Tellingly, when Raimunda needs to make her definitive dissolution of Paco's body, she enlists the help of the Cuban prostitute, Regina (María Isabel Díaz), to transport the body and to bury

---

[34] Juan A. Hernández Les, *Volver. Las películas de Almodóvar*, ed. Antonio Castro (Madrid: Ediciones JC, 2010), pp. 253–77 (p. 268).

[35] Critics have often noted that in casting Carmen Maura in the role of Irene, Raimunda's mother, after an absence of nearly 20 years from an Almodóvar film, the film's title suggests yet another level of return.

it in the Manchegan countryside. This seemingly minor detail suggests the collaboration between these parallel migrants in the forging of an emerging master Hispanic cultural narrative in which cultural specificities and personal experiences of Spaniards and Latin Americans merge to produce the effect of a common or shared experience.

The presence of Penélope Cruz is key to Almodóvar's conception of the film. On one level, she emblematises the Spanish tradition of the earthy woman of the *pueblo*, sexy but also maternal. We should recall that in her two previous appearances in Almodóvar films, *Carne trémula* (1997) and *Todo sobre mi madre* (2001), Cruz embodied the mother as martyr, thereby refiguring the Spanish tradition in markedly universal terms. At the same time, Cruz as a publicity icon has developed another international career that has effectively refigured her Spanish qualities into international Mediterranean Latina features. This comes through most notably in some of her Hollywood productions – (*All the Pretty Horses, Blow, Vanilla Sky* and most recently with Johnny Depp in *Pirates of the Caribbean*), and, paired with Mexican Salma Hyak in Luc Besson's Latina comedy, *Bandidas* (2006).

This rare combination of opposing features – folksy and cosmopolitan, Spanish and international – help to define Cruz's portrayal of Raimunda as an interstitial figure in the cultural transition toward modernity, yet deeply imbued with the traditional values of the village, moving gracefully between urban and rural milieus without any awareness of the essential contradiction between the two outlooks. She is rooted in her provincial past but accepting of the broader Hispanic world.

Almodóvar raises that profile to a higher meta-cinematic level when he aligns Raimunda/Cruz with the Italian neorealist screen legend, Anna Magnanni. In the Magnaniesque character, explicitly linked by a film text, *Bellísima* (Luchino Visconti, 1951) at the film's end, Raimunda is not merely the long-suffering mother of the Spanish and Latin American *culebrones* (soap operas), but also a universal 'Latin' figure with an appeal to a broad range of audiences.

As the construction of Raimunda suggests, it is not just one of these hybrid features that evokes the transnational texture of *Volver* but the accumulation of diverse and overlapping intertexts that enable the audience to perceive the cohesion of a collective cultural sensibility that recuperates and reunifies the otherwise fragmented historical and personal experience of a deterritorialised Hispanic community.

Co-producing a cinematic Latin America.

As the preceding discussion has proposed, the geopolitical project of *Volver* bears a powerful congruence with what Nuria Triana Toribio has called El Deseo's 'broad international profile'[36] with special distribution strategies for the circulation of their films in Latin America. It is not difficult to recognise the strategic coincidence of the filmmaker's geo-cultural aesthetic with the production company's transnational approaches to film distribution in the region. Triana Toribio in fact has identified Almodóvar as one of Spain's 'directores mediáticos',[37] that is, a media friendly, media-savvy film auteur. The basis of that designation derives in no small part from the operations of El Deseo, Almodóvar's own produc-tion company, which he has used as a platform both to distribute his own films beyond the normal circulation of Spanish films and also, strategi-cally, to engage in a series of co-production with Latin American auteurs. From a more theoretical perspective, Almodóvar's blurring of the usual distinction of filmmaker versus producer implies a critical revision of Walter Benjamin's famous aphorism of 'the author as producer'.[38]

The Benjaminian model suggests how the twin concepts of 'author' and 'producer' relate to the ideological deconstruction of nation-based cinema which is at the heart of the international marketing and reception of Almodóvar's films. For Benjamin, the concept of the producer was, of course, metaphorical. The filmmaker was defined as the producer of knowledge of ideology, rather than of purveyor of cultural objects. In fact, throughout his pivotal essay, Benjamin alludes to the manner in which the 'producer' intervenes to disrupt conventional consumption of culture by the bourgeoisie and in so doing achieves a 'functional transformation' (Benjamin, p. 228) of mass media. For him, production is 'conceived around the view of the artist who actively intervenes in the social, polit-ical and economic order that disrupt the status quo' and, through those works, promotes 'the exemplary character of production, which is able first to induce other producers to produce and, second, to put an improved apparatus at their disposal' (p. 233). The reciprocal nature of the author–

---

[36] Nuria Triana Toribio, 'Journeys of El Deseo between the Nation and the Transnational in Spanish Cinema', in *Studies in Hispanic Cinemas*, 4.3 (2007), 151–63 (p. 155).

[37] NuriaTriana Toribio, 'Auteurism and Commerce in Contemporary Spanish Cinema: Directores mediáticos', *Screen*, 49.3 (2008), 259–76 (p. 260).

[38] Walter Benjamin, 'The Author as Producer', in *Reflections: Essays, Aphorisms, Autobiographical Writings*, edited with an Introduction by Peter Demetz (New York: Schocken Books, 1978), pp. 220–38.

producer model at the heart of El Deseo's operation reflects that double focus of creativity and a form of cultural pedagogy.

Coloured by Almodóvar's own experience of transnational authorship, his production company's decision to support the production and distribution of films by a small but significant group of Latin American directors underscores the logic whereby auteur cinema has come to replace the logic of the nation. Elizabeth Ezra and Terry Rowden in fact argue that the 'auteur' as representative and bearer of national and/or ethnic identity has been central to the international reception and reputation of filmmakers.[39] Though Almodóvar has not actively engaged in any of the Latin American productions sponsored by El Deseo, it is clear from his statements that the films they choose to promote, reflect what executive producer Agustín Almodóvar has characterised as a special affinity with Latin America.

Against this macro-geographic conception, we note a counterpoint in specific film practices related to the peculiar authorial geography that emerges in the films in which El Deseo has engaged in co-productions: Guillermo del Toro's *El espinazo del diablo* (Mexico, 2000); Andrés Wood's 2001 *La fiebre del loco* (*Loco Fever*); *Cobrador* (*In God We Trust*) (Paul Leduc, 2007); Julia Solomonoff's *El último verano de la Boyita* (*Boyita's Last Summer*, 2010); finally, two Argentine films produced by Lita Stantic and directed by Lucrecia Martel: *La niña santa* (*The Holy Girl*, 2004) and *La mujer sin cabeza* (*The Headless Woman*, 2008). With fair consistency, these films exploit mises-en-scène in which rural settings predominate, affording something of a generic sense of Latin American space. This prototypical ruralism, as the model of *Volver* suggests, secures a form of spatial–cultural legibility that serves as a bridge between local and global spectatorship. The rural in these works is imbued with an intra-historical cluster of connotations within which the contemporary tensions of peripheral modernity mirror the historical depiction of Latin America's urban–rural conflicts.[40]

---

[39] Elizabeth Ezra and Terry Rowden, 'General Introduction', in *Transnational Cinemas: The Reader*, ed. Elizabeth Ezra and Terry Rowden (London: Routledge, 2006), pp. 1–12 (p. 3).

[40] It is interesting to note that the transnational Almodóvar of *Volver* coincides with the stages of what critics have noted as his mature auteurism, the cycle of films that begin with *La flor de mi secreto* (1995). This is a relevant context in that it is the mise-en-scene which locates the dominant urban space of his cinema as intimately linked to the nostalgia for the rural traditionalist past, a trope which more effectively coincides with a particular Latin American social and cultural reality than Almodóvar's formative period.

In this insistence on a geographical imaginary rooted in traditional rural societal practices and perceptions, it is worth noting the paradigmatic case of Lucrecia Martel's cinema and her preferred space, her native Argentine province of Salta. Its barren landscapes lend themselves to more global readings of her films as expressions of communities on the margins than is often the case with Argentine films that are set in the geographically recognisable cityscape of Buenos Aires. Almodóvar has himself commented on the significant rural space of Martel's *La mujer sin cabeza*, underscoring the ways that the film offers a heightened sense of the class conflict all but absent in his own films (Almodóvar, 'Colocar la cámara', p. 8).

Aesthetic choices that produce the erasure of the rigid markings of national, ethnic or political borders are common throughout all of El Deseo's Latin American collaborations. The focus in these films is, instead, on a more universal profile of characters on the margins of society, be they the exploited fishermen and dock workers in *La fiebre del loco*, the sexually marginalised heroine of *El último verano de la Boyita*, or the otherwise 'invisible' indigenous characters who shatter the psychological equilibrium of the title character of Martel's *La mujer sin cabeza*.

We may in fact look to Raimunda in *Volver* as crystallising a feature common to many of the characters in these co-production; that is the manner in which she embodies the psychological wounds of peripheral modernity. Like Raimunda, they inhabit a landscape of social marginality; through the intervention of the movie camera, however, they are made visible, and, at times, also provided with a striking auditory presence by means of off-screen sounds. Speaking in praise of Martel's's *La mujer sin cabeza*, Almodóvar has noted, for instance, her ability to 'colocar la cámara y llenar la pantalla con sonidos' (position the camera and to fill the screen with sounds) (Almodóvar, 'Colocar la cámara', p. 8). In this way these auteurist co-productions share a heightened audiovisual sense of the presence of marginalised communities who have traditionally been left off-screen and out-of-frame in Latin American cinema.

Genre, cutting across national borders, both in their rhetorical design and in their specific practices, appears to have helped shape at least two very different co-productions by Mexican filmmakers under the partial aegis of El Deseo. *El espinazo del diablo*, the first of the major forays into Latin American co-productions, was officially classified as a Spanish production since it was shot entirely in Spain, while Paul Leduc's *Cobrador* (*In God We Trust*) was less easily classifiable since it involved the Mexican filmmaker working with co-producers from five countries, including Spain and Britain. As a further expression of its inherent transnationalism, the film was shot in the USA, Mexico, Argentina and Brazil.

El espinazo was shot in Spain entirely under the aegis of El Deseo. Unable to find appropriate funding for a bloody, gothic genre film set in Mexico, Del Toro was supported by El Deseo under the key proviso that the film be shot with a Spanish production crew but with an international cast. Thus Del Toro's scenario, set during the Mexican Revolution, is replaced by the Spanish Civil War and the cast simply mixes up the national origin of the characters among Spaniards (Eduardo Noriega, Marisa Padres) and an Argentine lead (Federico Luppi). These aspects of the production dislodge the film from any appearance of historical or cultural specificity by constructing in their absence a mise-en-scène and plot rooted in a specific Spanish transnational narrative trope – the Spanish Civil War – but guided by gothic genre conventions (noir lighting and suspenseful music, etc.) that make the film legible for a broadly defined international market. It is, ultimately, the idiosyncrasies of genre, however, coupled with El Deseo's skill at international distribution, that enabled the film to circulate in a 'borderless' international film market more widely than might otherwise have been the case with a sole Latin American producer.[41]

The second genre film is considerably more problematic. *Cobrador* is the product of one of the most iconoclastic Latin American filmmakers of the previous generation, Paul Leduc. His earlier films of the 1980s – *Frida, naturaleza viva* (1983) and *Barroco* (1988) had combined many of the same transnational elements that effectively displaced the geopolitical borders with the sense of a common trans-Hispanic culture involving Europe, the Americas and Africa. The common feature of those earlier films had been the intense development of the sound-track which involved blockage of conventional dialogue in order to free his films from a Hollywood-constructive narrative structure and also to open the cinematic text to a broader engagement by diverse Hispanic audiences.

---

[41] It is worth noting here that *The Devil's Backbone* was a collaboration with Del Toro's producer, Bertha Navarro, a key figure in Latin American co-productions with Spain. A 2008 tribute to her at the Guadalajara International Film Festival was accompanied by a catalogue appropriately titled 'Bertha Navarro: cineaste sin fronteras' (Filmmaker without Borders). Navarro, whose production company, Tequila Gang, was also the key figure for two other co-productions with El Deseo: Andrés Wood's *La fiebre del loco* (*Loco Fever*, 2001) and Paul Leduc's *Cobrador* (*In God We Trust*). See Ana Cruz, *Bertha Navarro: cineasta sin fronteras* (Guadalajara: Universidad de Guadalajara, 2008).

Cobrador follows some of that same pattern with a paucity of connective dialogue to provide easy coherence to the often elliptical fragments of this multi-protagonist film. Promoted with the star billing of Peter Fonda, who is only seen in early sequences, the film exploits the formula of the multiple-protagonist plotting that has been a signature element of Mexican transnational filmmaker Alejandro González Iñárritu (*Amores perros, Twenty-one Grams, Babel*). The action is set in New York, Mexico, Brazil and Argentina and, besides El Deseo's modest investment of 15 per cent of the budget, the film was co-produced by Mexican, Brazilian, British and Argentine producers. Ostensibly a denunciation of multinational plundering of Latin American resources, *Cobrador* was generally acknowledged to be a weak film that failed to succeed artistically in the eyes of the critics or as a commercial property in any of its European or Latin American target markets, This failure may owe as much to the film's narrative unrootedness, noted in its lack of any one clearly defined cultural milieu or perspective, or, stemming from that textual flaw, from the failure to successfully market it.

The contrastive successes and failures of these two genre films, and of the more artistically acclaimed Martel films, helps further clarify the logic of Almodóvar's and El Deseo's Latin American project. As co-producer Agustín Almodóvar explains in public and private interviews,[42] the goal of El Deseo in terms of these Latin American projects is modest. It is less about box office profit than about the expenditure of cultural capital to promote promising Latin American filmmakers. El Deseo's interest in Latin American co-productions is built around the 'desire to communicate with those similar to us' through what Agustín Almodóvar calls 'una red de confianza' (a network of trust) in people Pedro knows and whose professional judgement he respects. The operating paradigm of El Deseo as a modestly sized 'artisanal' production company is like that of a family. Not surprisingly, therefore the *red de confianza* through which Latin American production evolves for El Deseo has been of a more familial nature. It is, for that reason, that through the work of Esther García, executive co-producer at El Deseo, contact was made with Bertha Navarro who, starting with Guillermo del Toro's *El espinazo del diablo*, in 2000, began a series of personal interactions with Agustín and Pedro that runs to the present.

---

[42] Personal conversation with the producer in Madrid, January 2011.

In much the same way that Almodóvar proposed the confining map of Spain as the geopolitical imaginary constraining the Spanish spirit in *La flor de mi secreto*, one may look at the portfolio of El Deseo as a reimagined cultural map of the region in which the inflexible political borders are dissolved through an emphasis on the historical commonalties of a shared cultural experience.

Finally, what we may discern beneath the surface of El Deseo's astute financial arrangements with Latin American co-productions is a deeper conceptual project involving the cinematic emphasis on cultivating a deterritorialised sensibility that dislodges films from their exclusively local environments and addresses broader audiences. In that model, questions of the geographic imaginary weigh heavily, as does a conception of authorial legibility as the voice of community. In this regard, *Volver* may be viewed as crystallising some of the essential elements of that shared cultural experiences of language, song and sound: the struggle of individuals who recognise themselves trapped in that peripheral modernity. While not all El Deseo co-productions fully adhere to this cluster of elements in every way, collectively they do provide a basis for understanding the conceptualisation of broader transnational cinematic audiences that is emerging as a cultural community in what is increasingly our own post-national age.

7

Transnational Film Financing and Contemporary Peruvian Cinema: The Case of Josué Méndez

SARAH BARROW

It seems clear that without the support of transnational collaborative funding and support initiatives, filmmakers from so-called 'small'
Hispanic countries such as Peru where 'everything would seem to be
against the idea'[1] would lack the means to create and release their works
in traditional formats even onto the specialist festival circuit let alone
via commercial exhibition networks. As Randal Johnson, in his study
on film policy, pointed out in 1996, in Latin America 'political turmoil,
economic instability, high inflation rates and debt crises have contributed
to the instability of national industries',[2] and the context for cinematic
activity emanating from Peru has changed little since he wrote that paper.
Even relatively established and internationally acclaimed directors from
(and based in) Peru such as Alberto Durant and Francisco Lombardi
have consistently struggled to access the small amounts of state-administered funding that is available via competition most years.[3] This essay

[1] Michael Chanan, 'The Economic Condition of Cinema in Latin America', in
New Latin American Cinema: Theory, Practices and Transcontinental Articulations, ed.
Michael T. Martin (Detroit: Wayne State University Press, 1997), pp. 185–200.
[2] Randal Johnson, 'Film Policy in Latin America', in *Film Policy: International,
National and Regional Perspectives*, ed. Albert Moran (London: Routledge, 1996), pp.
128–47.
[3] Durant is probably best known for his crime thriller of 1991 *Alias la Gringa*,
although he continues to direct films to this day. Lombardi's seminal work, *La boca
del lobo* (1988), is set amidst the crisis of the *Sendero Luminoso* conflict of the 1980s
and '90s. He has since directed 11 more films, many of which have been the result
of co-production deals. While Lombardi was among the first wave of Latin American
filmmakers who were successful in gaining support from Spanish TV in the 1980s and

argues that more complex financial networks than those relied upon by
Lombardi and Durant are now required by most Latin American directors, and that these in turn set up new relationships and power dynamics
that bring potential complications and interferences that hark back to the
concerns about imperialism that preoccupied their predecessors of the
1960s.[4] Despite such risks, new models of funding have emerged that
allow for a certain degree of freedom from the constraints and expectations of local politics, some of which rely on networks of state funding
devolved to other groups (such as festivals), while others have been established by businesses as philanthropic ventures. Most recently, the possibilities offered by so-called 'new' media via social networking sites have
been harnessed as opportunities for engaging audiences around the world
directly in the movie business(es) – funding, distribution, and exhibition
– many of which have been of benefit to filmmakers throughout Latin
America.

This chapter specifically explores the range of strategies adopted by
Josué Méndez in his mission to ensure the completion, distribution,
promotion and relatively widespread international exhibition of his first
two features, *Días de Santiago* (2004) and *Dioses* (2008). Having failed
to acquire substantial state backing for the first feature project, Méndez
was obliged at first to rely largely on the goodwill of friends and family
as well as on the associates and resources based at the TV station that
provided him with a regular income.[5] When experienced Lima-based
Swiss producer Stefan Kaspar came on board to back the project's development and link it into European schemes, the film was given access
to the complex European network of festivals and funds.[6] Having won

---

early 1990s, those sources have long since dried up or have been diverted to other more
reliable and potentially more lucrative projects. See 'Co-productions and Common Cause'
by Rob Rix on this era of Hispanic co-production in *Spanish Cinema: Calling the Shots*,
ed. Rob Rix and Roberto Rodríguez-Saona, Leeds Iberian Papers (Leeds: Trinity and All
Saints, University of Leeds, 1999), pp. 113–28.

4   See Michael Chanan's chapter 'Latin American Cinema: From Underdevelopment
to Postmodernism', in *Remapping World Cinema: Identity, Culture and Politics in Film*,
ed. Stephanie Dennison and Song Hwee Lim (London: Wallflower, 2006), pp. 38–54 for
a full discussion of this historical and ideological context.

5   Conacine is the national body that oversees film policy and funding for Peruvian
filmmakers. It reports directly to the government, currently via the Ministry of Culture.
For further information, see http://www.conacine.pe (Last accessed 11 December 2011).

6   Stefan Kaspar's own producer credits include successful 1980s co-productions with
Channel 4 such as *Gregorio* (1984) and *Juliana* (1988), made as part of the left-wing,
socially committed Grupo Chaski. See Sophia A. McLennen's article on their work for
a full account of the impact of these films, 'The Theory and Practice of the Peruvian

a host of awards at a Human Rights festival in Germany, it went on to garner further acclaim at both the Rotterdam and Cannes film festivals, ensuring financial support for a reasonably well-funded promotional campaign back in Peru as well as overseas, and culminating in a place for the director on the highly regarded script residency in Paris backed by the Cannes festival for new filmmakers from around the world. Méndez's success, coinciding with that of a noteworthy group of 'new' Latin American directors, suggests that the time may be right for an investigation into the impact of transnational funding and other support schemes on the development of a national cinema for Peru.

While this chapter does not presume to suggest that Peruvian cinema is now thriving and that its filmmakers have been awash with new opportunities since the early 2000s, it does attempt to explore the potential for sustained rejuvenation offered by taking a fresh approach to the negotiation of national schemes (state-backed initiatives and local support) alongside transnational collaborations (festivals, competitions, trans/multilateral projects) in the context of film financing, looking at both Hispanic and non-Hispanic sources. Moreover, the attempts made by Méndez and his production team to carve out a formula for success with his first two features provides us with a fascinating case study which points to the benefits and pitfalls of the vast array of funding possibilities that are on offer in the increasingly complex world of cinema production and distribution. Influenced to a certain extent by the work of John Tomlinson on the relations between culture and globalisation, and his concern for the power politics of transnational networks,[7] I am particularly interested in his exploration of the 'rapidly developing and ever-demeaning network of interconnections and interdependences that characterize modern social life [... and ...] the increasing flow of goods, information, people, and practices across national boundaries' (Tomlinson, p. 2). This essay argues that the speed of such developments underscores the need to negotiate these networks with great care in logistical as well as conceptual and ideological terms when it comes to cultural production, in order to sidestep the shadow of imperialism that has made such funding partnerships difficult to set up in the past.

Grupo Chaski', *Jump Cut: A Review of Contemporary Media*, 50 (Spring 2008). Available at: http://www.ejumpcut.org/archive/jc50.2008/Chaski/index.html (Last accessed 11 December 2011).

7   See John Tomlinson's study of the development of globalisation and its impact on culture in *Globalization and Culture* (Cambridge: Polity Press, 1999).

The survey and analysis that follow explore the new associations and, crucially, the interdependences (often uneven, whether intentionally or not) that are generated by transnational funding and support schemes set up to support the development of films such as those under discussion here. Such interconnections and interdependences that exist between film-makers and their producers, between different producers and funders, and/ or between films, filmmakers and their audiences are, as Catherine Grant and Annette Kuhn point out in the introductory essay to their volume on world cinema, fundamental to understanding the 'transnational aspects of the medium'.[8] These films become interesting as sites of exchange and as examples of cultural production in an increasingly complex filmmaking environment. As such, it could be argued that through participation in such schemes, filmmakers such as Méndez are unwittingly complicit in the ongoing pressures of cultural imperialism and commercial imperatives.[9] On the other hand, such examples may serve as cause for celebration in that there are production teams willing to negotiate the legislative, finan-cial and political minefields of transnational funding and award schemes that help bring these films to public screens, thereby contributing to the gradual creation of more interesting and nuanced networks and structures of power.

The case of Josué Méndez: *Días de Santiago* (2003) and *Dioses* (2008)

Josué Méndez was considered by several observers to be part of a new generation that led to a situation in 2003 that signalled, as Jeffrey Middents points out, 'a surge of interest and activity' for and in Peruvian cinema.[10] He was distinctive at that time for an apparent acknowledge-

---

[8]   Catherine Grant and Annette Kuhn, 'Screening World Cinema', in *Screening World Cinema: A Screen Reader*, ed. Grant and Kuhn (Oxford: Routledge, 2006), pp. 1–14 (p. 2). Grant and Kuhn distinguish usefully between the 'multinational' and the 'international', and argue that it is the latter – 'that is to say the international interconnectedness' (p. 2) – that is of greater relevance in any study of the transnational and cinema.

[9]   My focus on Méndez is partly to allow for a more detailed study of his films, but also because he lacks the family connections that peers such as Claudia Llosa enjoy and which would require acknowledgement as part of her own transnational network. Note that Llosa is the niece both of the internationally renowned novelist Maria Vargas Llosa and of the Hollywood-based director Luis Llosa.

[10]   Jeffrey Middents, *Writing National Cinema: Film Journals and Film Culture in Peru* (Hanover, NH: Dartmouth College Press; University Press of New England, 2009). Middents notes that in 2003, 'ten locally produced films opened in Lima; the Universidad Católica announced its seventh annual international film festival in Lima; and, after

ment that reliance on state funds for feature filmmaking alone would be futile and naive. He was born in 1976 and grew up in Lima, but went to the USA to study Film and Latin American Studies at Yale University. On the strength of three award-winning short films, he was selected to participate in the prestigious Producer's Workshop run by the *Festival des Trois Continents* (Nantes, France) in 2000.[11] His first feature, *Días de Santiago* (2003) was made on his return to Peru, after a period of establishing his craft as writer, director and editor for Peruvian television, advertising and theatre. As a result of its funding package, the film had its world premiere in competition at the Rotterdam International Film Festival (January 2004), and was selected for further screening in over one hundred festivals worldwide. In the end, it was distributed in more than 15 countries, it was Peru's Official Entry for the Academy Awards (2004), and it represented its country at the *Tous les Cinémas du Monde* selection at the Cannes Film Festival. The film won more than 35 international prizes, and thereby became Peru's most garlanded film to that date.[12]

In this section of the essay, I attempt to unravel and reveal the ingredients that led to the young filmmaker's apparently 'instant' success, taking into account the production and financial context as well as the distinctive narrative and stylistic qualities of the film itself. I hope to uncover the extent to which the interconnections and interdependences between director, production team and their broader network of contacts worked together to lead to an important turning point for Peruvian cinema in terms of a new way of exploiting the transnational dimension of film finance, especially at the levels of distribution, exhibition and marketing.

At the time of its release, *Días de Santiago* was regarded as probably the most accomplished film by a Peruvian director who was welcomed onto the domestic arena for attempting 'new narrative structures or styles

---

several years where new megaplexes were only being built in the very affluent parts of the capital, the Chilean company CinePlanet opened a new theater in Los Olivos, a lower-middle-class suburb far from ... the traditional centers of Peruvian cultural power' (p. 181).

[11] The young director established an early reputation for innovative filmmaking with his short films, namely the award-winning *Parelisa* (1999) and *Solo Buenos Amigos* (1997), both of which he also wrote and edited.

[12] Prizes included the FIPRESCI Award at the highly respected Fribourg International Film Festival in Switzerland which is granted by representatives of the International Cinematographic Press Federation and aims to encourage new cinema. The film's presence at this festival was partly secured by its Swiss producer's reputation and network of contacts throughout Europe.

that, while perhaps not innovative compared to what is happening in other cinemas around the world, brought a fresh perspective to Peruvian cinema' (Middents, p. 191). It is notable, however, that Méndez's first film received very little financial or other support for its preproduction and production stages from conventional national or transnational sources. Although the director was granted a small script development award in 2000 from Conacine, the state-run operation that until 2011 administered a small pot of money in support of the development of national cinema in Peru, he financed the shoot and most of the post-production himself. Continuing to work as an editor for national television, he shot the film on low-tech digital format over 24 days, pulling in favours from associates, friends and family in true guerrilla filmmaking fashion.[13] Completion was finally made possible by an award from the Hubert Bals Fund for world cinema established by the Rotterdam Film Festival in 1987 with the support of the Dutch Ministry of Foreign Affairs. As already noted, it premiered at that festival in January 2004, and thus became the first Peruvian film to be selected for Rotterdam's official competition. As Tamara Falicov remarks in her insightful essay on film festivals and their associated funding schemes, '[T]he Hubert Bals Fund is a key avenue for filmmakers from the developing world to gain funding and a space to screen their work ... [while] ... the most valuable aspect of the fund, besides the financial help, is the exposure in an international film festival setting'.[14] The festival screenings and awards that followed made it possible for the producers to draw up and implement a comprehensive distribution plan for commercial exploitation in cinemas and on DVD. The film was finally screened in Peru, at the main festival for world cinema, in August 2004, and thereafter enjoyed a profitable commercial run throughout the country. In fact, it remained on domestic screens in a competitive environment for an unprecedented six months from late 2004

[13] As Middents points out, *Días de Santiago* 'was only the third commercially released feature [from Peru] to be shot on digital video'. (*Writing National Cinema*, p. 191)

[14] Tamara Falicov, 'Migrating from South to North: The Role of Film Festivals in Funding and Shaping Global South Film and Video', in *Locating Migrating Media*, ed. Greg Elmer, Charles H. Davis, Janine Marchessault and John McCullough (Lanham: Lexington Books, 2010), pp. 3–21. Falicov also reveals that one of the main supporters of *Días de Santiago*, Stefan Kaspar, was granted funding from the Hubert Bals scheme to support the production of 10 DVDs of Latin American films and a microcinema network to provide sites for Peruvians to watch films outside the urban centres.

to early 2005, and was shown in a variety of provincial cities as well as on the commercial circuit in Lima.[15]

Días de Santiago was celebrated in Peru and beyond for taking a distinctive approach to the recurrent and familiar themes of violent conflict and national identity that had been explored by earlier filmmakers of renown from Peru such as Francisco Lombardi, Alberto Durant and Marianne Eyde. Perhaps the overwhelmingly positive reception by national critics, who considered it the best quality Peruvian film for several years, was even more surprising than the international success it enjoyed, given the negativity that usually greets a new film from a local director.[16] The critics praised the way it drew upon a more experimental approach to the codes of film language and adapted them to the representation of a dystopian vision of urban Peru. Many were impressed by the director's use of a nervous, jump-cutting non-linear editing style, edgy hand-held cinematography, and unpredictable switches between black-and-white and colour, as well as by the use of blue and orange tints to emphasise the inner turmoil of his main character. They also applauded its impressionistic approach to the use of sound: the sparing use of lamenting tones in a zither-based soundtrack, and the experimentation with everyday noises to evoke the tense, heightened reality of the moment. Moreover, credit was given for the tight composition and an intermittent voice-over which further ensure that the audience is positioned to experience the world from inside the protagonist's tormented mind. Most of all, they admired Méndez's obvious passion for cinema generally, and the implicit formal references in the film to the work of internationally renowned filmmakers such as Krzysztof Kieslowski and Wong Kar-Wei.

Set at the end of the 1990s, an increasingly repressive decade in political and social terms, Méndez's film follows the frustrated efforts made by Santiago (Pietro Sibille), its young working-class, mixed-race protagonist, to reinsert himself into family and civilian life after several years as a marine defending the integrity of his country in the remote Amazon and Andean areas of Peru. Particular sets of enemies mentioned in the film include the Ecuadorian Army, and remnants of insurgent groups such as the Sendero Luminoso (Shining Path), who had by this point

---

[15] By 2004, cinemas in Peru were run mainly by multinational companies and screened Hollywood blockbusters almost exclusively. It was difficult even for a successful European film to gain an exhibition slot, and almost impossible for a Peruvian feature to do so, given the poor performance of earlier national releases.

[16] The film won the critics award, as well as the best actor award, at the Lima Festival of Latin American Film, August 2004.

become linked, according to state-promulgated discourse, with traffickers of cocaine. Once home, Santiago tries hard to reintegrate himself into civilian life and to fulfil the expectations of others but is blocked at every turn. His relationship with his wife crumbles, his old army comrades try to draw him into a life of crime, and he fails to develop any emotional tie with his family. His professional options are restricted, and he becomes convinced that the only way to survive in the urban jungle of Lima is by applying the tactics he learnt as a marine to everyday life. Ultimately, though, he struggles to impose strict order on his life and on those around him. When he realises that his initial strategy is failing, he tries instead to imitate the middle-class youngsters he meets, who idle away their days by clubbing, drinking and shopping. Events spin wildly out of control when his violent brother's girlfriend begins to make seductive overtures and pleads with Santiago to kill her lover. In the end, Santiago cannot stop himself lashing out in frustration at those who confront and try to control him, and the narrative moves towards a disturbing and explosive ending.

Although the film focuses on the troubled inner world of one traumatised individual who cannot escape the cycle of violence in which he has become entrapped, his story may also be taken metaphorically and symbolically as a painfully realistic vision of a generation in crisis within a specific national context. It offers an effective prism through which issues of concern to young Peruvians at the turn of the twenty-first century may be understood, while at the same time it struck a chord with audiences around the world who appreciated it largely as an intricate portrayal of a young man returning from war. Santiago's story begins with his return to a place that he no longer recognises and the narrative centres on the painful process of reintegration into a society that has moved on without him. His years in the armed forces have obliged him to put certain ambitions on hold, only to have them cruelly dashed when he returns home. His world and his hopes crumble and disintegrate when he abandons the rigid structure of the armed forces; he faces an uncertain future without support and guidance from anyone who really understands what he has been through, or what he now lacks by way of psychological formation. His is an intensely personal struggle of re-assimilation into civilian life that draws attention to 'the struggle against dissolution and fragmentation'.[17]

The formal quality of Méndez's film is raw, intense, and fragmentary,

---

[17] Zygmunt Bauman, *Identity* (Cambridge: Polity, 2004), p. 77.

reinforcing the psychological trauma of Santiago by the use of cinematic strategies of dislocation that are strongly reminiscent of the French New Wave movement of the 1960s, revealing a little of the director's many influences from a wide range of 'world' cinemas. These dislocatory moments provide a discomforting viewing experience, and in so doing, they highlight the film's approach to identity as fractured, multi-layered, contradictory, complex and, to draw from Bauman once more, as 'fluid' (p. 77). It also focuses on the constant need to react and respond to changing social conditions and human emotions. *Santiago* strikes a far from optimistic note about humanity, contemporary Peruvian reality, and life for young people living in Lima by illustrating the tragic consequences of a society in meltdown. Moreover, although rejecting the traditional approach of flashback to depict directly Santiago's traumatic years in the jungle, the film nevertheless conveys a strong sense of an individual who cannot escape his past and who is paralysed by his own memories. As such, it deals more with the abstract concept of memory and the scars it can leave, than with individual concrete memories. As one Peruvian critic pointed out, this film offers 'una áspera y dolorosa exploración de las huellas que deja la guerra en los seres humanos que regresan a sus hogares a luchar por una "normalidad" que probablemente jamás recuperarán' (a vivid and painful exploration of the scars left by war on human beings who return home to fight for a 'normality' that they will probably never attain).[18]

The film pulls no punches. In terms of approach, Méndez's film is quite unlike another *opera prima* by one of his peers that appeared the same year: *Paloma de papel* by Fabrizio Aguilar, which handles the same broad themes of identity and conflict but takes a much more traditional turn in terms of style and narrative structure, as it focuses on a young boy's plight as he is taken by Sendero Luminoso insurgents to be trained as a 'freedom fighter'. While Aguilar's film unashamedly celebrates the power of humanity, and became the 'biggest local crowd-pleaser' (Middents, p. 191) of 2003, Méndez's work strikes a distinctly more pessimistic note about the future for those young Peruvians who were in some way caught up in a series of conflicts that were then largely forgotten or ignored by the media and society generally.[19] Santiago's story thus in many ways

[18] Raúl A. Cachay, 'Un francotirador en Lima', *El comercio*, 9 August 2004, p. 8 (Translation is mine).

[19] However, while *Paloma de papel* also attracted significant international attention including funding from a number of transnational schemes and North American projects such as USAID, and awards from globally significant bodies such as Amnesty International, its director failed to achieve similar success within the next decade.

serves to illustrate Anthony Smith's powerful contention that 'the importance of national amnesia and getting one's own history wrong [is essen-
tial] for the maintenance of national solidarity',[20] a sentiment that may
resonate with audiences of any nationality. But unlike the family and
friends around him who remained largely oblivious to the personal impact
of conflict, this protagonist cannot shake off the memories of the brutality
he engaged in, and his wheelchair-bound former comrade is so consumed
by the indelible psychological scars of war that for him the only way out
is by committing suicide. Santiago recalls time and again the early excite-
ment he felt at being sent out on a mission, a sentiment that was soon
dashed and replaced by disillusionment sparked by the harsh treatment
of recruits like him by the officers. However, even harder to confront is
the rejection of his worth by civilians who have no idea what he and his
comrades have been through on their behalf.

Indeed, the film is structured as a series of increasingly tense combats
between Santiago and all those he encounters in civilian society, with the
protagonist usually positioned as both victim and aggressor. As well as
drawing attention to the spiralling torment he suffers, these clashes also
serve to highlight the fragmented and disconnected nature of Lima society
at the end of the twentieth century. The city, like so many others across
the world, is presented as a complex environment that is completely
disjointed in terms of its racial groupings and their associated meanings.
Santiago is forced to learn that the capitalist values of wealth, individual
progress and private ownership are more important in this unfamiliar,
uncanny world that he returns to than the socialist values that marked
the country one decade before. This atmosphere of dislocation is highlighted, for example, when the intense, hyper-disciplined Santiago and
his lazy, self-serving brother are forced to confront each other; when the
struggling, inarticulate protagonist tries to join in the social whirl of the
young women in his IT class, whose hedonistic lifestyle both repulses
and seduces him; when the young man makes a hesitant enquiry about
his course options to the receptionist at the private college and is treated
with disdain; when the financially impoverished soldier is reminded of his
lack of status and wealth by the department store supervisor who shows
no respect for his military experience. In short, the more Santiago tries
to reinstate the sense of order, discipline, camaraderie and respect that

he appreciated about military life, the more he realises that his efforts to reintegrate as a civilian are doomed.

Despite resonating with such a pessimistic tone, the film was welcomed by domestic and international audiences for whom it appeared to offer a distinctive, albeit uncomfortable vision of everyday life in the metropolis for those who fail to conform to the demands and expectations of consumer society. The image of a dystopian city at the turn of the millennium that offered nothing but isolation and alienation for a returning military man certainly struck a chord with critics and general cinema-goers alike. Moreover, it won its director a scholarship from the Cannes Film Festival that gave him the opportunity to spend six months developing his next project in Paris at Cinéfondation, a residency programme created in 1998 'to inspire and support the next generation of international filmmakers'.[21]

For his next project, Méndez opted for a very different approach in terms of genre, style and theme, although he retained the trope of an outsider embodied in the main male character. However, *Dioses* (*Gods*) eschews the gritty realism of *Santiago* and adopts the tone of a dark satirical comedy which follows a set of characters from Peru's hermetic upper-class. The emphasis is again on a dysfunctional family but this time that family is wealthy and its members' lives are structured around a hollow series of meaningless, yet intriguing social events and sexual dalliances. Its protagonists are beautiful and privileged. They live in the most luxurious house by the most exclusive beach in Peru. The film offers a vision of a world where there appear to be no material problems or needs; a world of forms and beauty, an artificial world of appearances – not the stereotypical vision of Peru held by most outsiders, nor experienced by most 'insiders'. The family in *Dioses* represents a different sort of Peruvian social structure, the family that has everything, but which clings to a world of unbreakable and inflexible social customs, perhaps in fear of losing the privileged position attained or of having to acknowledge the unfairness of their situation. *Dioses* presents a story that centres on this family, its decadence, its rigid social mechanisms, and its efforts to conceal any interior ugliness under a veneer of physical perfection.

Four characters form the central focus of the film. Twenty-one year old

---

[21] http://www.festival-cannes.com/en/cinefoundation.html (Last accessed 11 December 2011). Cinéfondation, supported by the CNC (National Cinema Centre of France) and the City of Paris, offers up to six international directors a year the chance to develop their second feature from a base in Paris with the intensive support of industry professionals and with access to all the cinematic resources the city can offer.

Andrea (Anahí de Cárdenas) lives the life of a socialite until she discovers she is pregnant. Her brother Diego (Sergio Gjurinovic) is being pressured by his father to enter the family business rather than go to college, but is also struggling to overcome a sexual attraction to his own sister at the same time as trying to find a place for himself within a decadent upper-class society where all behave as if they are beyond rules and morality. Meanwhile, prospective stepmother Elisa (Maricielo Effio) is desperate to hide her lower-class, provincial roots and to ingratiate herself into a group of vapid trophy wives. Presiding over the clan is Agustín (Edgar Saba), whose defining characteristic is his oblivion to his family's intense dissatisfaction with their lot. Providing an important point of contrast is the family's maid who is kept on the periphery – present yet also always absent – representative of the servant class found in many upper-class Peruvian households.[22] The film's climax draws back at the last minute from escalating into the violence that lurks everywhere as a threat. Like the earlier film, the ending of *Dioses* is ambivalent, suggesting that the positive closure his characters seek remains out of their control and that their destinies are tied up with the constraints of social structure.

Study of both these films suggests that the director is motivated by an awareness of social injustice. In *Dioses*, the isolation of the Peruvian upper-class is emphasised literally through the location of the family's house in an exclusive gated beach community, and through their alcohol-sustained disinterest in the serious economic and social problems affecting their country. The impact of this situation on the lives of the young people at the heart of this narrative is almost as traumatic as the situation faced by Santiago from the first film, although invoking audience sympathy is far more of a challenge with the privileged characters of the second feature. Nevertheless, the core dilemma of a struggle by one young man to fit in and find a place for himself in a morally bankrupt society is loosely repeated. Likewise, the exploration of the hedonistic lifestyles of wealthy young women in Lima, at the periphery of the narrative of his first feature, is present again here. Moreover, just as that first film dealt with the sort of topical issues that resonated across national and cultural borders, so too

---

[22] This image of the household servant is a trope that has cropped up in a number of Peruvian films by socially committed directors of the 1980s and 1990s, notably *Ni con Dios ni con el Diablo* (Nilo Pereira del Mar, 1990) whose protagonist Jeremías (Marino León de la Torre) escapes from the violence threatening his Andean village, only to find himself entrapped by the strict hierarchies of an upper-class household in Lima.

does this one with its nuanced critique of racial and class-based divisions that are understood by the curious spectator the world over.

More could be explored in relation to the thematics of the film and the interplay of the topical with the perennial that, according to commentators such as Mette Hjort and Tamara Falicov, is part of what generates interest in films that fit the rubric of 'national', 'world' or even 'foreign' cinema. However, for the purposes of the remainder of this essay, and to shift the focus back to the world of transnational funding and support schemes, I want to focus now on investigating the story behind the making of this second film. For this other story would appear to exemplify the all-too-common paradox for any artistic venture that suggests that access to greater funds, time and resources may not always lead to a more successful project in either commercial or critical terms. The seductive nature of discovering and nurturing talent, somehow being able to lay claim to having contributed to the development of a new star, is shown here not to be the best path to success in the short term. The network of resources that helped bring this second project to fruition is far more complex than that which supported the first and leads one to wonder whether the various sources of advice that were offered as part of the schemes involved, as well as the requirements attached to them, may have resulted in a less confident film that lacked the sense of mission, focus and purpose that made *Santiago* stand out. It is also useful to consider whether the touristic, stereotypical perception of what is authentic, interesting and meaningful about Peruvian identity, its people and their stories would have led many potential or actual viewers (unaware of the complexities of Peruvian culture) to dismiss this film for its apparent dismissal of the Andean culture with which Peru is normally associated. Indeed, many may have found its focus on the upper-class either too localised or too Westernised and in any case lacking in the exotic qualities of Andean tradition and folklore that the typical art-house festival audience might expect.

The production context, in particular the funding strategy and model of this film are complex in the way that many films from small nations now are if they cost anywhere near the $600,000 budget of *Dioses*. The production company set up by Méndez in 1998, Chullachaki Cine, had declared its interest in producing films of international quality, with worldwide commercial appeal, and promoting co-productions between Peru and the rest of the world, and while *Santiago* had fulfilled the first two of those aims to a certain extent, *Dioses* offered the opportunity to move further into the world of co-production. In fact, Chullachaki negotiated resources and support from a range of schemes beyond those administered by the

Peruvian state in order to create a film with the same level of integrity and conceptual interest as the director's debut, but with higher production values. In the end, these resources came from Germany (with the help of Mil Colores Media and Cachoeira Films), Argentina (Lagarto Cine) and France (TS Productions), with financial input from all of the following: Conacine (Peruvian state film fund), Incaa (the national cinema fund for Argentina), Ibermedia (transnational Hispanic fund), World Cinema Fund (attached to Berlin Film Festival), Fonds Sud (French-financed scheme for filmmakers from countries where funds are otherwise difficult to access), Cinéfondation (attached to Cannes Film Festival), and the Hubert Bals Fund (attached to Rotterdam Film festival). The project was further affected by the involvement of an experienced British director as mentor, funded by another French scheme designed to bring together the worlds of business and art. The impact of the interventions and power dynamics brought into play by the requirements of some of the contributors will form the basis of the brief discussion that follows.[23]

The story of the film's creation began with the drafting of the script in Paris as part of the Cinéfondation scheme, during which time the proposal was submitted to the Berlinale: World Cinema Fund (WCF) in Autumn 2006. This fund is an initiative that had been established two years earlier by the German Federal Cultural Foundation, the Berlin International Film Festival, and the Goethe Institute with a mission to 'support filmmakers from transition countries' that have a weak film infrastructure of their own.[24] *Dioses* became one of only five projects (out of 82 submissions that year) to be granted €55,000 towards its production costs by a prestigious scheme that prides itself on supporting potentially award-winning projects. The scheme also offers guaranteed screening in Germany itself, in line with its exhibition-related remit of promoting cultural diversity in German cinemas.

One requirement of funding from the WCF is that a German partner should be involved, although not necessarily as co-producer. In fact, the scheme's guidelines explicitly avoid referring to the German affiliates as 'producers', partly because of their stated ideological aim to promote

---

[23] Note that despite this high level support, as a last-minute *Dioses* fundraiser, the producer organised a fiesta netting a much needed sum of $1,400 towards catering costs.

[24] These 'transition countries' eligible for support from the WCF include those in the regions of Latin America, Africa, the Middle East and Central Asia, South East Asia and the Caucasus. See the scheme's website for further details: http://www.berlinale.de/en/das_festival/world_cinema_fund/wcf_profil/index.html (Last accessed 11 December 2011).

intercultural dialogue within the film industry and a positive under-standing of globalisation that aims not to privilege one partner over the other, but also – more pragmatically – in order to provide the opportunity for co-operations with other film-related companies in Germany such as world sales agents or distributors. In the case of *Dioses*, the involvement of the Munich-based production company Mil Colores Media (together with Cachoeira Films, also located in Germany), set up in 2004 with a special interest in co-producing, distributing and promoting feature films and creative documentaries made by Latin American and Spanish film-makers, was crucial in this respect both as conduit to the German funds and as support for the Peruvian producers, Chullachaki Producciones.[25] However, the power dynamics created by the specific management of the funding is interesting in that it is the German partner who signs the agreement and who is the direct recipient of the financial support, and so becomes to an extent the dominant partner, controlling the finance and impacting thereby on creative decisions. This potentially uneven scenario is mitigated to a degree by the requirement on the part of the German partner to prove that the WCF funding (minus a possible handling fee for the German producer of 7.5% max) is spent entirely in the WCF region, but the relationship between funding and creative control remains crucial.

During the year after securing the WCF finance, Méndez benefited further from European support in the form of a period of mentoring from British director Stephen Frears. This was sponsored as part of the Rolex Mentor & Protégé Arts Initiative, which promotes itself as an international philanthropic programme created to assist extraordinary artists to achieve their full potential, and offers 'promising young artists from around the world unique access to renowned artistic masters'.[26] Méndez was selected from young directors all over the world and was awarded $50,000 as well as a year of mentoring during which Frears passed on his knowledge and artistic experience to Méndez at key stages of the filmmaking process, firstly by reading and commenting on the script and then by working at the young director's side during an editing workshop on the first cut in London. Early in the process – shortly before shooting began on set – Frears paid a visit to his 'protégé' in Lima, where he met the actors and the production team, and helped Méndez work through aesthetic and conceptual issues by acting as a critical friend and constantly emphasising

---

[25] See http://www.milcolores.info/milc.html (Last accessed 11 December 2011).
[26] See http://www.rolexmentorprotege.com/en/index.jsp (Last accessed 11 December 2011).

the need for precision and planning. Interestingly but perhaps not surprisingly given Frears' own wide-ranging body of work and his sometimes uneasy relationship with the cinematic establishment, he speaks in all his interviews on this project about taking a very hands-off approach and allowing Méndez to learn from his mistakes. In one report, he reflects for example that 'All you can do is ask questions ... Méndez has to provide the answers' (2007, rolexmentorprotege.com).

It is worth noting that, like many schemes linked to festivals, this project seeks out new artists from around the world (applications have to be invited after a form of scouting process) and brings them together with experienced artists, mostly European or North American, for a year of creative collaboration in a one-to-one mentoring relationship. Such an approach aims to ensure a level of quality with which the brand of Rolex would clearly wish to be associated, suggesting a relationship that is perhaps more symbiotic than one of dependence. At the same time, it propels the chosen artist into an élite world of even more privileged access to increased opportunities for funding, distribution, exhibition and travel. The value of networking that raises awareness amongst those whose job it is to seek new talent cannot be underestimated and brings to the fore the inequality and potential injustice for those who lack access to those networking situations. It is certainly a complex relationship that requires careful negotiation by both mentor and mentee, both with each other and with the company that makes the scheme possible.

The outcome of all these interventions was that *Dioses* was finally completed with a much larger budget than *Santiago* and the production team was more confident about the proposed release strategy. Undeterred this time by any potential hostility from the nation's top critics – renowned for expressing frustration and disappointment at their own national cinema –the film premiered first at the Lima Film Festival in August 2008. There it won the state-sponsored (Conacine) prize for best Peruvian feature, as well as the audience award supported by FX Design which ensured sound post-production support for Méndez's next project. Other festival screenings in Switzerland, Hong Kong, Italy, Spain and Canada followed and the film's commercial release launched in Peru in October 2008 throughout the national Cineplanet chain in Lima and five of the provinces. This unprecedented commercial exhibition activity was helped by the team's success in winning the new National Award for Distribution, Promotion and Exhibition in early August 2008. However, while it won a handful of awards, namely in Lima (best Peruvian film), Biarritz (best film) and Havana (best sound), it did not achieve anywhere near the level of recognition from the critics, nationally or internationally, that *Santiago* had enjoyed four years earlier.

The benefits and potential drawbacks of such varied and complex approaches to production finance and support may be appreciated even more fully by placing them into a broader national context by reference to this director's filmmaking peers who continue to acknowledge the power of transnational networks to bring their ideas to the screen. Take, for example, Barcelona-based Peruvian Claudia Llosa who stormed into the world cinema ring with the 2009 Berlin Festival winner, *La teta asustada (The Milk of Sorrow)*. This film received 80 per cent of its funding from a range of Spanish sources and the rest from a blend of national and international partners such as Ibermedia, Conacine, the European Union's Media programme, Berlin's World Cinema fund and Zurich's Visions Sud-Est scheme. With this follow-up to her well-received debut *Madeinusa* of 2006, she confounded the critics by winning such a prestigious festival award with a film that offered a slow-paced focus on a harrowing and very specific aspect of recent Peruvian history and Andean culture.[27]

Indeed, the rate of filmmaking in Peru had picked up by the end of the first decade of the twenty-first century to the extent that the Lima-based critics started to write about the future for national cinema in slightly less gloomy tones than had been the norm. Between 2006 and 2008, 15 features of a range of genres and styles were released commercially, a relative bonanza compared to previous years, and even the normally pessimistic Isaac León Frías suggested that 2009 might be a productive time for Peruvian cinema in his round-up of 2008 releases.[28] An increasing number of aspiring filmmakers recognise that shooting digital short projects of decent quality serves as a sign of emerging talent and as calling cards for the type of project mentioned in this essay which need to attract the funding scouts. Meanwhile, the direct involvement of more filmmakers in the administration of the Peruvian state's funding mechanisms for cinema, alongside civil servants, teachers and critics, gave rise to greater collaborative approaches between filmmakers and policy-makers. While

[27] The editor of *Sight and Sound*, Nick James, made the briefest reference to Llosa's winning film in his article on the Berlin festival in April 2009 as he had left the event before her film was screened. Nevertheless, she was named (and pictured) as one of the 'Nine Kings and Queens' of contemporary Latin American cinema in an article by Argentine critic and festival director Sergio Wolf in the September 2010 edition of the same publication.

[28] Isaac León Frías, 'Peru', *International Film Guide*, ed. Ian Haydn Smith (London: Wallflower, 2009), p. 251.

much of this activity remained located in Lima, video activity developed outside the centre that continues to access online opportunities for world-wide distribution and exhibition.

Although there is still a lack of effective financial and legal infra-structure within Peru to support its filmmakers compared with most of its neighbours, it does seem as if the new generation of directors and producers has become aware of the need to seek funds and other support beyond national borders as a matter of course, rather than dwelling on what is not available more locally. They may draw inspiration on this from the efforts of directors such as Josué Méndez and Claudia Llosa and their teams who are amongst those who have taken the leap into the choppy waters of transnational film production, targeting Hispanic and non-Hispanic schemes. Several projects have been achieved that are not excessively compromised – neither aesthetically nor thematically – by such collaborative arrangements, despite concerns about the need to guard against cultural hegemony from the 'West' or the 'North'. Michael Chanan argues in his essay on Latin American cinema's relationship to postmodernism and globalisation, that we see 'a continuing imperative to bear witness to local histories which takes us to the interstices, the margins and the peripheries' (2006, p. 49); and indeed Méndez and Llosa represent an exciting generation of twenty-first-century filmmakers who seem committed to doing just that.

8

The Silenced Screen:
Fostering a Film Industry in Paraguay

CATHERINE LEEN

En *Hamaca paraguaya*, el silencio es político, es cierto, pero yo quería que fuera también humano. Nosotros tenemos largas historias de guerras perdidas, otras ganadas (pero también perdidas), de dictaduras que nos han callado y que terminaron [...] pero no terminaron, y eso es algo que se siente en este país, y afecta principalmente a la humanidad de la gente.

In *Hamaca paraguaya* (*Paraguayan Hammock*), the silence is political, it's true, but I also wanted it to be human. We have long histories of lost wars, other wars that were won (but also lost), of dictatorships that have silenced us and that ended [...] but they haven't ended, and that is something that one feels in this country, and it fundamentally affects people's humanity.[1]

The above comments by Paz Encina on her internationally acclaimed debut feature *Hamaca paraguaya* (*Paraguayan Hammock;* 2006) suggest much about Paraguay as a nation and, by extension, the situation of film-making there. Paraguay's history has certainly been marked by war and poverty, but perhaps the event that has most marked recent decades is that it endured the longest-standing dictatorship in South America, which led to a repression that imposed an atmosphere of silence, fear, and isolation and whose effects reverberate to the present day, both in terms of the

---

[1] Paz Encina, 'Arrastrando la tormenta', in *Hacer cine: Producción audiovisual en América Latina*, ed. Eduardo A. Russo (Buenos Aires: Editorial Paidós, 2008), pp. 331–43 (p. 332). Unless otherwise stated, all translations are mine.

content of the films made in Paraguay and in terms of the ongoing battle for these films to be made and seen.

Filmmakers in Paraguay face unique challenges because their country has been culturally and economically marginalised for much of the twentieth century, with the result that it has virtually no presence at all in the realm of cinema. Very little has been written on cinema in Paraguay and so this chapter is largely based on interviews with filmmakers, as well as material from numerous websites showcasing the work of Paraguayan cineastes.[2] The reasons for the lack of a cinematic presence for Paraguay are many: General Alfredo Stroessner's dictatorship from 1954 to 1989 meant that any kind of cultural expression was stifled by fear of repression and widespread censorship; an enduring history of corruption protects the vested interests that control much local industry, including cinemas; and there is a huge black market in CDs and DVDs.[3] Local filmmakers also suffer from a lack of infrastructure, including film schools or a local market sufficient to sustain production, thus making the inherently costly business of filmmaking even more difficult. Moreover, there is no cinema law that would facilitate the organisation of co-productions or help to develop collaborations with international film production organisations, although, as we shall see later in this chapter, there are ongoing attempts to establish a cinema law and thus foster a national film industry.

Lack of funding or possibilities for distribution are not, of course, problems unique to Paraguay. Stam and Shohat note that lack of finance and possibilities for distribution are widespread in what they term Third World cinema, which they define mainly as Latin American, Asian and African cinema:

> [T]he global distribution of power still tends to make the First World countries cultural 'transmitters' and to reduce most Third World countries to the status of 'receivers.' [...] In this sense, cinema inherits the

2   I would like to express my sincere thanks to the filmmakers Joaquin Baldwin, Leticia Coronel, Paz Encina, Juan Carlos Maneglia, Silvana Nuovo, Ricardo Álvarez, and Tana Schémbori. Thanks are also due to all at Paraguay Cine, especially Cristina Rey, Cristian Nuñez, Érika Mesa and Javier López, for welcoming me on visits to Asunción in 2007 and 2008 and for their open and frank discussions on their work and the situation of filmmaking in Paraguay today. Warm thanks also to Carla Fabri. I am particularly grateful to Fabián Bozzolo of Canal 13, without whose generosity and support this research would have been impossible.

3   For a detailed study of the corruption during Stroessner's dictatorship, see Roberto L. Céspedes, 'Corrupción', in *Realidad Social del Paraguay*, ed. Javier Numan Caballero Merlo (Asunción: Biblioteca de Antropología, 1998), pp. 693–715.

structures laid down by the communication infrastructure of empire, the networks of telegraph and telephone lines and information apparatuses which literally wired colonial territories to the metropole, enabling the imperialist countries to monitor global communications and shape world events.[4]

While other nations in Latin America, particularly those without a history of cinematic production, such as Bolivia and Ecuador, are doubtless at a major disadvantage compared to countries such as Mexico, Argentina and Brazil, which have long-established film industries that have traditionally enjoyed strong state support, the lack of a cinema law and the fact that Paraguay is the only South American nation not to be a member of Ibermedia make filmmaking exceptionally challenging for local filmmakers.

The struggles faced by Paraguayan filmmakers in financing their work is a theme that emerges time and again in interviews with filmmakers. Tana Schémbori notes that:

> [E]l cine no se ha planteado como industria ni como un bien cultural. Todas las películas (entiéndase video o cine) se han hecho con inversiones independientes, coproducciones o ayudas mínimas del FONDEC, único fondo existente para la cultura. [...] En Paraguay no existe el audiovisual (cine o video) como negocio y mucho menos como una manifestación cultural.

> Cinema has not been established as an industry or as a valuable cultural asset. All (Paraguayan) films (whether video or film) have been made with private investments, co-productions or minimal support from FONDEC, the only existing fund for the arts [...] In Paraguay the audiovisual (film or video) does not exist as a business and much less as a reflection of culture).[5]

Commenting on the making of his documentary *Paraguay fue noticia* (*Paraguay in the News*), Ricardo Álvarez observes that during the two years that the making of the film took:

> [N]o cubrimos el presupuesto. Esos dos años nos buscamos la vida haciendo otros trabajos institucionales, dando clases en la universidad, el editor pidió prestado a sus padres etc. Uno sobrevive.

---

[4] Ella Shohat and Robert Stam, *Unthinking Eurocentrism: Multiculturalism and the Media* (New York: Routledge, 2003), p.30.

[5] Personal interview with Tana Schémbori, 8 July 2008.

We did not cover our costs. During those two years we tried to make a living doing other institutional work, teaching at the university, the editor got a loan from his parents and so on. You get by.[6]

Ramiro Gómez notes that financial difficulties can also mean that the distribution of completed films, including his, suffers:

La situación de los dos documentales (*Tierra roja* [*Red Earth*] y *Frankfurt*) es la siguiente; con los últimos fondos de Helvetas conseguimos pagar la confección de los DVDs con menú interactivo […], con traducción a 3 idiomas para poder hacer circular la obra como se debe, pero sólo conseguimos pagar lo que es la matriz o sea el original y algo así como 100 copias de cada documental, todo esto en Transeuropa, una empresa Argentina.

The situation of the two documentaries (*Tierra roja* [*Red Earth*] and *Frankfurt*) is this: with the last remaining funds from Helvetas we managed to pay for the manufacture of the DVDs with interactive menus, with subtitles in three languages to help distribute the work as it should be, but we could only pay for the master, that is the original, and about 100 copies of each documentary, all of which was done by Transeuropa, an Argentine company.[7]

The problems outlined above, which have greatly impeded the development of a film industry in Paraguay, are examined in this chapter, as are the history of Paraguayan cinema and some productions made in recent years. The campaign to establish a cinema law in the country, the contribution made by FONDEC to national cinema, and the outlook for the future of Paraguayan cinema are also addressed.

Paraguay: an invisible cinema?

In the draft document of the proposed Ley de Cine, the veteran Paraguayan filmmaker Hugo Gamarra notes that Paraguay is, in terms of cinema, 'un país invisible, sin rostro ni identidad en el mundo' ('an invisible country,

---

6   Interview with Ricardo Alvarez. Available at: http://elpororo.com/category/03-entrevistas/ (Last accessed 3 June 2010).

7   Interview with Ramiro Gómez. Available at: http://elpororo.com/category/03-entrevistas/ (Last accessed 20 July 2010). In this interview, Gómez notes that Helvetas Paraguay was an NGO that supported the making of *Tierra roja* but that has since withdrawn from Paraguay.

without an image or an identity in the world').[8] Paraguay is one of the least known Latin American countries, largely due to the enduring and extremely repressive dictatorship of General Alfredo Stroessner. The celebrated Paraguayan writer Augusto Roa Bastos, who spent most of his life in exile for criticising Stroessner's government, as did many intellectuals, is best known for his 1975 novel *Yo, El Supremo* (*I, The Supreme*), a satire that centres on an authoritarian dictator.[9] Roa Bastos notes that Stroessner's regime made artistic expression almost impossible:

> The fragmentation of Paraguayan culture, together with the imbalance of its forces of production and this paralysing fear which has taken on the characteristics of both a public and a private, an individual and a collective consciousness, has had a profound effect [...] on the creative forces of [...] society. Brutality and terror have dried up the sources which feed those works of writers and artists that illustrate the originality of a people.[10]

Aníbal Orué Pozzo, in his study of journalism in Paraguay, confirms that it was only in 1992, when a new Constitution was written, that censorship and repression ceased to be the norm, as they were under Stroessner's dictatorship:

> La censura y autocensura era 'normal'. Se perseguía y reprimía a diversos sectores sociales y políticos, incluyendo a periodistas y medios de comunicación.
>
> Censorship and self-censorship were 'normal'. Diverse social and political sectors were persecuted, including journalists and communications media.[11]

The Washington Post's obituary of Stroessner, published on 17 August 2006, notes that under his rule Paraguay became 'a haven for Nazi war criminals, deposed dictators and smugglers'.[12] James Cockcroft adds that

---

8   'Pre-proyecto de ley del cine y el audiovisual paraguayo'. Available at: http://www.recam.org/_files/documents/pre_proyecto_ley_de_cine.doc.pdf. (Last accessed 30 May 2010).
9   Efraím Cardozo, *Breve historia del Paraguay* (Asunción: Servilibro, 2007), p. 158.
10 Quoted in John King, *Magical Reels: A History of Cinema in Latin America* (London: Verso, 1990), pp. 101–2.
11 Aníbal Orué Pozzo, *Periodismo en Paraguay: estudios e interpretaciones* (Asunción: Arandurá Editorial, 2007), p. 184.
12 Adam Bernstein, 'Alfredo Stroessner, Paraguayan Dictator', *The Washington*

for those who attempted to oppose the regime 'fear of kidnapping, torture or death was a daily reality' (p. 440).

Stroessner's Colorado Party ruled Paraguay for 61 years, the longest uninterrupted rule of any party in the world.[13] Following his election as president for the sixth consecutive time in 1983, with over 90 per cent of the vote, the newspaper *ABC Color*, which had attempted to investigate state corruption, was closed down in March 1984. Humberto Rubin, the director of Radio Ñandutí, which had also been openly critical of the government, was arrested on numerous occasions, and the station was closed in 1987.[14] Stroessner's successor, General Andrés Rodríguez, was not a promising candidate for reform, given that he had links with drug trafficking and black market trade in livestock, coffee, arms and precious stones. The fact that Juan Carlos Wasmosy, who took up office on 15 August 1993, was the first civilian president to be elected after the end of Stroessner's dictatorship, did not mean an end to corruption. In 2008, Lambert summed up the situation since the end of Stroessner's dictatorship as follows:

> Since 1989 Paraguay has suffered three attempted coups d'etat (1996, 1999, 2000), the assassination of a Colorado vice president (1999), and sustained economic recession and stagnation (1996–2003), during which yearly per capita income dropped below $1,000. It has also seen the growth of pervasive, institutionalized corruption, reflected in the indictment on corruption charges of two former presidents, Juan Carlos Wasmosy (1993–98) and Raul Gonzalez Macchi (1998–99). A third, outgoing president Nicanor Duarte Frutos, may soon face similar charges.[15]

The campaign of the former bishop Fernando Lugo finally seemed to bring the promise of a real transition government, almost 20 years after the supposed return to democracy in Paraguay. Since 2005, Lugo has led the APC, a coalition that relies heavily on the support of the Liberal Party

---

Post, 17 August 2006. Available at: http://www.washingtonpost.com/wp-dyn/content/article/2006/08/16/AR2006081601729.html (Last accessed 10 February 2007).

[13] Benjamin Dangl and April Howard, 'New vs. Old Right in Paraguay's Election', *NACLA Report on the Americas*, 41 (2008), p. 14.

[14] Frank O. Mora and Jerry W. Cooney, *Paraguay and the United States: Distant Allies* (Georgia: University of Georgia Press, 2007), p. 208.

[15] Peter Lambert, 'A New Era for Paraguay', *NACLA Report on the Americas*, 41 (2008), pp. 5–8 (p. 5).

(PLRA). On 15 August 2008, Lugo delivered his inaugural address, partly in Spanish and partly in Guaraní, saying:

> Today [...] marks the end of an exclusive Paraguay, a Paraguay of secrets, a Paraguay known for its corruption; today is the start of a Paraguay whose government and whose citizens will have no truck with those who steal from the people, with actions which cloud over transparency in public life and with those few feudal lords of a strange country of yesteryear which has somehow survived to the present day.[16]

As well as tackling corruption, Lugo sought to bolster the nation's economy by renegotiating contracts with Brazil so that Paraguay could sell its surplus energy to its partner at prices closer to market rates, rather than at cost, as a contract signed into law by Stroessner stipulated.[17]

Since his election, Lugo has faced criticism over what many see as the slow pace of the promised reform, although he has achieved some successes, such as tackling corruption in Customs and the Port Administration and creating a five-year plan that combines sustainable growth with social justice.[18] He has also consolidated Paraguay's partnership in the Mercosur by assuming the presidency of the organisation for six months and reaffirming the country's commitment to the free-trade association in Brussels in May 2011.[19] The significance of this affirmation cannot be overlooked, because, as Ligia García Béjar points out, the association has cultural as well as trade provisions, and she sees membership of the Mercosur as a key way in which a film industry could develop in Paraguay:

> Probably, the only possibility for Paraguay, as with other small Latin American countries, in developing a motion-picture industry is to give

[16] Quoted in Hugh O'Shaughnessy, *The Priest of Paraguay: Fernando Lugo and the Making of a Nation* (London: Zed Books, 2009) pp. 6–7.

[17] Alexei Barrionuevo, 'Ex-Cleric Wins Paraguay Presidency, Ending a Party's 62-Year Rule', *New York Times*, 21 April 2008. Available at: http://www.nytimes.com/2008/04/21/world/americas/21paraguay.html?_r=1&ref=paraguay. (Last accessed 21 July 2010).

[18] Diego Abente-Brun, 'Paraguay: The Unraveling of One-Party Rule', *Journal of Democracy*, 20 (2009), 143–56 (p. 152).

[19] EFE, 'Paraguay y CE insisten en ventajas de pacto UE_Mercosur', *ABC Color*, 24 May 2011. Available at: http://www.abc.com.py/nota/paraguay-y-ce-admiten-obstaculos-pero-insisten-en-ventajas-pacto-ue-mercosur/. (Last accessed 29 May 2011).

an incentive of international co-production in collaboration with neigh-
boring countries and especially members of Mercosur.[20]

On 15 August 2010, Lugo issued a statement on the second anniversary
of his election confirming that the revision of the Itaipú contract with
Brazil, which would result in Brazil paying three times more for energy
bought from Paraguay, would be signed into law soon. He also reaffirmed
his commitment to reforming the country's infrastructure, education,
health system, and employment creation and suggested that the improve-
ment in Paraguay's international image would lead to more investment
in the country.[21] This last claim seems to be supported by the fact that
he announced on 13 June 2010, that he had granted 5,520 million guaraníes from the funds resulting from the newly renegotiated contract to the
Ministry for Culture, with a view to financing bicentennial celebrations
and establishing a National Centre for Culture.[22] The monies from this
fund were partly allocated to a new project by Paz Encina, the director
of *Hamaca paraguaya* (*Paraguayan Hammock*), which screened to great
acclaim at the Cannes Film Festival in 2006. Encina was awarded €70,000
by the Bicentennial Programme, but she ultimately failed to make up the
remaining funds needed for a shoot projected to cost €350,000 overall,
despite having a shortfall of only €50,000 as a result of securing funding
from Fonds Sud of France, Hubert Bals of Holland and FONDEC. She
has subsequently re-applied to the Bicentennial Programme to get funding
for the making of a short film instead. While this is clearly a substantial
investment from Paraguay in her work, it falls far short of Lugo's promise
to give her his full support when they met for a press conference in 2008,
soon after Encina's first feature premiered at Cannes.[23]

It may seem churlish to suggest that Lugo should prioritise the development of a film industry over economic reform or the tackling of corrup-

---

[20] Ligia García Béjar, 'The Media in Paraguay: A Locked Nation in Times of Change',
in Alan B. Albarran, *The Handbook of Spanish Language Media* (London: Routledge,
2009), p. 186.

[21] 'El mensaje de Lugo por sus 2 años de Gobierno', *Ultima hora*, 15 August 2010.
Available at: http://www.ultimahora.com/notas/349059-El-mensaje-de-Lugo-por-sus-2-
anos-de-Gobierno. (Last accessed 11 August 2010).

[22] Cardozo, José, 'Lugo aprobó donar G. 5520 millones de Itapú', *ABC Color*, 13 June
2010. Available at: http://www.abc.com.py/nota/134133-lugo-aprobo-donar-g-5–520-
millones-de-itaipu/. (Last accessed 25 May 2011).

[23] Marlene Aponte Branco, 'Pese a reconocimientos, Paz Encina no puede filmar',
ABC Color, 14 June 2010. Available at: http://www.abc.com.py/nota/134639-pese-a-
reconocimientos-paz-encina-no-puede-filmar/. (Last accessed 2 May 2011).

tion in a country where it was estimated in 2007 that up to 20 per cent of the population live in extreme poverty, but it has to be said that this limited support may well reflect a lack of understanding of how film could benefit Paraguay not only in terms of its culture but also economically.[24]

Paraguayan film history: An overview

Despite Gamarra's comment that Paraguayan cinema is invisible, it does in fact have a long history. Juan Carlos Maneglia and Tana Schémbori in their unpublished 2001 MA thesis on Paraguayan film history, make it clear that far from having no film culture, Paraguay has, despite a complete lack of state support until very recently, produced an extraordinary number of documentaries, features, and shorts:

> Si bien es cierto que en una primera lectura la actividad cinematográfica en el Paraguay pareciera no tener una historia, la realidad demuestra otra cosa.

> While it is true that at first glance filmmaking in Paraguay seems not to have a history, the reality is quite different.[25]

This view is substantiated by Juan Manuel Salinas Aguirre, who notes that, although the fact that a film shot using 35 mm film can easily cost up to $1 million makes filmmaking almost prohibitively expensive for local producers, there has been a sporadic but significant history of film production in Paraguay.[26]

According to journalist Manuel Cuenca's 2005 essay on Paraguayan film history, the first film shows were held in Paraguay in 1900, when a programme of ten black-and-white shorts, on subjects including 'Juegos de niños' (Children's Games) and 'Artistas del circo' (Circus Artists) was presented. Filmmaking began in Paraguay in 1905, only a decade

[24] O'Shaughnessy, p. 8.

[25] Juan Carlos Maneglia and María Rossana (Tana) Schémbori, 'El video de ficción en la década de los '80', MA thesis, Departamento de Ciencias de la Comunicación, Facultad de Filosofía y Ciencias Humanas, Universidad Católica Nuestra Señora de la Asunción, Asunción, 2001, p. 35.

[26] Juan Manuel Salinas Aguirre, 'El cine en Paraguay'. Available at: http://www. paraguaycine.com/cine_nacional.html#3. (Last accessed 12 June 2010).

after the first film projections in Paris.[27] The initial period of filmmaking in Paraguay was entirely focused on documentaries, normally made by foreigners, such as the group of French filmmakers who, in the early 1920s, failed in their attempt to make a film about the Chaco War and because of financial difficulties, were forced to sell their camera. It found a buyer in Hipólito Jorge Carrón, who, with his brother-in-law Guillermo Quell and his nephew Nicolás Carrón Quell, made the first films by Paraguayans in the country. En 1925 their 35 mm film *Alma paraguaya* (*The Soul of Paraguay*) portrayed a traditional religious pilgrimage to the town of Caacupé. Another important figure in local filmmaking was Agustín Carrón Quell, who made a 16mm film in 1947 that portrayed an operation carried out by Dr Héctor Blas Ruiz, who removed a tumour weighing 16 kilos from the body of a young woman. Before the Chaco War broke out, Agustín Carrón Quell also filmed the first aerial scenes of Asunción (Maneglia and Schémbori, p. 21).

While Stroessner undoubtedly stifled any creative or critical filmmaking, he did support the idea of the Noticioso Nacional, which from 1954 to the 1980s showed 35 mm documentary films about political events to cinema audiences. The head of this newsreel was Jorge Peruzzi, with technical support from the Brazilian Domingo Soares. In its early years, the films were made in Buenos Aires and Rio de Janeiro, but later Soares built a laboratory in Asunción, so that for the first time film was processed and edited in the country (Maneglia and Schémbori, p. 23). The 1960s saw a strong influence from the New Argentine Cinema and also European auteur cinema that led to the foundation of the group 'Cine Arte Experimental' by director Carlos Saguier in 1964. The movement had little chance of survival in such a repressive atmosphere, however; a reality underlined by the censorship of Saguier's 1969 film *El Pueblo* (*The People*), which portrays life in a remote village and is considered by many to be a cornerstone of national cinema (J. King, p. 101). Another key development in this decade was the foundation by the Jesuit Francisco de Paula Oliva of the Departamento de Ciencias de la Comunicación in the Universidad Católica de Asunción (Maneglia and Schémbori, p. 31).

The 1970s and 1980s saw the rise of video, which led to the production of numerous amateur films, but the most significant film to be produced was *Cerro Corá* (1978), directed by Guillermo Vera y Rendía, a propaganda film described by the dictatorship as the first colour feature made

[27] Manuel Cuenca, 'El cine en Paraguay'. Available at: http://www.paraguaycine.com/cine_nacional.html#3. (Last accessed 10 August 2010).

in Paraguay and as a homage to Stroessner on his birthday. The film made explicit links between Stroessner and the nineteenth-century military hero General Solano López (Getino, pp. 140–1). A positive outcome of this film was the return to Paraguay of Hugo Gamarra, who would become a key figure in developing a national film culture. Gamarra is a journalist, scriptwriter and director who received a Masters degree in film and television from the School of Communications of the University of Austin, Texas, in 1980. In an interview, Gamarra notes that in 1980, as he was graduating from Austin, the team who made *Cerro Corá* invited him to Paraguay to make a film about the Chaco War. He accepted the opportunity to return and oversee a Paraguayan film studio but was confronted with a harsh reality:

> During my first five years back I was disappointed to realize that the people from the Paraguayan government were trying to use filmmaking for their own political–economic purposes, to support certain political attitudes rather than try to foster a real national cinema. Film production was being used for corrupt purposes, to make money for some individuals and to confirm the idolatry of the Paraguayan dictator, Alfredo Stroessner.[28]

Gamarra went on to make several documentaries, as well as a 45-minute drama called *Marcelina*, and when Stroessner's 35-year dictatorship ended in 1989, he was among the founders of the Fundación Cinemateca y Archivo Visual del Paraguay. He also established the Festival Cinematográfica Internacional de Asunción. Among his best known works are *El portón de los sueños* (*The Gateway to Dreams*, 1988), a documentary following Augusto Roa Bastos' return from exile; his script for *El toque del oboe* (*The Call of the Oboe*, 1998), a feature co-produced with Brazilian director Claudio McDowell; and the more recent documentary about a film projectionist in Paraguay, *Profesión cinero* (*Profession Cineaste*, 2007).

---

[28] Noel King, 'Film Culture in Paraguay: An Interview with Hugo Gamarra Etcheverry', *Senses of Cinema.* Available at: http://archive.sensesofcinema.com/contents/02/21/echeverry_interview.html. (Last accessed 6 July 2010).

La Ley del Cine, FONDEC and Ibermedia

Octavio Getino notes that cinema screenings in Paraguay have increased in recent years because of the investments of film companies in installing new cinemas in shopping centres. The growth of this cinema industry is also the result of investment by North American distribution companies in marketing and advertising. Getino cites Gamarra's comment about how the overwhelming dominance of US filmmaking in Paraguay has a profoundly negative impact on local filmmakers:

> La gran mayoria del público está [...] definitivamente colonizada por los relatos audiovisuales norteamericanos, a tal punto que le cuesta aceptar otro estilo y ritmo narrativo. (Getino, p.143)

> The vast majority of the public is thoroughly colonised by North American audiovisual narrative, to the point where it is difficult for them to accept another style or narrative rhythm.

The limited possibilities for distribution also remains a severe obstacle in Paraguay and other countries without a strong national film industry, as Deborah Shaw points out:

> Filmmakers from all over Latin America have produced interesting work that [...] audiences should have access to, however, because of the nature of the market and the difficulties in ensuring distribution deals with globally powerful companies, many high-quality films are never seen outside the countries in which they are made, and even then, many are shown in very few theatres for a limited time.[29]

Paraguayan filmmakers have sought to address these and other difficulties by establishing a Cinema Law. The draft proposal for this law is based on the cinema laws of Argentina, Brazil and Chile and was co-written by Ray Armele, Richard Careaga, Leticia Coronel, Renate Costa, Gustavo Delgado, Hugo Gamarra, Juan Carlos Maneglia, Claudia Rojas, Billy Rosales, Carlos Saguier, Tana Schémbori and Tatiana Uribe. The main provisions of the proposed law are the development and recognition of the work of filmmakers in Paraguay and the establishment of a Film Institute. The first aim of the law is outlined in Article 2:

---

[29] Deborah Shaw, *Contemporary Cinema of Latin America: Ten Key Films,* (London: Continuum, 2003), p. 1.

La presente ley tiene por objeto el desarrollo, fomento, difusión, protección y preservación de las obras cinematográficas y artes audiovisuales nacionales, como así también el reconocimiento de una industria cinematográfica y audiovisual, incentivando a la investigación y el desarrollo de nuevos lenguajes.

This law seeks to develop, foster, distribute, protect and preserve national cinematographic works and audiovisual arts, as well to achieve the recognition of a cinematographic and audiovisual industry, providing incentives for research and the development of new languages.[30]

The responsibilities of the Instituto del Cine y el Audiovisual Paraguayo (ICAP) are outlined in Article 7 and include allocating the new funds available for film and audiovisual production, known as the Fondo de Fomento Audiovisual; supporting audiovisual education through grants, residencies, and other means; proposing the necessary legislation for the development of cinematic and audiovisual culture; supporting technical education; collaborating with the Ministry of Education to incorporate the audiovisual into the education system; and establishing relationships with governmental institutions from other countries.

It is envisaged that the finance required for the Fondo de Fomento Audiovisual would come from taxes on film screenings of national and international films. Five years have passed since this first draft was written, however, and the government has yet to act to sign it into law. Christian Núñez, president of the Organización de Profesionales del Audiovisual Paraguayo (OPRAP), notes that the tax would mean that cinemas would pay 12,000 guaraníes (about $2.50) per film opening, while cable channels would pay 5,000 guaraníes (about $1) per viewer. He adds that the approval of the law has been frustrated by the opposition of powerful interest groups who refuse to pay the tax. The businesses opposed to the law include communications regulator Cerneco, advertising agency APAP and Argentine-owned video and cable company Multicanal. During a recent tribute to her work, Paz Encina called on the government to keep dialogue about the law open, noting that the best tribute the government can pay to filmmakers is to allow them to produce their work and tell their stories.[31] Juan Carlos Maneglia also emphasises the importance of having a cinema law:

---

[30] 'Pre-proyecto ley del cine', http://recam.org/_files/documents/pre_proyecto_ley_de_cine.doc.pdf.
[31] Marisol Ramírez, 'Cineastas piden diálogo en torno a la Ley de Cine ', *Última*

Puede contribuir a fortalecer los fondos para el cine, para proteger a sus directores, técnicos, actores y todos los que intentan vivir de este arte. Puede contribuir a organizar a los extranjeros que quieran realizar sus proyectos en este país, y también para proteger lo poco que se ha realizado.

It could help to boost funds for cinema, to protect directors, technicians, actors and everyone trying to make a living in this field. It could contribute to organising foreigners who want to film in this country, and also to protect the little (cinema) that has been produced.[32]

Silvana Nuovo echoes Maneglia's insistence on the need for the law, but she notes that the prioritisation of short-term financial gain over long-term investment in the arts presents a formidable obstacle to its passing:

Los políticos no se dan cuenta de la importancia de que haya una industria cultural, de que exista un cine paraguayo, que además en el inmediato no va a retribuir económicamente, es una inversión a largo plazo. Para que haya cine tiene que haber escuelas de cine aquí todavía no hay, la inversión tiene que empezar en la formación. Las salas de cine y los canales de TV son inversiones privadas, no parece que les interese el desarrollo cultural del país, solo las ganancias en el inmediato.

Politicians don't realise the importance of having a culture industry, of having a Paraguayan cinema, which moreover will not give an economic return immediately, it's a long-term investment. In order to have cinema one must have cinema schools here, which don't exist; the investment has to begin in education. Cinemas and TV stations are private investments, and it appears that they are not interested in the country's cultural development but in immediate returns.[33]

In September 2011, *7 cajas* won the San Sebastián Film Festival's 20th Films in Progress award, which covers the expenses of post-production to allow the film to be screened in cinemas. Coronel notes that the draft proposal of the law was rewritten in 2009, although the content is substantially the same as the original document, and that it is hoped that it will finally be passed into law in 2011.[34] In the absence of the law, the only

hora, 10 October 2009. Available at: http://www.ultimahora.com/notas/263099-cineastas-piden-di%E1logo-en-torno-a-la-ley-de-cine. (Last accessed 10 July 2009).

32 Personal interview with Juan Carlos Maneglia, 8 July 2008.
33 Personal interview with Silvana Nuovo, 17 August 2010.
34 Personal interview with Leticia Coronel, 5 August 2010.

source of national funding available to filmmakers at present is FONDEC (Fondo Nacional de la Cultura y las Artes), which as Schémbori notes, does not acknowledge that filmmaking is a particularly expensive discipline that requires far more funding than a ballet or an art exhibition.[35]

Nor is FONDEC in a position to fully finance a film. Coronel notes that she only received funding from the agency for *Yo, mujer sola* (*I, A Woman Alone*) after already securing finance from France, Spain, Mexico and Argentina.[36] The case of Encina's *Hamaca paraguaya* is also illustrative of the constraints under which the fund operates. The total budget for the film was $624,589, of which the French organisation Fonds Sud Cinema contributed $120,000. [37] FONDEC's investment of 102,000,000 guaraníes (just over $21,500), although the largest single sum awarded to any national cultural project in that year, was still substantially less than the funding provided for the film by foreign partners.[38] When one considers that the total budget for all arts projects available from FONDEC in 2004 was 1,301,646,995 guaraníes, which is approximately $275, 480, or not much more than double the contribution of Fonds Sud Cinema to a single project, one begins to appreciate just how limited the resources for filmmaking are in Paraguay. Questions have also been raised about the way in which FONDEC allocates its funding. Nuovo comments that its management could be greatly improved and that its selection criteria seem arbitrary.[39] Gómez has reported on his very negative experience with the funding agency:

Yo tuve un problema con el FONDEC, hice una denuncia de corrupción que no fue atendida, sólo la prensa le dio divulgación y ahí quedó, como todo en Paraguay. *Tierra roja* fue un proyecto que no fue adjudicado por esta institución, no le vieron futuro [...] *Frankfurt* si recibió el apoyo de la institución, pero no como pensé que debieron haberlo hecho, entonces los denuncié. De ahí en adelante todo fue más difícil para mí en este país.

35 Personal interview with Tana Schémbori, 25 August 2010.
36 Personal interview with Leticia Coronel, 5 August 2010.
37 France Diplomatie website.http://www.diplomatie.gouv.fr/en/france-priorities_1/cinema_2/cinematographic-cooperation_9/production-support-funding_10/films-benefiting-from-aid_13/film-listby-country_15/paraguay_2688/hamaca-paraguaya_2834/index.html. (Last accessed 1 August 2010).
38 FONDEC website, http://www.fondec.gov.py/recursos/f12082009-adj-2004.pdf. (Last accessed 6 June 2010).
39 Personal interview with Silvana Nuovo, 17 August 2010.

I had a problem with FONDEC, I made a complaint about corruption that was not addressed, only the press reported it and that was it, like everything in Paraguay. *Tierra roja* was a project that was not supported by this institution, they did not think it had a future [...] *Frankfurt* did receive the institution's support but not in the way I thought it should have, so I filed a complaint. From then on, everything became more difficult for me in this country.[40]

This experience suggests that corruption is not a distant memory in Paraguay and that even the success of former projects brings no guarantee of increased funding. Moreover, the fact that Paraguay does not belong to Ibermedia, the largest filmmaking body in Latin America, is hugely detrimental to the development of projects with other nations.

Globalisation, co-productions and their discontents: the case of *Hamaca Paraguaya* (*Paraguayan Hammock*)

Notwithstanding the aforementioned problems in securing finance both nationally and internationally, a younger generation of filmmakers has produced a diverse body of work that reflects their international backgrounds and exchanges and that encompasses several genres. Tana Schémbori and Juan Carlos Maneglia are perhaps the best known of this new generation. The pair studied Communications at the Universidad Católica in Asunción and first worked together in the 1990s at the production company Alta Producciones, where they made over 100 advertisements and TV series including 'El ojo' ('The Eye') and 'Río de fuego' ('River of Fire'). In 1996, they formed Maneglia Schémbori Realizadores, producing advertisements and short films, including *Artefacto de primera necesidad* (*An Essential Artefact*, 1995), which has been shown to great acclaim at film festivals nationally and internationally, winning first prize in the category of Short Fiction Films at the Tercer Festival Internacional de Rosario in 1995 and for Best Experimental Short at the International Film and Drama Fest of Oklahoma in 1997. In 1999, they were granted scholarships to study at the New York Film Academy, where Schémbori made *Extraños vecinos* (*Strange Neighbours*) and Maneglia made *Say Yes*, both short fiction films that were screened in New York at the Museum of Modern Art. In 2002, their short *Amor basura* (*Love*

40 Personal interview with Ramiro Gómez, 25 August 2010.

is Rubbish) (35 mm) was screened before major films in Asunción and was so popular that it remained in cinemas for two and a half months. Their first digital short, *Horno ardiente* (*Burning Oven*) was completed soon after this. They have just completed the shooting of their first feature-length film on 35 mm, a thriller entitled *7 cajas* (*Seven Crates*) set in Asunción's Mercado 4, which, despite lacking minimal standards of hygiene and health, according to Elisa Ferreira, is extremely popular with locals.[41]

The Colombian Silvana Nuovo and her Cuban filmmaking partner Ricardo Álvarez have focused on documentaries and are the producers and directors of the Paraguayan–French co-production *Ogwa* (2006), which charts the story of the renowned Paraguayan artist. This film has received national and international recognition, including being featured as the Official Selection at the Festival de Cine Bogotá in 2007 and receiving the award for the best documentary about visual arts at the Festival de Cine Documental de Asunción in 2007. Their most recent work, the feature-length *Paraguay fue noticia* (*Paraguay in the News*, 2008), debuted on Canal 13 in 2009. This film exposes the corrupt practices of the owners of the Ycua Bolaños supermarket in Asunción, which was burned down by a fire on 1 August 2004, killing some 400 people and injuring 500. *Paraguay fue noticia* follows the trials that followed after it was revealed that the doors were deliberately shut after the fire broke out to prevent people from leaving without paying for their shopping.[42] Ramiro Gómez, another filmmaker in his thirties, is the director of the documentaries *Tierra roja* (*Red Earth*, 2006) and *Frankfurt* (2008). Like Saguier's groundbreaking *El pueblo* (*The People*), *Tierra roja* represents everyday life in Paraguay through the stories of four families living in the countryside. *Frankfurt*, meanwhile, follows the fortunes of the players in a rural football league in Paraguay. The Paraguayan filmmaker Érika Mesa and her Cuban filmmaking partner Javier López produce what they term 'videoperformances'. One such example is *Haciendo mercado* (*Making a Market*), which features a Guaraní shaman who preaches the

---

[41] Elisa Ferreira, *Las mujeres productoras de alimentos en Paraguay: Tecnología y comercialización* (Venezuela: IICA Biblioteca, 1996), p. 54. In September 2011, *7 cajas* won the San Sebastián Film Festival's 20th Films in Progress award, which covers the expenses of post-production to allow the film to be screened in cinemas: see http://www. variety.com/article/VR1118043228?categoryid=13&cs=1&cmpid=RSS%7CNews%7CFil mNews. (Last accessed 15 December 2011.)

[42] Kinemultimedia website: http://www.kinemultimedia.com/en/documentales/ paraguay-fue-noticia. (Last accessed 2 July 2010).

words of economist Philip Kotler, thus raising questions about globalisation, post-colonial economic dependencies and the tensions between indigenous cultures and the New World Order.

A younger generation of filmmakers, still in their twenties, has generally studied outside Paraguay but continues to develop a film practice that relates to the nation's history and socioeconomic concerns. Leticia Coronel studied Communications at the Universidad Católica de Asunción, Paraguay, and continued her studies in Argentina, Madrid and Cuba. She is the director of short films including *Ingravidez y Gravidez* (*Weightlessness and Pregnancy*), a film based on the life of María de la Cruz, a 30-year-old mother of nine from the town of San Joaquín, some 200 km from Asunción. This film has been screened to much acclaim at festivals including the Primer Ciclo de Videoarte Latinoamericano, Valencia, Spain, in 2006 and at the 9 Mostra del Cinema Latinoamericano di Cremona, Italy, in the same year. She is currently producing the feature *Yo, mujer sola* (*I, A Woman Alone*), which presents the interweaving stories of five Paraguayan women, including a 52-year-old artist returning from exile and a 40-year-old indigenous woman who lives on a reservation outside Asunción. Joaquín Baldwin, a Paraguayan filmmaker based in Los Angeles, has won over 100 awards for his animated films *Papiroflexia* (2007) and *Sebastian's Voodoo* (2008), the latter of which won a student Academy Award in 2009. He was also the South American winner of Pangea Day, an international event that celebrated filmmaking as a means of erasing borders between peoples, in 2008.[43]

Co-productions are a key element in what Deborah Shaw terms the 'internationalization process' of Latin American film.[44] Since the 1990s, co-productions in Latin America have increased dramatically, and there has been an increase in the distribution and availability of films by Latin American directors. As Ambrosio Fornet notes, 'with limited budgets, devalued currencies, and soaring production costs, few filmmakers in Latin America enjoy the luxury of single-source local financing',[45] thus co-productions offer a valuable opportunity to get finance for films that otherwise could not be made.

The financial operations of co-production agencies are not always

[43] For further information on this event, see Pangea Day website, http://www.pangeaday.org/aboutPangeaDay.php. (Last accessed 2 May 2011).

[44] Deborah Shaw (ed.), *Contemporary Latin American Cinema: Breaking into the Global Market* (Lanham: Rowman and Littlefield, 2007), p. 1.

[45] Quoted in Ann Marie Stock, *Framing Latin American Cinema: Contemporary Critical Perspectives* (Minneapolis: University of Minnesota Press, 1997), p. xxiii.

straightforward, however. Libia Villazana, in her study of the role of Ibermedia in co-productions with Latin America, notes that the 14 member
countries are obliged to pay at least $100,000 a year to the fund, while
Spain contributes $2 million, thus making it the major financial partner.
She also observes that the fund is controlled by Spain, as its offices are
based in Spain, most of its staff is Spanish, and the selection of projects
to be funded is overseen by the Spanish head of the Technical Unit of
Ibermedia, Elena Villardel.[46] Villazana concludes that Ibermedia's rigid
control over its co-productions and privileging of its own goals over those
of Latin American co-producers amounts to a subtle 'form of neo-colonialism' (Villazana, p. 66). Falicov also expresses some reservations about
the fund, noting that, like its European counterparts, it has not avoided
'problems of paternalism and the inherent power dynamics that surface
when there are inequalities of power and resources'.[47] Notwithstanding
this caveat, she notes that the fund is important because it has remained
stable from year to year, unlike national funding agencies. She adds that
it also promotes distribution as well as helping to finance film production, and many of the films it has produced have achieved international
success.

Several Paraguayan filmmakers have expressed concerns about the fact
that Paraguay is not a member of Ibermedia. Coronel suggests that this
decision is again the result of a lack of political will, as Salvador Vayá,
the former director of the Centro Cultural de España en Asunción invited
representatives from Ibermedia to Asunción in 2007. Coronel and other
members of the group Gente de Cine addressed the Chamber of Deputies
in a bid to convince them that joining Ibermedia was an important move,
but they were not interested and no agreement was made.[48] As Nuovo
asserts, the lack of an agreement with Ibermedia hampers possibilities
for filmmakers:

> El artista necesita tiempo para crear, y es difícil crear cuando se está
> pensando en como ganarse la vida ... el cine es trabajo en equipo que
> necesita inversiones importantes, a falta de interés a nivel nacional
> hay que acudir a los fondos internacionales, que muchas veces no
> apoyan pues no tenemos el suficiente nivel, porque no hay ejercicio
> cinematográfico ni inversiones en tecnología.

---

[46] Libia Villazana, 'Hegemony Conditions in the Coproduction Cinema of Latin
America : The Role of Spain', *Framework*, 49 (2008), 65–85 (p. 78).
[47] See chapter 3.
[48] Personal interview with Leticia Coronel, 5 August 2010.

Artists need time to create their work, and it's difficult to create when one is thinking of how to make a living … cinema is team work that needs significant investment, because of the lack of interest on a national level, one has to apply for international funds, which often don't support us because we do not achieve the required level, because there is no cinematographic training or investment in technology.[49]

The lack of an agreement with Ibermedia means that the lack of a cinema law is even more detrimental to the film industry in Paraguay, as the experience of Paz Encina illustrates. Set in 1935 in rural Paraguay, *Hamaca paraguaya* is a poetic, almost static account of an elderly couple, Candida and Ramón, who await the return of their son from the Chaco War. This co-production with Argentina, France and Holland has been widely screened and distributed, and has received several prestigious international awards, including the FIPRESI Prize at Cannes and the Buñuel Award for Best Latin American Film at the San Sebastián Film Festival. In the interviews that accompany the DVD release, Argentine co-producer Lita Stantic suggests that the film may be the catalyst needed to develop a film industry in Paraguay:

La historia del cine paraguayo es casi inexistente. Por eso, *Hamaca paraguaya* va a ser una especie de inicio de una historia, ya que existe en Paraguay una idea de armar algo así como un instituto de cine y hay jovenes que tienen proyectos. Por eso es importante lo que puede generar esta película en su país.

Paraguayan film history scarcely exists. Therefore, *Hamaca paraguaya* will be a kind of beginning of a history, since there exists in Paraguay an idea of establishing something like a cinema institute and there are young people working on projects. Consequently, what this film could give rise to in its country is important.[50]

While the suggestion that Paraguay lacks a film history is inaccurate, it is perhaps a fair representation of the image that people have of Paraguay outside the country, and it also reflects its complete lack of a presence in the international film world until very recently. Encina describes her experience of working with the co-producers of *Hamaca paraguaya* in resolutely positive terms:

---

[49] Personal interview with Silvana Nuovo, 17 August 2010.

[50] Interview in the DVD release of *Hamaca Paraguaya* (TransEuropa Video Entertainment, 2006).

Fue un sueño. *Hamaca* fue una película que con una rapidez extrema consiguió todos los fondos para ser filmada, y tuvo un circuito bellísimo, pero creo que es una experiencia que no se va a repetir en mucho tiempo.

It was a dream come true. *Hamaca* got all the funds needed for filming extremely quickly, and its reception was wonderful, but I think it's an experience that won't be repeated for a long time.[51]

Given that Stantic and the film's other co-producer Marianne Slot are known for producing alternative and even subversive films, it would seem likely that they allowed Encina to follow her vision and to direct her film, which is based on her own script, in her own way. The hopes that Stantic expressed about the film giving rise to a new era where a film institute and other long-held dreams could be realised have proved to be unfounded, however. As Encina notes, her attempts to film a script entitled *Un suspiro* (*A Sigh*) have come to nothing, thanks in part to the difficulties she encountered in finding co-producers because of the lack of a cinema law in Paraguay. Moreover, when asked about the fact that I could not find a copy of the film for sale in Paraguay and that the copy I bought in Argentina is marked 'Cine Argentina' she responded that:

Ese es un doble juego, porque yo no encontré en Paraguay alguien que quería editar la película, por lo tanto, no se puede comprar una copia en Paraguay, por lo tanto la única forma de que *Hamaca* llegue a todo el mundo fue la piratería.

That's a Catch 22, because I couldn't find anyone in Paraguay who wanted to release the film on DVD, so you can't buy a copy of it in Paraguay, with the result that the only way people saw the film was through pirated copies.[52]

The fact that a filmmaker whose work was recognised at Cannes has given up on filming her next project suggests that while co-productions are extremely important to Latin American filmmakers, they are not a panacea and cannot overcome difficulties that are particularly stark in the case of Paraguay – lack of finance and infrastructure, rampant piracy that stifles any hope of a market for DVDs, the lack of a cinema law, and a

[51] Personal Interview with Paz Encina, 2 April 2010.
[52] Personal interview with Paz Encina, 2 April 2010.

lack of interest on the part of the government in supporting young film-makers.

Projecting the future

A further issue to consider when discussing the topic of film finance and Paraguayan cinema is the possibilities offered by digital technology. All of the filmmakers interviewed agreed that digital technology offered significant opportunities for the development of filmmaking in Paraguay. Nuovo asserts that it is an excellent option for a developing cinema, as does Gómez, who notes that, as well as allowing filmmakers to experiment and make mistakes without wasting a lot of money, digital technology represents

> el paso más importante e inteligente que puede dar el cine paraguayo, la falta de recursos y oficio no nos permite filmar en celuloide, además que al hacerlo estaríamos dependiendo de otras industrias (para los procesos de revelado y demás que sólo en un laboratorio son posibles) y del cambio del dólar y de la disponibilidad de éstos.

> The most important and intelligent step that Paraguayan cinema can take, the lack of resources and training prohibits us from filming on celluloid, as well as the fact that doing so would make us dependent on other industries (for developing film and other steps that can only be carried out in laboratories) as well as on the value of the dollar and access to that currency.[53]

Coronel has some reservations about the medium, noting that it has been used to make features that have been successful in local cinemas, but that on an international level, many festivals do not show digital films, while the possibilities for international distribution of digital films are limited.[54] Undoubtedly the most successful experiment with digital film by a Paraguayan filmmaker is Joaquin Baldwin's multiple award-winning *Sebastian's Voodoo*, which as well as winning a student Academy Award was the recipient of the Short Film Corner Award at Cannes. Baldwin's animated film about a voodoo doll who sacrifices himself to save his friends from a torturer is based on contemporary torture chambers and was mainly

---

[53] Personal interview with Ramiro Gómez, 25 August 2010.
[54] Personal interview with Leticia Coronel, 5 August 2010.

inspired by events such as Guantánamo Bay. He concedes, however, that he may have been subconsciously influenced by the repressive atmosphere of Stroessner's dictatorship.[55] Baldwin believes that for animators in particular, digital filmmaking is the future: 'You need a computer, no crew, no cameras, no lights, nothing but a computer, and you can get an Academy Award if you use it correctly. Zero budget films are everywhere now, and so are the learning resources.'[56] Baldwin's opportunity to study at UCLA was made possible because of scholarships he received, which he acknowledges were the only way that he could have completed a BA in the USA, although he adds that his funding was for tuition rather than specifically for his films and that while film festivals have been instrumental in his success, participating in them can be costly: 'Even with just the submission fees, applying to festivals can be slightly prohibitive for many. There's other costs involved, such as shipping, DVD duplication, creating tapes in different formats for exhibition, promotional materials, etc.'[57]

Baldwin is currently preparing a DVD release of his films which has been the result of a laborious process where he creates all aspects of the DVD, from the menus to the labels and then sells them one by one. He adds that he is not expecting to make money from the DVDs and that they are intended for fans and for promotional purposes.[58] The main reason why he expects to make very little money from this DVD is that his films are available online, a clear downside of the global dissemination of materials through the Internet. Moreover, when asked whether he would set an animated film in Paraguay, he noted that the average costs involved in making an animated feature are generally about $120 million, and so it would be impossible to make such a film in the country, although he observes that there is a market on the Internet for animated shorts, no matter where the director lives.[59]

The online distribution of films is constrained, however, by access to the Internet, which is not within reach of the majority of people living in Paraguay. In 2007, a study by Fundación Telefónica noted that only 3.6 per cent of Paraguayans use the Internet (García Béjar, p. 187). While a similar study conducted by the UN's International Telecommunications

55 Personal interview with Joaquín Baldwin, 14 May 2010.
56 Personal interview with Joaquín Baldwin, 14 May 2010.
57 Personal interview with Joaquín Baldwin, 14 May 2010.
58 Personal interview with Joaquín Baldwin, 14 May 2010.
59 Sergio Colman, Interview with Joaquín Baldwin. Available at: http://elpororo.com/category/03-entrevistas/ (Last accessed 3 June 2010).

Union in November 2008 cited usage figures of 7.8 per cent of the population, this figure is still extremely low.[60] Apart from the issue of access to the Internet, the prevalence of illegal downloading of films online also complicates the issue of making money from films distributed solely in this manner.

When asked whether the success of Encina and Baldwin's films had changed the situation of filmmaking in Paraguay, the filmmakers interviewed were unanimous in praising their work, but they ultimately felt that little had changed. There was little optimism either that Lugo's government would bring dramatic changes in the area of culture. Moreover, when asked what the biggest obstacle they faced was, all of them mentioned financial constraints. Schémbori stressed the need for a dedicated cinema fund that would address the particular financial demands of the medium. She estimates that her first feature, co-directed with Juan Carlos Maneglia, has cost approximately $435,000 and could not have been made without the support of numerous sponsors, including Yacyreta (a dam between Argentina and Paraguay). Maneglia believes that the future of cinema in Paraguay is very uncertain, though he notes that the fact that so many talented people are now working in the area may be reason for optimism. While Gómez is also less than optimistic about the future, he is clear about what needs to be done:

> Debemos empezar con lo básico. Una escuela que genere cineastas paraguayos, una escuela nacional de cine que todavía no la hay, en pleno 2010.

> We must start with the basics. A school that would produce Paraguayan filmmakers, a national cinema school that still does not exist, even in 2010.[61]

While this less than rose-tinted vision of the future is only to be expected, the achievements of Paraguayan filmmakers are such that there is much reason to suppose that they will continue to make films in a wide range of genres that tell uniquely Paraguayan stories or that deal with Paraguay's position in a world that largely ignores it. Baldwin has recently released his new film, *The Windmill Farmer*, *7 cajas* is in post-production, and Coronel is on the way to completing *Yo, mujer sola*. The establishment of

[60] Fundación Telefónica, http://www.internetworldstats.com/sa/py.htm. (Last accessed 20 April 2011).
[61] Personal interview with Ramiro Gómez, 25 August 2010.

a permanent exhibition that documents Paraguay's cinema history in the Museo del Barro is also a tribute to the achievements of local filmmakers, while the venue provides an invaluable space for cinema screenings and festivals. Festivals nationally, such as the annual Ta'anga, and internationally have also been hugely important in promoting Paraguayan film. The silenced screen is no more, and it is to be hoped that the eventual passing of a cinema law may lead to an increased presence internationally for Paraguayan cinema and an improved situation for its filmmakers.

9

Finance and Co-productions in Brazil

ALESSANDRA MELEIRO

The purpose of this chapter is to present an up-to-date (as of 2011) account of the funding available to filmmakers in Brazil, with particular consideration being given to the advantages and disadvantages to be gained from making co-productions.

From an economic perspective, the audiovisual industry plays a strategic role in the dissemination of information and therefore in the decision-making process of the world economy, not to mention the capacity of generating products, employment and income. It was estimated that the revenue of the audiovisual industry in Brazil in 1997 was about $5.5 billion, equivalent to approximately 1 per cent of Gross Domestic Product, compared with 1 per cent in Argentina, 0.5 per cent in Mexico, 1.1 per cent in Europe and 2.7 per cent in the USA.[1]

The four main American distributors enjoy the largest slice of the Brazilian market while the remaining market share is occupied by small independent distributors. From time to time, the major players, such as Columbia, Sony, Fox, Warner and UIP, have also invested in the distribution of Brazilian products. In this case, the company also acts as the producer, profiting from fiscal exemption in the remittance of foreign currency used in the co-production of Brazilian films (through Article 3A, resources secured through fiscal renouncement). Examples of this practice include *Tropa de elite 2* (*Elite Squad 2*, 2010), with over 11 million

---

[1] Iafa Britz, 'Brazil–Europe: Notes on Distribution, Finance and Co-Production', in *Exploiting European Films in Latin America,* Media Business file, n. 09 (Spain: MEDIA Business School, 2002), pp. 21–8.

viewers in Brazil, *Se eu fosse você 2* (*If I Were You 2*, 2009) *and Dois Filhos de Francisco* (*Two Sons of Francisco*, 2005). See Table 1.

Table 1: Biggest Box Office Intakes since 1995[2]

	Film	Year	Admissions	Box Office (R$)	Studio	Distributor
1	*Tropa de elite 2* (*Elite Squad 2*)	2010	11,023,475	89,277,934.02	Zazen Produções Audiovisuais Ltda.	Zazen Produções Audiovisuais Ltda.
2	*Se eu fosse você 2* (*If I Were You 2*)	2009	6,112,851	50,543,885.00	Total Entertainment	Fox Film do Brasil
3	*Dois filhos de Francisco* (*Two Sons of Francisco*)	2005	5,319,677	36,728,278.00	Conspiração Filmes	Columbia TriStar do Brasil
4	*Carandiru* (*Carandiru*)	2003	4,693,853	29,623,481.00	HB Filmes	Sony e Columbia
5	*Nosso lar* (*Astral City: A Spiritual Journey*)	2010	4,060,304	31,820,375.748	Cinética Filmes e Produções Ltda	Fox Filmes do Brasil
6	*Se eu fosse você* (*If I Were You*)	2006	3,644,956	28,916,137.00	Total Entertainment	Fox Filmes do Brasil
7	*Cidade de Deus* (*City of God*)	2002	3,370,871	19,066,087.00	O2 Filmes	Lumière e Miramax Filmes
8	*Lisbela e o prisioneiro* (*Lisbela and the Prisoner*)	2003	3,174,643	19,915,933.00	Natasha Enterprises	Fox Filmes do Brasil
9	*Cazuza – o tempo não para* (*Cazuza: Time Doesn't Stop*)	2004	3,082,522	21,230,606.00	Lereby Produções	Columbia TriStar do Brasil
10	*Olga* (*Olga*)	2004	3,078,030	20,375,397.00	Nexus Cinema e Video	Lumière
11	*Os normais* (*So Normal*)	2003	2,996,467	19,874,866.00	Missão Impossível Cinco Produções Artísticas	Lumière
12	*Xuxa e os duendes* (*Xuxa and the Elves*)	2001	2,657,091	11,691,200.00	Diler & Associados	Warner Bros.

---

[2] The source for this information is Ancine, 2010; see www.ancine.gov.br (Last accessed 4 October 2011).

13	Tropa de elite (Elite Squad)	2007	2,417,754	20,395,447.00	Zazen Produções Audiovisuais Ltda.	Universal Pictures do Brasil
14	Xuxa pop star (Xuxa Popstar)	2000	2,394,326	9,625,191.00	Diler & Associados	Warner Bros.
15	A mulher invisível (The Invisible Woman)	2009	2,353,136	20,498,576.00	Conspiração Filmes	Warner Bros.
16	Maria, mãe do filho de Deus (Mary, Mother of the Son of God)	2002	2,332,873	12,842,085.00	Diler & Associados	Columbia TriStar do Brasil
17	Xuxa e os duendes 2 (Xuxa and the Elves 2)	2002	2,301,152	11,485,979.00	Diler & Associados	Warner Bros.
18	Sexo, amor e traição (Sex, Love and Betrayal)	2004	2,219,423	15,775,132.00	Total Entertainment	Fox Filmes do Brasil
19	Xuxa abracadabra (Xuxa in abracadabra)	2004	2,214,481	11,677,129.00	Diler & Associados	Warner Bros.
20	Os normais 2 (So Normal 2)	2009	2,202,640	18,978,259.88	Globo Filmes	Imagem Filmes

Every audiovisual activity in Brazil is regulated and supervised by the National Film Agency (ANCINE), a special and independent autarchy linked to the Ministry of Culture that acts as a strategic unit in fomenting film production in Brazil, lending support to foreign co-productions and creating and implementing public policies and specific funds in order to meet the increasing demands of this constantly developing market.

It is important to note that all foreign screen productions carried out in Brazil must be reported to ANCINE and will require the participation of a national production company which will be responsible for production to the agency and other federal, state and municipal bodies. There is a clear distinction between the business models followed by Brazilian and foreign producers: one is production services and the other is international co-production. The term Production Services refers to when an international producer only wants to carry out his work at a location or studio in Brazil, without the use of the national partner's resources, simply hiring a national company that will be responsible for carrying out the work and providing the necessary support for recruitment, logistics, lease of equipment, and so on. For US and European producers, offshore deals are a means of lowering costs and hedging their financial bets at a time when the banking crisis has made film production loans at home harder to come by.

An International Co-production takes place when there is an association of one or more companies in the joint production, with the following types of partnerships:

- When the co-production involves a Brazilian company and a partner originating from a country with which Brazil maintains a diplomatic co-production relationship. The minimum compulsory nature of the Brazilian partner´s participation in the patrimonial rights of the work will be specified by the abovementioned diplomatic agreement;
- When the co-production involves a Brazilian company and a partner originating from a country with which Brazil does not maintain a diplomatic co-production relationship. In this case, there is a minimum compulsory nature of the Brazilian partner´s participation in at least 40 per cent of the patrimonial rights of the work.

The international co-productions are also protected by two different procedures regarding the resources invested by the Brazilian partner and which will guarantee its participation in the enterprise: when there is an intention of securing funds by using mechanisms of fiscal renouncement for the financial participation in the project; or when one simply wants to obtain Brazilian Product Certification without receiving incentive funds.

It is worth recalling that, in both cases, the works carried out under the terms of the co-production agreement will be considered as national works in all the participant countries and, therefore, will consider all the benefits stated in the effective country legislation of each co-producer.[3]

It is also worth noting that an international co-production is an effective way to accumulate a large production budget and share other resources, experience and knowledge. Thus, as long as content regulations, tax incentives and government agency funding are in place, it makes sense to have special arrangements that enable international co-production to qualify. The fear with international co-productions is that they end up being mid-Atlantic or 'Euro-puddings' without artistic merit or national orientation, unlikely to contribute to external benefits in the country of

---

[3] Aliança Brasileira de Film Commissions (Abrafic), *Manual de Exportação de Locações e Serviços Audiovisuais Brasileiros* (2008). Available at: www.abrafic.org. (Last accessed 11 June 2009).

either of the partners. This concern does seem to have largely abated in recent years, however.

Projects qualified through bilateral and multilateral international co-production treaties are recognised as national productions for both partners. They count as domestic content for quota purposes and are eligible for investment from any government funding agency in place, while private investors are eligible for any tax incentives. In this case, a co-production undertaken under a bilateral or multilateral treaty is considered a 'treaty co-production'. International co-productions that are not undertaken under the auspices of a co-production agreement are sometimes knows as 'co-ventures' or 'non-treaty co-productions'. Even where there is a co-production agreement, some international co-productions will not be made under its auspices. This may be because the way the project is structured does not allow it to qualify under the terms of the treaty, or because the benefits derived from having the project qualify are judged not worth the cost of the bureaucratic hurdles to be surmounted.

It is considerably more difficult for a non-treaty co-production than a treaty co-production to qualify as a domestic production for quota purposes. The non-treaty co-production must typically meet the same content and expenditure requirements as domestic productions, and the home partner must have equal decision-making responsibility for all creative elements.

Producers may not always eagerly embrace the co-production mode; it adds cost, complexity, and a need to compromise. However, it is often the only strategy which allows producers to accumulate the large budgets necessary to produce films that can compete effectively on the international market.

Regarding international co-productions, the following potential benefits can be identified:

1. **Pooling of financial resources**: increasingly, producers are unable to raise the funds necessary for a 'world class production' from the domestic market. An international co-production may generate this level of funding through financial contributions from a foreign partner.
2. **Access to a foreign government's incentives and subsidies**. If a project is structured so that it counts as domestic content in the market of each partner, it will be eligible for foreign as well as domestic government subsidies and perhaps tax incentives. International co-production treaties facilitate this.

3. **Access to partner's market**. Improved access is likely to occur for several reasons. First, the foreign partner is likely to have better knowledge regarding the distribution process in his/her domestic market and better connections to key players. Secondly, the foreign partner will have superior knowledge of the features demanded by viewers in his/her market and can help ensure the film possesses such attributes. Thirdly, where quotas are in effect, a treaty co-production will qualify.
4. **Access to a third-country market**. The partner may enjoy superior knowledge regarding the distribution system of the third-country market and better connections with key players in it.
5. **Learning from partner**. Learning opportunities may be anticipated if the partner has greater experience in marketing, film production processes or general management.

Brazilian production funding mechanisms

Co-productions are a sign of the Brazilian film industry's growing prestige and its emergence from two decades in the financial doldrums. Once among the most active in Latin America, the nation's filmmaking industry was decimated by devaluations, hyperinflation and shifting government policies.[4]

A neoliberal influx began to figure on the horizon in 1990 with the election of Fernando Collor de Melo. Ironically an heir to the traditional methods of right-wing populism, Collor demagogically assumed a 'dismantling of the state apparatus', which was basically a ruinous blow to the public sector. This proved particularly disastrous in the cultural area, where institutions and budgets were wiped out, staff laid off and a whole project-funding system effectively torn down overnight. The determination was that the market should be the criterion for sustaining artistic production.[5]

After making just two movies in 1991, the federal government launched its fiscal incentives policy, which allowed for the gradual resumption

[4]   Chris Kraul, 'Brazilian Film Industry's Resurgence Aided by Foreign Co-producers', *Los Angeles Times*, 22 December 2008. Available at: http://articles.latimes.com/2008/oct/23/business/fi-brazfilm23 (Last accessed 10 September 2011).
[5]   Isaura Botelho, *Marketing cultural: um investimento com qualidade* (São Paulo: Informações Culturais, 1998).

of Brazilian cinematographic production, and Brazilian filmmakers completed 90 productions in 2008, of which a part were partnered by Italian, Portuguese, Canadian and Spanish-American producers.

During the administration of President Luis Inácio Lula da Silva, the incentive laws remained a key to the competitiveness of the Brazilian film industry. Annual national film output rose progressively as a result of this incentive policy, and we are seeing favourable new structural parameters for the development of a film industry in Brazil, such as the Audiovisual Sector Fund. With US$ 18,981,503 available in 2008, this Fund is directed to all the links in the productive chain and the single most important innovation in comparison with the existing policies is the introduction of loans with sound perspectives for financial returns.

Figure 1: Brazilian production funding mechanisms

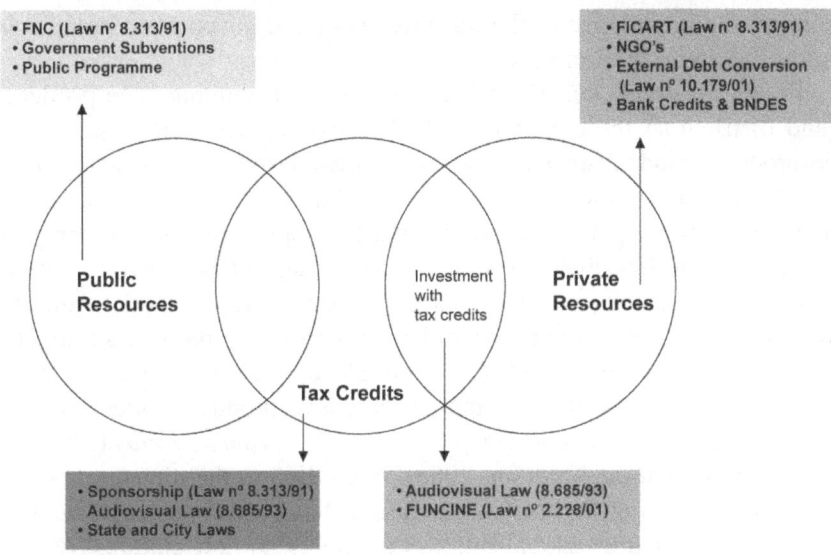

Source: Anders, 2008

The structure of Brazilian resources of funding (see Figure 1) is basically composed of Public Resources (FNC, Government Subventions and Public Programmes), Tax Credits (Sponsorship, Audiovisual Law and State and City Laws) and Private Resources (FICART, NGOs, External Debt Conversion and Bank Credits & BNDES [the Brazilian Development Bank]).

Although these funding mechanisms are greatly diversified, Brazilian film is still completely dependent on two resources, both of which come from the Audiovisual and Rouanet laws. Both the Audiovisual and Rouanet laws allow companies to tax deduct sums invested in Brazilian films. The Audiovisual Law has two core devices: Article 1 determines that companies can deduct up to 3 per cent of total tax returns on condition that the money is channelled into audiovisual production; and Article 3, which provides incentives for foreign distributors to invest in national film production (as co-producers), offering up to 70 per cent tax rebate on profits remitted abroad.[6]

To cite an example, of the R\$7 million it cost to produce Fernando Meirelles' *Cidade de Deus* (*City of God*, 2002), R\$5.5 million was invested by O2 Filmes, while the remaining R\$1.5 million was raised through the incentive laws. This parcel of R\$1.5 million came through Article 3 of the Audiovisual Law, which made the distributer Lumière a co-producer and exclusive rights-holder for nationwide distribution. Cases like this confirm the importance of the incentive laws and government policies in nurturing domestic film production.[7]

Breno Silveira's *Dois filhos de Francisco* had Columbia as co-producer (and distributor) through Article 3. This is an interesting case, as the co-producer and distributor actually *invited* the Brazilian producer Conspiração Filmes to come on board, and he was involved in the script and production right down to the master copy. This is not common practice at the Brazilian division of Columbia, but proved effective in producing a mass-interest film – and ran counter to the market rule, by which co- and associate producers have no power to interfere so directly in the creative process.[8] Another example of participation by a major player – in this case Disney – that became a co-producer under Article 3 is Cao Hambúrger's *O ano em que meus pais saíram de férias* (*The Year My Parents Went on Vacation*, 2005). According to the director, 'People seem to be looking for fresh ideas and different environments', and 'It probably comes from globalization, the interest in new cultures' (Kraul, 2008, n.p.). Other sources of funding, such as distributor advances, State

---

6 Paulo Sérgio Almeida and Pedro Butcher, *Cinema: desenvolvimento e mercado* (Rio de Janeiro: Aeroplano, 2003).

7 João Paulo Rodrigues Matta and Elizabeth Regina Loiola da Cruz Souza, 'Cidade de Deus e Janela da Alma: um estudo sobre a cadeia produtiva do cinema brasileiro', *Revista ERA/FGV*, 49 (2009), 27–37.

8 Belisa Figueiró, 'O desafio de lucrar com o cinema', *Revista de CINEMA* (2007). Available at: http://www.cenacine.com.br/?p=404.

and Municipal Laws for cultural incentives, municipal tax (fiscal) exemption laws and risk investors, are usually marginal in the film´s budget.

In addition to fiscal incentives, it is also necessary to stress the importance of direct promotion policies implemented through competitions and edicts from the Ministry of Culture, the State oil company Petrobrás, the Brazilian Development Bank (BNDES) and ANCINE, as can be seen from Table 2. A new investment alternative for the film industry comes in the form of the National Film Industry Financing Fund (Fundos de Financiamento da Indústria Cinematográfica Nacional – FUNCINES). This resource allows financial institutions duly accredited with the Central Bank to set up funds for investment in independent Brazilian film and audiovisual products, as well as undertakings associated with the film production chain. The first FUNCINE – BB CINE, managed by Banco do Brasil – was launched in 2004. FUNCINE funds are expected to inject credit into both distribution and screening, filling the gaps in the commercialisation of national cinema.

Recently, the Brazilian Development Bank (BNDES) created the Audiovisual Productive Chain Support Programme (PROCULT), whose general objective is to support the development of the Brazilian Audiovisual Industry, considering the specificities of the sector. PROCULT covers the lines of production, distribution, marketing, exhibition and infrastructure services.

As illustrated in Figure 2, a co-production can be eligible for Brazilian Tax Credit benefits when:

- A Brazilian independent production company submits the coproduction agreement, signed according to the treaty, for ANCINE'S approval;
- A Brazilian production company presents the project to ANCINE describing content, budget, and desired funding mechanisms;
- A national producer has, according to its curricula, to raise tax credit funds;
- ANCINE performs a technical analysis and approves the project; from there on, the national producer sets about raising funds directly with investors/sponsors. Investors/Sponsors deposit funds in the project's bank account under the producer's management.

Basically, there are two modalities for Co-Production Public Funding: Investments or Sponsorships. *Investments* are when a company purchases ownership rights of the audiovisual product with tax credit money (equity acquisition), and *Sponsorships* are when tax credit money does not allow

Table 2: Direct ANCINE Incentives (2003–2009)

Direct ANCINE Incentives	2003 (R$)	2004 (R$)	2005 (R$)	2006 (R$)	2007 (R$)	2008 (R$)	2009 (R$)
Development	500,000.00	1,020,000.00	–	–	–	–	–
Production	4,490,000.00	–	–	–	3,695,370.26 *	–	–
Completion	1,906,049.00	6,819,984.00	1,948,500.00	–	–	–	–
Turnover Bonus	–	–	4,162,000.00	7,500,000.00	8,380,065.00	8,176,052.24	9,300,000.00
Quality Bonus	–	–	–	1,000,000.00	500,000.00	700,000.00	700,000.00
Universalization of Access	–	–	–	–	–	542,986.00	–
Audiovisual Sector Fund	–	–	–	–	–	–	29,485,586.80
Sub Total – ANCINE Edicts (R$)	6,896,049.00	7,839,984.00	6,110,500.00	8,500,000.00	12,575,435.26	9,419,038.24	39,485,586.80
Ibermedia (contribution Fund in US$)	450,000.00	596,550.79	600,000.00	788,068.05	1,041,148.49	1,073,949.58	798,092.45
Brazil-Argentina Distribution	500,000.00	180,000.00	240,000.00	–	–	–	–
Brazil-Portugal Co-production (em US$)	300,000.00	300,000.00	300,000.00	300,000.00	300,000.00	300,000.00	300,000.00
Brazil-Galicia Co-production	–	–	–	–	–	R$ 300.000,00	100.000,00
International Total (em R$)	2,803,025.00	2,802,321.41	2,429,970.00	2,367,962.50	2,611,886.68	2,823,533.19	2,288,168.83
Total Direct Incentives (R$)	9,699,074.00	10,642,305.41	8,540,470.00	10,867,962.50	15,187,321.94	12,242,571.43	41,773,755.63

Figure 2: System workflow for a co-production which intends to take advantage of Brazilian Tax Credit benefits

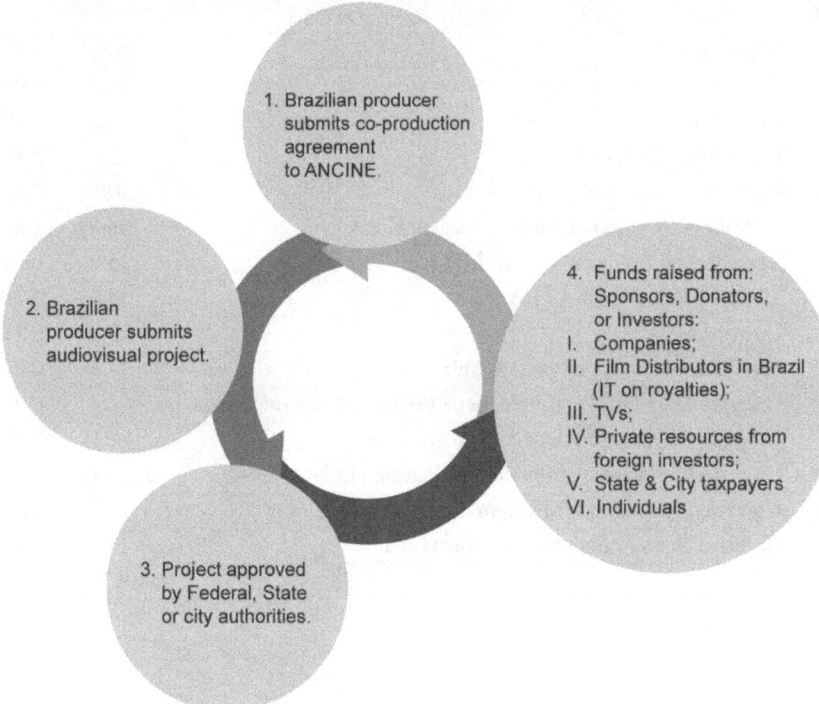

1. Brazilian producer submits co-production agreement to ANCINE.

2. Brazilian producer submits audiovisual project.

3. Project approved by Federal, State or city authorities.

4. Funds raised from: Sponsors, Donators, or Investors:
   I. Companies;
   II. Film Distributors in Brazil (IT on royalties);
   III. TVs;
   IV. Private resources from foreign investors;
   V. State & City taxpayers
   VI. Individuals

Source: Anders, 2008

ownership rights to be purchased by the investing/sponsor company. Among the Sponsorship Mechanisms we can find the Rouanet Law, the Audiovisual Law and State and City regulations. Among the Investment Mechanisms there are FUNCINES, the Audiovisual Law (Article 3) and Article 39.

Brazilian producers are frequently accused of having a 'subsidy trap' mentality, spending most of their time chasing public funds. They are dependent on the state and secure funding through connections and lobbying. State investments in cultural projects can be seen in Table 3 (a–c): in 2010, the biggest investor in Brazilian cinema through the Rouanet Law as well through the Audiovisual Law was the state-owned company Petrobrás (investments from Petrobrás account for 56 per cent of all such monies invested in nationally produced projects).

Table 3: Sums invested by Supporters/2010 – Rouanet Law – 8313/91 (R$ Thou)

(a)

#	Supporter	Sum	%
1	Petrobrás – Petróleo Brasileiro S/A	1,620	56.06
2	Redecard S/A	930	32.18
3	Linha Amarela SA – Lamsa	150	5.19
4	Dyfry do Brasil Duty Free Shop Ltda	100	3.46
5	Eletrobrás – Centrais Elétricas Brasileiras S.A.	46.3	1.60
6	Serra do Mar Produtos de Petróleo Ltda.	15.5	0.54
7	TORIBA VEÍCULOS LTDA	14.0	0.48
8	Lismar Ltda	7.0	0.24
9	Rio Preto Produtos de Petróleo Ltda.	2	0.07
10	Unipetro Dourados Distribuidora de Produtos de Petróleo Ltda	1	0.03
11	Unipetro MS Distribuidora de Petróleo Ltda	1	0.03
12	Unipetro Ourinhos Distribuidora de Petróleo Ltda.	1	0.03
13	Unipetro Prudente Distribuidora de Petróleo Ltda.	1	0.03
14	Unipetro Nova Andina Dist. Petróleo Ltda	1	0.03
Total		2,889.79	100

Source: Ancine (2010)

(b)

Sums Raised per Incentive Mechanism – R$ Thou – 2010

Incentive Mechanism	2009	2010	Variation (%)
Article 1 A – Law 8,685/93 (Audiovisual Law)	50.576,8	64.710,4	27.9%
Article – Law 8,685/93 (Audiovisual Law)	36.684,8	24.266,1	-33.9%
Article 3 – Law 8,85/93 (Audiovisual Law)	23.540,9	29.686,9	26.1%
Article 3 A – Law 8,685/93 (Audiovisual Law)	2.500,0	28.201,0	1028%
Article 39 – Law 2,228–1/01	11.801,4	12.474,6	5.7%
FUNCINES – Article 41 – Law 2,228–1/01	1.850,0	6.600,0	256.8%
Law 8,313/91 (Rouanet Law)	8.549,6	2.889,8	-66.2%
Total	135.503,46	168.828,87	24.6%

Source: Ancine (2010)

(c)

Sums Allocated per Supporter – Art.1 A of Law 8,685/93 –
R$ Thou – 2010

Rank	Supporter	Sum	%
1	Petrobrás - Petróleo Brasileiro S/A	18,180.63	28.1%
2	CIA de Saneamento Básico do Estado de São Paulo – SABESP	7,564.96	11.7%
3	Cia Vale do Rio Doce	3,874.28	6%
	VALE S/A	290.92	0.4%
4	Banco Nacional de Desenvolvimento Econômico e Social – BNDES	2,386.38	3.7%
5	NATURA COSMETICOS S.A.	1,758	2.7%
6	AMBEV BRASIL BEBIDAS LTDA.	1,200	1.9%
7	Tetra Pak Ltda.	1,100	1.7%
8	Banco BMG S.A.	1,050	1.6%
9	CEMIG GERAÇÃO E TRANSMISSÃO S/A	625	1%
	CEMIG DISTRIBUIÇÃO S/A	425	0.7%
10	CIA Brasileira de Metalurgia e Mineração	1,009.2	1.6%

Source: Ancine (2010)

The film and audiovisual market in Brazil has an annual turnover of 8 to 10 billion dollars, which puts it somewhere between eighth and tenth in the world ranking.

If TV productions are well positioned when it comes to exportation, especially given the high level of industrialisation the made-for-TV business has achieved in Brazil, the same cannot be said for Brazilian cinema. According to data from Ancine, the national film board, there are currently an estimated 170 feature films ready for release or in production. This has led Brazilian filmmakers, producers and public administrators to draw the same conclusion reached by former president Fernando Henrique Cardoso when he famously declared that it was time to 'export or die'. For Silvio Da-Rin, former Audiovisual Secretary at the Ministry of Culture, the present co-production policy does not simply aim to increase investment in Brazilian productions, but also broaden the range of market possibilities for those films. This government stance has found expression in policies such as the Cinema of Brazil Programme, created in 2006 through a partnership formed of the Ministry of Culture (MinC), the Audiovisual Secretariat (SAV), the Brazilian Trade and Investment Promotion Agency (Apex) and the Audiovisual Industry Union of São Paulo State (Siaesp).

Between the launch of the Cinema of Brazil Programme[9] and July 2009, 73 of the 147 participant companies indicated that business between Brazil and other countries had exceeded R$ 64 million, with the sale of 239 audio-visual products. During this period, the most significant business was done with Germany, Canada, Spain and France. In 2010, business volume stood at US$45.8 million, with 25 co-production agreements closed, 23 films selected for important festivals and 540 international sales generated. Many of these films were sold and distributed on the commercial circuit.[10]

Through the participation of Brazilian producers at the most prestigious international film festivals (Rotterdam, Cannes, Clermont-Ferrand, among others), as well at Brazilian film festivals, business meetings have yielded agreements that attract external investments in new audiovisual projects. An initiative of a Brazilian Association, the Brazilian Film Commissions Alliance (Abrafic), and Apex, recently released a manual that contains a description of the relevant entities, the main rules, norms and procedures to be observed in the development of transnational productions and co-productions in Brazil (Abrafic, n. p.).

Co-production is a much abused term: it may refer to any form of co-financing (a pre-sale to a television channel, theatrical distributor or foreign territory) or creative and financial collaboration between various producers (including broadcasters). In recent years, co-financing arrangements have been more popular than inter-governmental co-production agreements.[11] Tables 4 and 5 and Figures 3 and 4 provide an indication of the number and types of co-production.

---

[9] The Cinema of Brazil programme has 95 associate companies, including the biggest Brazilian production companies, such as 02, LC Barreto, Gullane, Tambelini, Conspiração and Casa de Cinema de Porto Alegre.

[10] See the Agência Brasileira de Promoção de Exportações e Investimentos (Apex) website. Available at: http://www.apexbrasil.com.br/portal/publicacao/engine.wsp?tmp.area=426&tmp.texto=7803. (Last accessed 15 August 2011).

[11] Anne Jäckel, *European Film Industries* (London: International Screen Industries/British Film Institute, 2003).

Table 4: Number of international co-productions made per year

(a)

Year	Number
1995	1
1996	0
1997	1
1998	3
1999	3
2000	5
2001	2
2002	4
2003	4
2004	8
2005	5
2006	9
2007	9
2008	15
2009	10
Total	**79**

Source: Ancine (2009)

(b)

Number of international co-productions underway in 2008

Stage	Number
Post-Production	13
Filming	4
Pre-Production	1
Fund-raising	9
Total	**27**
Grand Total	**106**

Source: Ancine (2009)

Figure 3: International co-productions year by year

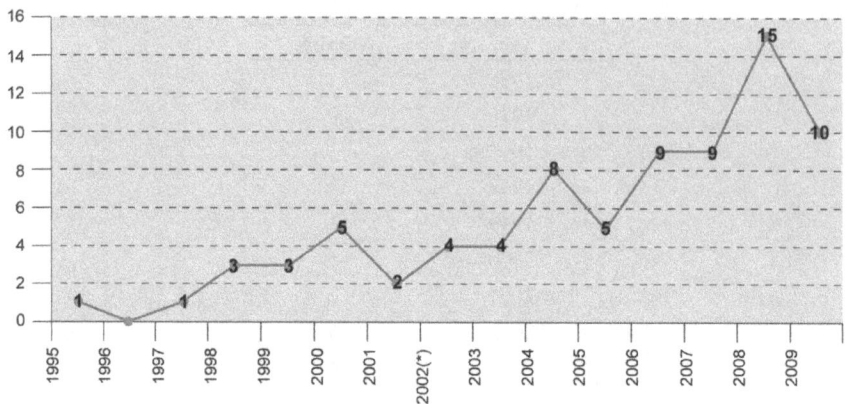

Source: Ancine (2009)

Figure 4: Number of international co-productions underway in 2008 and the share of Brazilian patrimony involved (minority, equal and majority share)

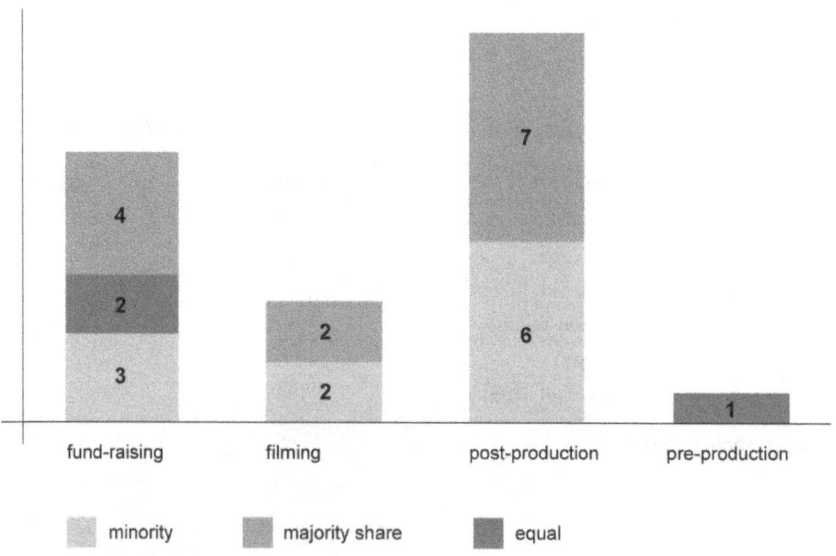

Source: Ancine (2009)

Of these international co-productions 49 per cent involve partners from other Latin American countries. In addition to the Latin American Film Co-production Agreement and the Ibermedia Programme, the creation of the 'Mercosul Audiovisual' programme, in partnership with the European Union (EU), has strengthened audiovisual co-production ties between Brazil and Europe through the injection of some €1.8 million.[12]

The phenomenon of co-productions in Brazil is quite recent. However, everything suggests that this will be the future production format. The Brazilian government has as policy of stimulating co-productions through the expansion of institutional relationships among film institutes and bilateral and multilateral agreements. (See the lists below.)

Brazil's bilateral agreements in the audiovisual sector
- Film Co-production Agreement Brazil–Germany (2005)
- Cooperation and Film Co-Production Agreement Brazil–Chile (1996)
- Co-production Agreement Brazil–Canada (1995)
- Co-production Agreement Brazil–Argentina (1988)
- Co-production Agreement Brazil–Venezuela (1988)
- Co-production Agreement Brazil–Portugal (1981)
- Co-production Agreement Brazil–Italy (1970)
- Co-production Agreement Brazil–France (1969)
- Co-production Agreement Brazil–Spain (1963)

Brazil's multilateral agreements in the audiovisual sector
Latin American Film Co-production Agreement (1989) – Argentina, Cuba, Mexico, Panama, Venezuela, Colombia, Ecuador, Nicaragua, Peru, Dominican Republic and Brazil

Cooperation between ANCINE and other institutions[13]
Ibermedia Fund
Portuguese–Brazilian Film Co-production Protocol
Galician Audiovisual Consortium Cooperation Protocol

---

[12] Programme orchestrated by MINC in September 2008, during a special meeting of Recam (Mercosul Board of Film and Audiovisual Authorities) at the Rio Film Festival, and implemented by the Audiovisual Secretariat (SAV) in 2009.

[13] Co-production 'Protocols', under an umbrella agreement, are simpler and establish more concrete measures, such as financial support. The Brazil–Portugal Protocol, which launched the *Edital Luso Brasileiro*, is a case in point, with awards of up to US$ 150,000 for Portuguese/Brazilian productions.

Co-production cases

Blindness, by the director Fernando Meirelles, a co-production by O2 Filmes (Brazil), Rhombus Media (Canada) and Bee Vine Pictures (Japan), had a budget of CDN 27,975,000.00, and was the first feature film to come out of the Brazil–Canada Agreement. In addition to a $25 million budget for this adaptation of the novel by José Saramago – a sum hitherto unthinkable for a film produced exclusively with funds from Brazilian fiscal incentive laws, Meirelles' partnership also ensured the movie's distribution through the powerful Fox. The result: besides the 630,000 tickets sold in Brazil, the film's release abroad, in countries like the USA, Canada and Japan, was also assured.[14] Table 5 gives details of the overall funding structure for *Blindness*.

Co-production agreements hold various benefits for Brazilian producers. Cláudia da Natividade, who produced the film *Estômago* (*Estomago: A Gastronomic Story*, 2007), by Marcos Jorge, highlights that 'co-production ensures that a Brazilian film will be released in at least one other country', adding that, 'in the case of European partnerships, European certification helps a lot in terms of access to the international market' (Rodrigo, n. p.). These comments are corroborated by the fact that two-thirds of the Latin American output that secured European distribution between 2002 and 2006 were co-productions with European countries. For other Brazilian producers, co-production gives the film the marketing advantage that goes with mixed-nationality movies; provides access to production funding and international distribution; facilitates an exchange of experiences and allows for the division of costs and fundraising. As long as the important matter of accessing all the conceivably relevant sources of public funding is not the one-and-only all-important reason for taking the co-production route, collaboration can be extremely fruitful. Project content is the most fundamental and relevant factor in cementing such partnerships. If the film's story genuinely requires the involvement of producers from different countries because of location or talent, then other advantages are likely to emerge in due course: a 'division of labour', with each co-producer tackling not just the public funding sources, but also the distributors, television channels, banks and insurance companies in their own terrain.[15] The film *Jean Charles* (2009), by the

---

[14] Márcio Rodrigo, 'O cinema brasileiro mira o exterior', *Gazeta Mercantil*, São Paulo, 10 October 2008, p. 8.

[15] Pardo, Alejandro, *The Audiovisual Management Handbook* (Madrid: MEDIA Programme, 2002).

Table 5: Financing Structure for *Blindness*

	Equity US$	Soft US$	Loan US$	Advance US$	Total US$	Totals US$
Canada – Telefilm and Corus	4,500,000				4,500,000	
Canada – Alliance Atlantis				1,375,000	1,375,000	
Canada – Tax credits		1,500,000			1,500,000	
Canada – OMDC			400,000		400,000	7,775,000
Brazil – Article 3°.		1,500,000			1,500,000	
Brazil – Article 1°. e 1A (BNDES, FIAT, C&A)		1.950,000			1,950,000	
Brazil – Pref. Paulínia		150,000			150,000	3,600,000
Japan – Cinema Investment			10,000,000		10,000,000	
Japan – Cinema Investment	3,000,000				3,000,000	13,000,000
Advances Italy and Scandinavia				2,500,000	2,500,00	
Producers and Director deferrals	1,100,000				1,100,000	3,600,000
Total (US$)	**8,600,000**	**5,100,000**	**10,400,000**	**3,875,000**	**27,975,000**	**27,975,000**

Source: O2 Filmes, 2008

Brazilian director Henrique Goldman, is a case apart, because it did not have the support of a formal coproduction agreement between the two countries – hence it is an 'agreement-free coproduction' or 'co-venture'. The executive producer was Stephen Frears. While the funding process involved both the Brazilian film agency (Agência Nacional do Cinema) and the UK Film Council, the movie was financed through transnational financial operations conducted by the Brazilian and British production team, rather than through any political or diplomatic effort on the part of the respective competent organs.

Under Brazilian law, a film is considered national when the director is Brazilian, when two-thirds of the team is Brazilian (including the cast) and when 40 per cent of the rights belong to a Brazilian producer. However, even when a film is 100 per cent Brazilian, the Brazilian producer rarely holds 40 per cent of the rights – this is because these are shared with the distributor (in the case of *Jean Charles*, the distributor Imagem), the investors, co-producers and actors, and so on. In order to obtain Brazilian funding for the film *Jean Charles*, the director and producer Henrique Goldman had to donate a percentage of his rights to the Brazilian production company, which meant that the latter held over half of the rights.

Today, to make international co-productions viable, the legal instruments that guarantee and legalise the flow of funds and the tapping of international markets need to be broadened. A formal agreement between Brazil and England would greatly facilitate these financial, taxation and legal matters, as a single system would be adopted by two countries that normally follow radically different procedures.

Table 6 shows forms of co-production funding provided by Intermedia in 2009.

Table 6: Intermedia funding 2009

Ibermedia 2009 Co-Production Modality – Majority Share Brazil			
Project	Brazilian Production Company	Director	US$
Peso da massa, leveza do pão (Weight of the Dough, Lightness of the Bread)	Taiga Filmes e Video	Julia Murat	150,000
Entre vales e montanhas (Between Valleys and Mountains)	Polo de Imagen Ltda.	Phillipe Barcinski	140,000
Amor sujo (Dirty Love)	Bananeira Filmes	Paulo Caldas	110,000
Carta para o futuro (Letter to the Future)	Urca Films Ltda.	Renato Martins	50,000
Total			450,000
Co-Production Modality – Minority Share Brazil			
Project	Brazilian Production Company	Director	US$
El facilitador (The Facilitator)	Tambke Filmes Ltda	Victor Arregui (Equador)	70,000
O manuscrito perdido de Fradique Mendes (The Lost Manuscript of Fradique Mendes)	Refinaria Produções Ltda	José Barahona (Portugal)	40,000

Mundialito (Gold Cup)	V2 Cinema	Sebastian Bednarik (Uruguai)	25,000
Embargo (Embargo)	Diler &Associados	Antônio Ferreira (Portugal)	100,000
Exilados (Exiles)	Polo de Imagen Ltda.	Mariana Viñoles (Uruguai)	12,000
Total			**247,000**

Development Modality			
Project	**Brazilian Production Company**	**US$**	
A marcha (The March)	Geral Ltda.	14,087	
Getulio, meu pai (Getulio, My Father)	Elimar Produções	14,977	
D. Felix e o tempo redondo (D. Felix and Round Time)	TIJD Produções Artísticas	15,000	
Sempre em outro lugar (Always Somewhere Else)	Bananeira Filmes	15,000	
Sobre rodas Latinoamerica (On the Wheel Latinoamerica)	Abbas Filmes	15,000	
Tudo isto me parece um sonho (All of This Looks Like a Dream)	Sarue Filmes Ltda	15,000	
Clandestinos (Clandestines)	Hkauffmann Produções Ltda.	12,000	
Total		**101,064**	

Screening Modality			
Cinema	**Company**	**State**	**US$**
Usina Unibanco de Cinema	Usina de Cinima Ltda.	MG	48,000

Table 7 shows co-production funding from Brazil and Portugal.

Table 7: Brazil–Portugal Co-productions – 2009

Coproduction Projects Brazilian Minority Share			
Project	**Brazilian Production Company**	**Director**	**Sum (US$)**
O grande kilapy (The Great Kilapy)	Raiz Produções Cinematográficas Ltda.	Zezé Gambôa	150,000
José e Pilar (Jose and Pilar)	O2 Cinema Ltda.	Antônio Miguel Gonçalves Mendes	150,000
Total			**300,000**

Coproduction Projects Brazilian Majority Share			
Project	Brazilian Production Company	Director	Sum (US$)
Quase memória (Near-memory)	J. Sanz Produção Audiovisual Ltda.	Ruy Guerra	150,000
Cresci na Mangueira (Raised in Mangueira)	Bossa Nova Filmes Criações e Produções Ltda.	Geórgia Guerra Peixe	150,000
Total			300,000
Total Brazil–Portugal Co-Production			600,000

Table 8 shows types of films with Brazilian–Galician co-funding.

Table 8: Brazil–Galicia Co-productions – 2009

Documentary – Co-Production Project Brazilian Minority Share				
			Sums Approved	
Project	Brazilian Production Company	Director	Agência Nacional do Cinema	Consórcio Audiovisual da Galícia
Brasil somos nós (We Are Brazil)	Bossa Nova Films Criações e Produções Ltda.	Robert Bellsolà	R$ 100,000	€40,000

Fiction – Co-Production Project Brazilian Galician Minority Share			
Project	Brazilian Production Company	Director	Sums Approved
Onde está a felicidade? (Where is the Joy?)	Pulsar Produções Artísticas e Culturais S.A.	Carlos Alberto Riccelli	€12,000

Concluding Remarks

In 2008, the total invested through local, regional and national incentives, subsidies and support programmes in the audiovisual sector was US$ 182 million (see Table 9). Meanwhile, the sums invested through international agreements (Ibermedia, Brazil–Portugal Co-production Agreement, Brazil–Galicia Co-production Agreement) during the same period totalled US$ 2 million (see Tables 6–8).

Table 9: Totals invested by Brazilian sources[16]

Supporter	Sum (R$)
BNDES	113 million
Fund raising Article 3 Audiovisual Law	63.4 million
Festivals	59.9 million
Audiovisual Sector Fund	37 million
Cultural Petrobrás Programme	30.3 million
MINC (SAV)	13.6 million
Rio Grande do Sul	12 million
São Paulo (State)	8.5 million
São Paulo (City)	8.4 million
Paulínia	5 million
Cinema of Brasil Programme	5 million
Brasília	4.3 million
Rio de Janeiro (City)	3.5 million
Bahia	1.3 million
Total	365.2 million

Brazil has a cinema network that does not surpass two thousand theatres – the vast majority being occupied by Hollywood fare. As such, transnational financing programmes are important not so much for the sums invested in nurturing national output, but for the chance they give Brazilian filmmakers to reach audiences outside the limited circuit of their home country (Rodrigo, n.p.). As such, international co-productions through Article 3 of the Audiovisual Law have enhanced film industry performance, with foreign players in charge of distribution (the majors) and exhibition (Cinemark and UCI). This amounts to an internationalisation of the Brazilian film market, with the denationalisation of control over the economics of national film.[17] National film performance has come to depend directly upon partnerships between producers and distributors in order to assure the minimum conditions to compete for screen space.[18]

---

[16] Source: Figueiró, Belisa, 'Cinema terá R$ 365,2 milhões em 2008', *Revista de CINEMA* (2008).

[17] André Gatti, *Distribuição e exibição na indústria cinematográfica brasileira (1993/2003)* (Campinas: Universidade Estadual de Campinas, 2005).

[18] João Paulo Rodrigues Matta, *Análise competitiva da indústria cinematográfica brasileira no mercado interno de salas de exibição de 1994 a 2003* (Salvador:

Both the Audiovisual Law and the Rouanet Law are tax exemption laws, meaning the collection of financial resources for the production of a film depends on the profits of Brazilian companies. Very few producers are able to raise funds from a single source and most films entail a multiplicity of deals. The diversification of sources of funding would appear to be one of the possible ways of guaranteeing minimum stability for the area, especially in this time of global economic crisis. This diversification is healthy for any sector, as it gives the professionals more room to manoeuvre and, given the resulting 'broader spectrum of taste', it increases their chances of having their projects accepted.

Although the Brazilian film market is the tenth largest in the world in terms of box-office intake and the seventh largest in terms of audience, it could not be described as self-sustaining.[19] Such a dependence on resources coming from these laws, as well as the de-structuring of production, represents the main problems for the definitive establishment of a film industry in Brazil.

Universidade Federal da Bahia, Faculdade de Administração, Núcleo de Pós-Graduação em Administração, 2004).

[19] André Klotzel, *O potencial da indústria cinematográfica no Brasil*, 2 vols (Campinas: Inovação Uniemp, 2006), vol. 2, pp. 18–19.

AFTERWORD

The nine essays in this collection, researched and written between 2008 and 2011, provide a 'snapshot' of transnational filmmaking practices in the imagined community of nations that we define as the Hispanic world roughly between the years 2005 and 2010. With its emphasis on film festivals, international funding agencies, and co-productions, we have concentrated on films that circulate 'abroad', but it is perhaps worth underscoring once more the fact that many films are both financed and circulate within Latin America without any recourse to 'foreign assistance'. These range from the Globofilmes-produced (or marketed) popular comedies and TV spin-offs in Brazil,[1] to genre films in Venezuela, to the kind of recent exploitation films discussed in a number of chapters in Tierney and Ruétalo's ground-breaking *Latsploitation* collection.[2]

In the year we go to press (2012), 'Hispanic' films continue to attract international attention and praise: for example, the current severe funding crisis in Portuguese cinema has been overshadowed in the press by the critical success of feature-length and short films, while the *Hollywood Reporter* declared this year, as a result of box-office and production increases and the notable presence of Latin American films at Cannes 2012, 'It's a good time to be part of the Latin American film industry'.[3]

What is evidently missing in this narrative, and what has become clear during the editing of this book, is the speed with which the economic and political landscape of Hispanic countries is changing, and the impact that such changes stand to have on cultural production. The continued financial crisis, and the extent to which this is hitting Spain (with 25%

---

[1]   For more information see the Globofilmes website: www.globofilmes.globo.com (last accessed 1 September 2012).

[2]   Dolores Tierney and Victoria Ruétalo (eds), *Latsploitation, Exploitation Cinemas and Latin America* (Abingdon and New York: Routledge, 2009).

[3]   Agustin Mango, 'Cannes 2012: Latin American Film Sector is on the Rise', *Hollywood Reporter* 19 May 2012. Available at: http://www.hollywoodreporter.com/news/cannes-film-festival-latin-american-film-326811 (last accessed 1 September 2012).

unemployment at time of going to press), is perhaps inevitably affecting funding of cultural agencies such as the Instituto Cervantes. This is of particular concern for film given that, as Núria Triana Toribio points out in chapter 5, cinema is considered to be one of the Instituto Cervantes' most successful cultural activities. As Tamara Falicov observes in chapter 4, to date the MPAA, France and Italy have not been permitted to join Ibermedia, in a supposed attempt to preserve the organisation's Ibero-American spirit. It remains to be seen how long such a desire will win out over pressing financial imperatives. Meanwhile, Brazil's rising economy and attendant use of soft power,[4] mirrored in the strength of and investment in the Brazilian film industry provide us with a telling indication of the complexity of power relations within this so-called Hispanic world. This complexity is recognised by the authors included in this volume, in which we have sought to look beyond reductive readings of Spanish-led initiatives such as Cine en Construcción, Ibermedia and co-productions with Latin American film industries as being exclusively neo-imperial in intentions and results.

Stephanie Dennison

---

[4] A good example of this use of Brazilian soft power can be seen in the advantages being taken in relation to both the hosting of the soccer World Cup in 2014 and the Olympic Games in 2016. Seemingly as part of a series of cultural events linked to the handing over of the Olympic flag between London and Rio de Janeiro, an audio-visual co-production agreement, the lack of which is referred to in chapters 1 and 9, was recently signed (September 2012) between the UK and Brazil.

WORKS CITED

'23 coproducciónes: acuerdo para promover el cine iberoamericano', *La nación* (Espéctaculos), 23 October 2000.

Abente-Brun, Diego, 'Paraguay: The Unraveling of One-Party Rule', *Journal of Democracy*, 20 (2009), 143–56.

Acland, Charles R, *Screen Traffic: Movies, Multiplexes, and Global Culture* (Durham NC: Duke University Press, 2003).

Agência Brasileira de Promoção de Exportações e Investimentos (Apex). Available at: http://www.apexbrasil.com.br/portal/publicacao/engine.wsp?tmp.area=426&tmp.texto=783.

Aliança Brasileira de Film Commissions (Abrafic). *Manual de Exportação de Locações e Serviços Audiovisuais Brasileiros*, 2008. Available at: www.abrafic.org.

Allatson, Paul, *Key Terms in Latino/a Cultural and Literary Studies* (Malden, MA and Oxford: Blackwell, 2007).

Almeida, Paulo Sérgio, and Pedro Butcher, *Cinema: desenvolvimento e mercado* (Rio de Janeiro: Aeroplano, 2003).

Almodóvar, Pedro, 'Colocar la cámara, llenar la pantalla de sonidos', in *La propia voz: el cine sonoro de Lucrecia Martel* (Gijón: Festival Internacional de Cine de Gijón, 2008), p. 8.

——, *La flor de mi secreto* (Barcelona: Plaza y Janés Ave Fénix/Serie Mayor: 1995).

——, *Volver: Guión* (Madrid: Ochoymedio/Libros de Cine, 2006).

Alvarez, Ricardo, Interview in *El pororo cine*. Available at: http://elpororo.com/category/03-entrevistas/

ANCINE (Agência Nacional do Cinema). *Relatório de acompanhamento financeiro 2006*, Superintendência de Acompanhamento de Mercado, 10/05/2007. Available at: www.ancine.gov.br.

ANCINE (Agência Nacional do Cinema). *Relatório de co-produções internacionais 1995–2007*. April 2008. Available at: www.ancine.gov.br.

Anders, Guilherme, *Brazilian Audiovisual Market In Depth Overview and the Official Financing Mechanisms*, Cesnik, Quintino & Salinas Advogados, Rio de Janeiro International Film Festival 2008. Available at: www.cenacine.com.br.

Andrew, Dudley, 'An Atlas of World Cinema', in *Remapping World Cinema: Identity, Culture and Politics on Film*, ed. Stephanie Dennison and Song Hwee Lim (London: Wallflower, 2006), pp. 19–29.

Apaolaza, Jon, 'Latin American Actors in Spain: The Vanguard in the Artistic

Exchange', *The Thinking Eye: Latin American and Spanish Cinema Online* 0 (August 2003). Available at: http://www.elojoquepiensa.udg.mx/ingles/revis_06/index.html.

Aponte Branco, Marlene, 'Pese a reconocimientos, Paz Encina no puede filmar', *ABC Color*, 14 June 2010. Available at: 'http://www.abc.com.py/nota/134639-pese-a-reconocimientos-paz-encina-no-puede-filmar/.

Appadurai, Arjun and Carol Breckenridge, 'On Moving Targets', *Public Culture*, 2 (1989), i–iv.

Armatage, Kay, 'The Festival in the City: The Geo-Politics of International Film Festivals', unpublished paper given at the Film Studies Association of Canada Conference, York University, Toronto, 29 May 2006.

Assmann, Aleida, 'Canon and Archive', in *Cultural Memory Studies: An International and Interdisciplinary Handbook*, ed. Astrid Erll and Ansgar Nünning (Berlin: Walter de Gruyter, 2008), pp. 97–107.

Avila, Oscar, 'Movie Piracy in Mexico', *ChicagoTribune*, 21 February 2009. Available at: http://www.pvscene.com/3287/movie-piracy-in-mexico/.

Baer, Hester and Ryan Long, 'Transnational Cinema and the Mexican State in Alfonso Cuaron's *Y tu mama tambien*', *South Central Review*, 21.3 (Fall 2004), 150–68.

Baldwin, Joaquín, Personal Interview with Catherine Leen, 14 May 2010.

Baltruschat, Doris, 'International TV and Film Co-Production: A Canadian Case Study', in *Media Organization and Production*, ed. Simon Cottle (Thousand Oaks, CA: Sage Publications, 2003), pp. 181–207.

Banco Itaú webpage. Available at: www.itau.com.

Barcia, Manuel, 'A Star is Born: Enter the CELAC', *The Huffington Post*, 28 December 2011. Available at: http://www.huffingtonpost.co.uk/manuel-barcia/a-star-is-born-enter-the-_b_1172484.html#es_share_ended.

Barden, Andrew J. and Katia Cortes, 'Brazil's Piracy under Fire as Lula Caught with Contraband Film', *Bloomberg*, 14 November 2005. Available at: http://www.bloomberg.com/apps/news?pid=newsarchive&sid=aiVz7vok1v5A.

Barnabé, Diego, 'Uruguay puede quedar fuera del fondo Ibermedia para la producción audiovisual si no paga sus deudas', Interview with José Sanchez Varela (Taxi Films) with participation by Elena Villardel (head of Programa Ibermedia), *Radio El Espectador,* Uruguay, 17 May 2000. Available at: http://www.espectador.com/text/clt05171.htm.

Barrionuevo, Alexei, 'Ex-Cleric Wins Paraguay Presidency, Ending a Party's 62-Year Rule', *New York Times*, 21 April 2008. Available at: http://www.nytimes.com/2008/04/21/world/americas/21paraguay.html?_r=1&ref=paraguay.

Barros, Leonardo Monteiro de, *Seminário de Coprodução Internacional*, Rio de Janeiro International Film Festival 2008. Available at: www.cenacine.com.br.

Basch, Linda, Nina Glick Schiller and Cristina Szanton-Blanc, *Nations Unbound: Transnational Projects, Postcolonial Predicaments, and Deterritorialized Nation-states* (Langhorne: Gordon and Breach, 1994).

Bauman, Zygmunt, *Identity* (Cambridge: Polity, 2004).

Benjamin, Walter, 'The Author as Producer', in *Reflections: Essays, Aphorisms, Autobiographical Writings,* edited with an Introduction by Peter Demetz (New York: Schocken Books, 1978), pp. 220–38.

Bergfelder, Tim, 'National, Transnational or Supranational Cinema?: Rethinking European Film Studies', *Media, Culture & Society*, 27.3 (2005), 315–31.

Bermúdez Barrios, Nayibe (ed.), *Latin American Cinema: Local Views and Transnational Connections* (Calgary: University of Calgary Press, 2010).

Bernstein, Adam, 'Alfredo Stroessner, Paraguayan Dictator', *The Washington Post*, 17 August 2006. Available at: http://www.washingtonpost.com/wp-dyn/content/article/2006/08/16/AR2006081601729.html.

Berry, Chris, 'What is Transnational Cinema? Thinking from the Chinese Situation', *Transnational Cinemas*, 1.2 (2010), 111–27.

Bethell, Leslie, 'Brazil and "Latin America"', *Journal of Latin American Studies* 42 (2010), 457–85.

Birri, Fernando, *Por un nuevo cine latinoamericano 1956–1991* (Madrid: Ediciones Cátedra, 1996).

Bologna Declaration of 19 June 1999. Available at: http://www.bologna-bergen2005.no/Docs/00-Main_doc/990719BOLOGNA_DECLARATION.PDF

Bonet, Lluís, 'Industrias culturales y desarrollo en Iberoamérica: Antecedentes para un debate', in *Iberoamérica 2002. Diagnóstico y propuestas para el desarrollo cultural*, ed. Néstor García Canclini (México: Santillana, OEI, 2002).

Bonet, Lluis and Alberto de Gregorio, 'La industria cultural española en América Latina', in *Las industrias culturales en la integración latinoamericana*, ed. Néstor García Canclini and Carlos Moncloa (Mexico City: Grijalbo, 1999), pp. 87–128.

Boquerini, Francisco Blanco, *Pedro Almodóvar* (Madrid: Ediciones JC, 1989).

Botelho, Isaura, *Marketing cultural: um investimento com qualidade* (São Paulo: Informações Culturais, 1998).

Britz, Iafa, 'Brazil–Europe: Notes on Distribution, Finance and Co-Production', in *Exploiting European Films in Latin America*, Media Business file, n. 09 (Spain: MEDIA Business School, 2002), pp. 21–8.

Burton, Julianne, *Cine y cambio social en America Latina* (Mexico City: Diana Editorial, 1991).

Cachay, Raúl A., 'Un francotirador en Lima', *El Comercio*, 9 August 2004, p. 8.

Cannes festival website. Available at: http://www.festival-cannes.com/en/cine-foundation.html.

Cardozo, Efraín, *Breve historia del Paraguay* (Asunción: Servilibro, 2007).

Cardozo, José, 'Lugo aprobó donar G. 5520 millones de Itapú', *ABC Color*, 13 June 2010. Available at: http://www.abc.com.py/nota/134133-lugo-aprobo-donar-g-5-520-millones-de-itaipu/.

Casanova, Lourdes, *Global Latinas: Latin America's Emerging Multinationals* (London: Palgrave Macmillan, 2009).

—— (ed.), 'From Multilatinas to Global Latinas: The New Latin American Multinationals'. Available at: www.iadb.org/intal/intalcdi/PE/2009/03415.pdf.

Castells, Manuel, The Rise of the Network Society (Oxford: Blackwell, 1996).

Castillo, Debra A., 'The New New Latin American Cinema: *Cortometrajes* on the Internet', in *Latin American Cyberculture and Cyberliterature*, ed. Claire Taylor and Thea Pitman (Liverpool: Liverpool University Press, 2007), pp. 34–49.

Céspedes, Roberto L., 'Corrupción', in *Realidad social del Paraguay*, ed. Javier Numan Caballero Merlo (Asunción: Biblioteca de Antropología, 1998).

Chanan, Michael, 'The Changing Geography of Third Cinema', *Screen*, 38.4 (1997), 372–88.

——, 'The Economic Condition of Cinema in Latin America', in *New Latin American Cinema: Theory, Practices and Transcontinental Articulations*, ed. Michael T. Martin (Detroit: Wayne State University Press, 1997), pp. 185–200.

——, 'Economic Conditions of Early Cinema', in *Cinema 1900–1906, FIAF* 1982; revised version in *Early Cinema: Space Frame Narrative*, ed. Thomas Elsaesser and Adam Barker (London: BFI, 1990).

——, 'Latin American Cinema: From Underdevelopment to Postmodernism', in *Remapping World Cinema: Identity, Culture and Politics in Film*, ed. Stephanie Dennison and Song Hwee Lim (London: Wallflower, 2006), pp. 38–54.

—— (ed.), *Twenty-five Years of the New Latin American Cinema* (London: BFI and Channel Four Television, 1983).

Chang, Justin, 'Porfirio' (review). Available at: http://www.variety.com/review/VE1117945262/.

Chavarrías, Antonio, 'La coproducción con Latinoamérica: Cambiar es posible', *Academia: Revista del cine español*, 34 (2004), 12–13.

Cheung, Ruby, 'Corporatizing a Film Festival: Hong Kong', in *Film Festival Yearbook 1: The Festival Circuit*, ed. Dina Iordanova with Ragan Rhyne (London: Wallflower, 2009), pp. 99–115.

Cine en Construcción website. Available at: http://www.clubcultura.com/cineenconstruccion/home.html

Cinema en Construction/Cine en Construcción Facebook page. Available at: http://www.facebook.com/pages/Cinema-en-Construction-Cine-en-Construccion/169484588554.

Clavín, Patricia, 'Defining Transnationalism', *Contemporary European History*, 14.4 (2005), 421–39.

Cohen, Robin, 'Diasporas and the Nation-state: From Victims to Challengers', *International Affairs*, 72 (1996), 507–20.

Collier, Simon, *Carlos Gardel: su vida, su música, su época*, translated by Carlos Gardini (Buenos Aires: Plaza & Janés, 2003).

Colman, Sergio, Interview with Joaquín Baldwin. Available at: http://elpororo.com/category/03-entrevistas/.

Conacine website. Available at: ttp://www.conacineperu.com.pe/acerca1.htm.

Coronel, Leticia, Personal Interview with Catherine Leen, 5 August 2010.

Cortés, María Lourdes, Personal Interview with Tamara Falicov, 24 November 2005.

——, email correspondence with Tamara Falicov, 31 January 2011.

Cotter, Robert Michael 'Bobb', *The Mexican Masked Wrestler and Monster Filmography* (Jefferson, NC: McFarland & Company, 2005).

Cousins, Mark, 'Widescreen on Film Festivals', in *Film Festival Yearbook 1: The Festival Circuit*, ed. Dina Iordanova with Ragan Rhyne (London: Wallflower Press, 2009), pp. 155–8.

Crofts, Stephen. 'Concepts of National Cinema', in *The Oxford Guide to Film*

Studies, ed. John Hill and Pamela Church Gibson (Oxford: Oxford University Press, 1998), pp. 385–94.

Cruz, Ana, *Bertha Navarro: cineasta sin fronteras* (Guadalajara: Universidad de Guadalajara, 2008).

Cuenca, Manuel, 'El cine en Paraguay'. Available at: http://www.paraguaycine.com/cine_nacional.html#3. (Last accessed 10 August 2010).

Czach, Liz, 'Film Festivals, Programming, and the Building of a National Cinema', *The Moving Image*, 4.1 (2004), 74–88.

Dangl, Benjamin and April Howard, 'New vs. Old Right in Paraguay's Election', *NACLA Report on the Americas*, 41.1 (January 2008).

Dapena, Gerard, 'In Search of Gardel's Guitar: Representing the Transhispanic Musical Nation', paper delivered at the Second International Conference on Latin(o)American and Iberian Cinemas, University of Hawaii-Manoa, November 2005.

Dawtrey, Adam, 'Universal pacts with Mexican trio Cuaron, del Toro, Inarritu to make five pics', *Variety*, 18 May 2007. Available at: http://www.variety.com/index.asp?layout=cannes2007&jump=story&articleid=VR1117965227.

DeGuzmán, María, *Spain's Long Shadow: The Black Legend, Off-Whiteness and Anglo-American Empire* (Minneapolis: University of Minnesota Press, 2005).

Dennison, Stephanie and Song Hwee Lim, 'Situating World Cinema as a Theoretical Problem', in *Remapping World Cinema: Identity, Culture and Politics in Film*, ed. Stephanie Dennison and Song Hwee Lim (London: Wallflower, 2006), pp. 1–15.

De Valck, Marijke, *Film Festivals: From European Geopolitics to Global Cinephilia* (Amsterdam: Amsterdam University Press, 2007).

De Valck, Marijke and Skadi Loist, 'Film Festival Studies: An Overview of a Burgeoning Field', in *Film Festival Yearbook 1: The Festival Circuit*, ed. Dina Iordanova with Ragan Rhyne (London: Wallflower Press, 2009), pp. 179–215.

DGA Quarterly. Available at: http://www.dgaquarterly.org/BACKISSUES/Spring2010/PiracyByTheNumbers.aspx.

Díaz López, Marina. Personal Interview with Nuria Triana Toribio, 1 December 2008.

D'Lugo, Marvin, 'Across the Hispanic Atlantic: Cinema and its Symbolic Relocations', *Studies in Hispanic Cinemas*, 5.1–2 (2009), 3–7.

——, 'El cine de la inmigración: crónicas de un género anunciado', introduction to *Fotogramas para la multicuturalidad: migraciones y alteridad en el cine español contemporáneo*, ed. Móncia Cantero-Exojo, María Van Liew and José Carlos Suárez (Valencia: Tirant lo Blanch, 2011), pp. 9–21.

——, 'The Geopolitical Aesthetic in Recent Spanish Films', *Post Script*, 21.2 (2002), 1–8.

Douglas, Mary and Isherwood, Baron C, *The World of Goods: Towards an Anthropology of Consumption* (New York: Basic Books, 1979). Reprinted with a new introduction (London: Routledge, 1996).

Durovicová, Natasa, 'The Hollywood Multilinguals 1929–1933', in *Sound Theory Sound Practice*, ed. Rick Altman (New York and London: Routledge: 1992), pp. 138–53.

Durovicová, Natasa and Kathleen E. Newman (eds), *World Cinemas, Transnational Perspectives* (Abingdon: Routledge, 2009).

EFE, 'El Festival de Cine de Donostia exhibirá sus filmes en el Instituto Cervantes', *Deia*, 3 February 2006, p. 68.

——, 'Paraguay y CE insisten en ventajas de pacto UE_Mercosur', *ABC Color*, 24 May 2011. Available at: http://www.abc.com.py/nota/paraguay-y-ce-admiten-obstaculos-pero-insisten-en-ventajas-pacto-ue-mercosur/.

Elsaesser, Thomas, *European Cinema Face to Face with Hollywood* (Amsterdam: Amsterdam University Press, 2005).

Encina, Paz, 'Arrastrando la tormenta', in *Hacer cine: Producción audiovisual en América Latina*, ed. Eduardo A. Russo (Buenos Aires: Editorial Paidós, 2008).

——, Personal Interview with Catherine Leen, 2 April 2010.

Espinosa, Julio García, 'Cuban Cinema: A Long Journey toward the Light', in *When was Latin America Modern?*, ed. Nicola Miller and Stephen Hart (New York and London: Palgrave Macmillan, 2007), pp. 167–76.

Estrada, Julio, *El sonido en Rulfo: 'el ruido ese'* (Mexico City: Universidad Nacional de México, 2009).

Europa Cinema. Available at: http://www.europa-cinemas.org/en/index.php.

Evans, Chris, 'Latin Lovers', *Screen International*, 1612, 21–27 September 2007, 19–21.

'Extortion-like Mass Automated Copyright Lawsuits Come to the US: 20,000 Filed, 30,000 More on the Way', *Techdirt*. Available at: http://www.techdirt.com/articles/20100330/1132478790.shtml.

Ezra, Elizabeth and Terry Rowden, 'General Introduction: What is Transnational Cinema?', in *Transnational Cinema: The Film Reader*, ed. Elizabeth Ezra and Terry Rowden (London: Routledge, 2006), pp. 1–12.

Ezra, Elizabeth and Terry Rowden (eds), *Transnational Cinema: The Film Reader* (London: Routledge, 2006).

Faist, Thomas, *The Volume and Dynamics of International Migration and Transnational Social Spaces* (Oxford: Oxford University Press, 2000).

Falicov, Tamara, *The Cinematic Tango: Contemporary Argentine Film* (London: Wallflower, 2007).

——, 'Migrating from South to North: The Role of Film Festivals in Funding and Shaping Global South Film and Video', in *Locating Migrating Media*, ed. Greg Elmer, Charles H. Davis, Janine Marchessault and John McCullough (Lanham: Lexington Books, 2010), pp. 3–21.

Fermín, Zuri, Ibermedia administrator. Personal Interview with Tamara Falicov, 30 May 2003.

Ferreira, Carolin Overhoff, 'The Limits of Luso-Brazilian Brotherhood: *Fortress Europe in Terra Estrangeira* by Walter Salles and Daniela Thomas', *Third Text*, 20 (2006), 731–41.

Ferreira, Elisa, *Las mujeres productoras del alimentos en Paraguay: Tecnología y comercialización* (Venezuela: IICA Biblioteca, 1996).

'Festival Frenzy: Exhausted Executives Are Starting to Question which Autumn Festivals to Attend, Forcing Events to Define their Role', *Screen International*, 1612, 21–27 September 2007, cover and 10–11.

FIAPF website. Available at: http://www.fiapf.org/.

Figueiró, Belisa, 'Cinema terá R$ 365,2 milhões em 2008', *Revista de CINEMA* (2008). Available at: http://www.cenacine.com.br/?p=411.

——, 'O desafio de lucrar com o cinema', *Revista de CINEMA* (2007). Available at: http://www.cenacine.com.br/?p=404.

——, 'Programa Cinema do Brasil impulsiona coproduções em 200%', *Revista de CINEMA*, Edição Internacional (2008). Available at: http://www.cenacine. com.br/?p=421.

Finney, Angus, *The State of European Cinema: A New Dose of Reality* (London: Cassell, 1996).

Fond Sud Cinéma. Available at: http://www.diplomatie.gouv.fr/en/france-priorities_1/cinema_2/cinematographic-cooperation_9/production-support-funding_10/fonds-sud-cinema_11/index.html.

FONDEC website. Available at: http://www.fondec.gov.py/recursos/f12082009-adj-2004.pdf.

France Diplomatie website: http://www.diplomatie.gouv.fr/en/france-priorities_1/cinema_2/cinematographic-cooperation_9/production-support-funding_10/films-benefiting-from-aid_13/film-listby-country_15/paraguay_2688/hamaca-paraguaya_2834/index.html.

Foner, Nancy, *From Ellis Island to JFK: New York's Two Great Waves of Immigration.* (New Haven: Yale University Press, 2000).

'Forma en que Uruguay cumplirá con Ibermedia no satisface a cineastas', *El Espectador*, 11 August 2003. Available at: http://www.espectador.com/principal/noticias/ind0311182.htm.

Fornet, Ambrosio, *Alea, una retrospectiva crítica* (La Habana: Editorial Letras Cubanas, 1987).

Fra-Molinero, Baltasar, 'The Suspect Whiteness of Spain', in *At Home and Abroad: Historicizing Twentieth-century Whiteness in Literature and Performance*, ed. La Vinia Delois Jennings (Knoxville: University of Tennessee Press, 2009), pp. 147–69.

Francia, Aldo, *Nuevo Cine Latinoamericano en Viña del Mar* (Santiago, Chile: CESOC, Ediciones ChileAmerica and ARTECIEN, 1990).

Fundación Telefónica website. Available at: http://www.internetworldstats.com/sa/py.htm.

Gabilondo, Joseba, 'Introduction' to the Special Section: The Hispanic Atlantic, *Arizona Journal of Hispanic Cultural Studies*, 5 (2001), 91–113.

——, 'One-Way Theory: On the Hispanic Atlantic Intersection of Postcoloniality and Postnationalism and its Globalizing Effects', *Journal of Iberian and Latin American Literary and Cultural Studies* 1 (2001). Available at: http://arachne. rutgers.edu/vol1_1gabilondo.htm.

Gabriel, Teshome H, *Third Cinema in the Third World: The Aesthetics of Liberation* (Ann Arbor: UMI Research Press, 1982).

García Béjar, Ligia, 'The Media in Paraguay: A Locked Nation in Times of Change', in *The Handbook of Spanish Language Media*, ed. Alan B. Albarran (London: Routledge, 2009).

Garcia Canclini, Néstor, *Consumidores y ciudadanos: conflictos multiculturales de la globalización* (Mexico City: Grijalbo, 1995).

——, 'Cooperación, Diálogo: ¿Son las palabras más apropiadas?' V Campus Euroamericano de cooperacão cultural, Almada, Portugal, 2007, 9. Available at: http://www.redculturalmercosur.org/docs/Garcia-Canclini.pdf.

——, *La globalización imaginada* (Buenos Aires: Paidós, 2005 [1999]).

Garcia Ferrer, Alberto, 'Cine, televisión y cooperación iberoamericanos', lecture given at the Universidad 3 de Febrero, Buenos Aires, 30 August 2006.

Gatti, André, *Distribuição e exibição na indústria cinematográfica brasileira (1993/2003)* (Campinas: Universidade Estadual de Campinas, 2005).

Getino, Octavio, 'Some Notes on the Concept of a "Third Cinema"', in *New Latin American Cinema. Vol. 1: Theory, Practices, and Transcontinental Articulations,* ed. Michael T Martin (Detroit: Wayne State University Press, 1997), pp. 99–107.

Glick Schiller, Nina, 'Terrains of Blood and Nation: Haitian Transnational Social Fields', *Ethnic and Racial Studies*, 22.2 (1999), 340–66.

Globofilmes website: www.globofilmes.globo.com.

Gómez, Ramiro, Interview in *El Pororo Cine*. Available at: http://elpororo.wordpress.com/category/03-entrevistas/.

Gonzáles, Velda (Sub-Director of Programming, Puerto Rico Film Commission), email correspondence with Tamara Falicov, 30 October 2006.

González, Reynaldo, *Llorar es un placer* (La Habana: Editorial Letras Cubanas, 1988).

González Acevedo, Juan Carlos, *Che, qué bueno que vinisteis: el cine argentino que cruzó el charco* (Barcelona: Editorial Dieresis, 2005).

Grant, Catherine and Annette Kuhn, 'Screening World Cinema', in *Screening World Cinema: A Screen Reader*, ed. Catherine Grant and Annette Kuhn (Oxford: Routledge, 2006), pp. 1–14.

Gratius, Susanne, 'La vocación iberoamericana de España', *El país*, 17 May 2010.

Grillo, Ralph D, 'Transnational Migration and Multiculturalism in Europe', in *Oxford: ESRC Transnational Communities Working Paper*, WPTC-01–08, 2001.

Guarnizo, Luis E., 'On the Political Participation of Transnational Migrants: Old Practices and New Trends', in *E Pluribus Unum? Contemporary and Historical Perspectives on Immigrant Political Incorporation*, ed. Gary Gerstle and John Mollenkopf (New York: Russell Sage Foundation, 2001), pp. 213–63.

Haddu, Miriam, 'The Power of Looking: Politics and The Gaze in Salvador Carrasco's *La otra conquista/The Other Conquest*', in *Contemporary Latin American Cinema: Breaking into the Global Market*, ed. Deborah Shaw (Lanham: Rowman and Littlefield, 2007), pp. 153–72.

Harbord, Janet, *Film Cultures* (London: Sage, 2002).

Hayward, Susan, 'Framing National Cinema', in *Cinema and Nation*, ed. Mette Hjort and Scott Mackenzie (London: Routledge, 2000), pp. 88–102.

Hedetoft, Ulf. 'Contemporary Cinema: Between Cultural Globalisation and National Interpretation', in *Cinema and Nation*, ed. Mette Hjort and Scott MacKenzie (London: Routledge, 2000), pp. 278–97.

Hernández Les, Juan A, *Volver. Las películas de Almodóvar*, ed. Antonio Castro (Madrid: Ediciones JC, 2010), pp. 253–77.

Higbee, Will and Song Hwee Lim, 'Concepts of Transnational Cinema: Towards a Critical Transnationalism in Film Studies', *Transnational Cinemas*, 1.1 (2010), 7–21.

Higson, Andrew, 'The Limiting Imagination of National Cinema', in *Cinema and Nation*, ed. Mette Hjort and Scott Mackenzie (London: Routledge, 2000), pp. 63–74.

——, 'Transnational Developments in European Cinema in the 1920s', *Transnational Cinemas*, 1.1 (2010), 69–82.

Higson, Andrew and Richard Maltby (eds), *'Film Europe' and 'Film America': Cinema, Commerce and Cultural Exchange, 1920–1939* (Exeter: University of Exeter Press, 1999).

Hind, Emily, 'Provincia in Recent Mexican Cinema, 1989–2004', *Discourse*, 26.1–2 (2004), 26–45.

Hirsch Hadorn, Gertrude, Holger Hoffmann-Riem, Suzette Biber-Klemm, Walter Grossenbacher-Mansuy, Dominique Joye, Cristina Pohl, Ure Wiesmann and Elizabeth Zemp (eds), *Handbook of Transdisciplinary Research* (Bern: Springer, 2008).

Hjort, Mette, 'On the Plurality of Cinematic Transnationalism', in *World Cinemas, Transnational Perspectives*, ed. Natasa Durovicová and Kathleen Newman (London: Routledge, 2009), pp. 12–33.

——, 'Themes of Nation', in *Cinema and Nation*, ed. Mette Hjort and Scott Mackenzie (London: Routledge, 2000), pp. 103–17.

Hjort, Mette and Scott Mackenzie (eds), *Cinema and Nation* (London: Routledge, 2000).

Hoefert de Turégano, Teresa, 'The International Politics of Cinematic Coproduction: Spanish Policy in Latin America', *Film and History: An Interdisciplinary Journal of Film and Television Studies*, 34.2 (2004), 15–24.

Hoskins, Colin, Stuart McFadyen and Adam Finn, *Global Television and Film: An Introduction to the Economics of the Business* (New York: Oxford University Press, 1997).

Howard, April, 'Saying No to Soy: The Campesino Struggle for Sustainable Agriculture in Paraguay', *Monthly Review*, 61 (2009), 37–46.

Hubert Bals Fund website. Available at: http://www.filmfestivalrotterdam.com/en/about/hubert_bals_fund/

Ibermedia website. Available at: www.programaibermedia.com

'Ibermedia aprueba ayudas a la coproducción para 32 títulos, 13 de ellos con participación Española', *CINEinforme* 45 (February 2005), 34.

'Ibermedia financiará cinco películas uruguayas', *La República*, 25 November 2005. Available at: http://asoprod.org.uy/Ibermedia_financiara_cinco_peliculas_uruguayas.php.

'Ibermedia inicia una nueva etapa con la intención de dar mayor protagonismo a la distribución', *CINEinforme*, 43.762 (October 2003), 24.

Jäckel, Anne, *European Film Industries* (London: International Screen Industries/ British Film Institute, 2003).

Jerónimo, Miguel Bandeira, 'An Enduring Global Imperial Imagination: Lusotropicalism, Lusophonia and the Remnants of the Third Portuguese Empire', paper given at *London Debates 2010: How does Europe in the 21st Century*

Address the Legacy of Colonialism? Available online at http://commonwealth. sas.ac.uk/events/event-details.html?id=7431.

Johnson, Randal, 'Film Policy in Latin America', in *Film Policy: International, National and Regional Perspectives*, ed. Albert Moran (London: Routledge, 1996), pp. 128–47.

Jones, Gareth A., 'Latin American Geographies', in *The Companion to Latin American Studies*, ed. Philip Swanson (London: Arnold, 2003), pp. 5–25.

Kaminsky, Amy, 'Argentina White', in *At Home and Abroad: Historicizing Twentieth-century Whiteness in Literature and Performance*, ed. La Vinia Delois Jennings (Knoxville: University of Tennessee Press, 2009), pp. 1–28.

Kearney, Michael, 'Borders and Boundaries of State and Self at the End of Empire', *Journal of Historical Sociology*, 4.1 (1991), 52–74.

——, 'The Local and the Global: The Anthropology of Globalization and Transnationalism', *Annual Review of Anthropology*, 24 (1995), 547–65.

Kinemultimedia website: http://www.kinemultimedia.com/en/documentales/paraguay-fue-noticia.

King, John, *Magical Reels: A History of Cinema in Latin America* (London: Verso, 1990).

King, Noel, 'Film Culture in Paraguay: An Interview with Hugo Gamarra Etcheverry', *Senses of Cinema*. Available at: http://archive.sensesofcinema.com/contents/02/21/echeverry_interview.html.

Klady, Leonard, 'Not the Whole Picture', *Screen International*, 1614, 5–11 October, 2007, 28.

Klotzel, André, *O potencial da indústria cinematográfica no Brasil*, 2 vols (Campinas: Inovação Uniemp, 2006).

Knegt, Peter, 'CANNES '07 / Cuaron, Del Toro, and Inarritu Form 'cha cha cha'; Trio Ink 5 Film Pact With Universal/Focus', *Indiewire* (May 18, 2007). Available at: http://www.indiewire.com/article/cannes_07_cuaron_del_toro_and_inarritu_form_cha_cha_cha_trio_ink_5_film_pac/.

Kogan, Lauren, 'The Spanish Film Industry: New Technologies, New Opportunities', *Film Historia*, XVI.1–2 (2006). Available at: http://www.publicacions. ub.es/bibliotecaDigital/cinema/filmhistoria/2006/Ensayo_TheSpanishFilmIndustry_NewTechnologies_5.htm.

Kraul, Chris. 'Brazilian Film Industry's Resurgence Aided by Foreign Co-producers', *Los Angeles Times*, 23 October 2008. Available at: http://latimesblogs.latimes.com/laplaza/2008/10/brazilian-film.html.

Lachmann, Renate, 'Mnemonic and Intertextual Aspects of Literature', in *Cultural Memory Studies: An International and Interdisciplinary Handbook*, ed. Astrid Erll and Ansgar Nünning (Berlin and New York: Walter de Gruyter, 2008), pp. 301–10.

Lambert, Peter, 'A New Era for Paraguay', *NACLA Report on the Americas*, 41 (2008), pp. 5–8.

Lambert, Peter, and Ricardo Medina, 'Contested Discourse, Contested Power: Nationalism and the Left in Paraguay', *Bulletin of Latin American Research*, 26.3 (2007), 339–55.

Larkin, Brian, 'Itineraries of Indian Cinema: African Videos, Bollywood, and Global Media', in *Multiculturalism, Postcoloniality and Transnational Media*, ed. Ella Shohat and Robert Stam (New Brunswick: Rutgers University Press, 2003), pp. 170–92.

'A Latin American Decade?', *The Economist Special Report on Latin America*, 11 September 2010.

Lavretskii, I. R., 'A Survey of the Hispanic American Historical Review 1956–1958', *Hispanic American Historical Review* 40.4 (1960) 340–60.

Lee, Hyangjin, *Contemporary Korean Cinema* (Manchester: Manchester University Press, 2000).

León Frías, Isaac, 'Peru', in *International Film* Guide, ed. Ian Haydn Smith (London: Wallflower, 2009).

Levitt, Peggy, *The Transnational Villagers* (Berkeley and Los Angeles: University of California Press, 2001).

Levitt, Peggy and Nina Glick Schiller, 'Conceptualizing Simultaneity: A Transnational Social Field Perspective on Society', *International Migration Review*, 38.3 (2004), 1002–39.

Lieberman, Evan, 'Mask and Masculinity: Culture, Modernity, and Gender Identity in the Mexican *Lucha Libre* films of El Santo', *Studies in Hispanic Cinemas*, 6.1 (2009), 3–17.

López, Ana M, 'Are All Latins from Manhattan? Hollywood, Ethnography and Cultural Colonialism', in *Mediating Two Worlds: Cinematic Encounters in the Americas*, ed. John King, Ana M. López, Manuel Alvarado (London: BFI Publishing, 1993), pp. 67–80.

Lu, Sheldon Hsiao-peng, 'Historical Introduction: Chinese Cinemas (1896–1996) and Transnational Film Studies', in *Transnational Chinese Cinemas: Identity, Nationhood, Gender*, ed. Sheldon Hsiao-peng Lu (Honolulu: University of Hawaii Press, 1997), pp. 1–31.

Maneglia, Juan Carlos, Personal Interview with Catherine Leen, 8 July 2008.

Maneglia, Juan Carlos and María Rossana (Tana) Schémbori, 'El video de ficción en la década de los 80', MA thesis, Departamento de Ciencias de la Comunicación, Facultad de Filosofía y Ciencias Humanas, Universidad Católica Nuestra Señora de la Asunción, Asunción, 2001.

Mango, Agustin, 'Cannes 2012: Latin American Film Sector is on the Rise', *Hollywood Reporter*, 19 May 2012. Available at: http://www.hollywoodreporter.com/news/cannes-film-festival-latin-american-film-326811.

Marsh, Steven, 'Missing a Beat: Syncopated Rhythms and Subterranean Subjects in the Spectral Economy of *Volver*', in *All about Almodóvar: A Passion for Cinema*, ed. Brad Epps and Despina Kakoudaki (Minneapolis and London: University of Minnesota Press, 2009), pp. 339–56.

Martín-Barbero, Jesús, *De los medios a las mediaciones: comunicación, cultura y hegemonía* (Mexico City: GG, 1987).

——, 'La telenovela en Colombia: antecedentes y situación actual', in *El espectáculo y la pasión: las telenovelas latinoamericanas*, ed. Nora Mazziotto (Buenos Aires: Ediciones Colihue, 1995), pp. 43–62.

Martin-Jones, David and Soledad Montáñez, 'Bicycle Thieves or Thieves on Bicycles? *El bano del papa* 2007', *Studies in Hispanic Cinemas*, 4.3 (2007), 183–98.

Matta, João Paulo Rodrigues, *Análise competitiva da indústria cinematográfica brasileira no mercado interno de salas de exibição de 1994 a 2003* (Salvador: Universidade Federal da Bahia, Faculdade de Administração, Núcleo de Pós-Graduação em Administração, 2004).

——, *Políticas públicas federais de apoio à indústria cinematográfica brasileira: um histórico de ineficácia na distribuição.* Centro de Análise do Cinema e do Audiovisual. Available at: www.cenacine.com.br.

Matta, João Paulo Rodrigues and Elizabeth Regina Loiola da Cruz Souza, 'Cidade de Deus e Janela da Alma: um Estudo sobre a Cadeia Produtiva do Cinema Brasileiro', *Revista ERA/FGV*, 49 (2009), 27–37.

Mazziotti, Nora, 'Intertextualidades en la telenovela argentina: melodrama y costumbrismo', in *El espectáculo de la pasión: las telenovelas latinoameri-canas*, ed. Nora Mazziotti (Buenos Aires: Colihue, 1995), pp. 153–64.

McLennen, Sophia A., 'The Theory and Practice of the Peruvian Grupo Chaski', *Jump Cut: A Review of Contemporary Media*, 50 (Spring 2008). Available at: http://www.ejumpcut.org/archive/jc50.2008/Chaski/text.html.

McDonald, Paul and Janet Wasko (eds), The Contemporary Hollywood Film Industry (Malden, MA: Blackwell, 2007).

'El mensaje de Lugo por sus 2 años de Gobierno', *Ultima Hora*, 15 August 2010. Available at: http://www.ultimahora.com/notas/349059-El-mensaje-de-Lugo-por-sus-2-anos-de-Gobierno.

Meyero, Paché, 'Agustín Almodóvar, productor de cine', *La voz de Avilés*, 21 November 2001, n.p.

Middents, Jeffrey, 'Ibermediating National Cinemas.' paper delivered at the Society for Cinema and Media Studies (SCMS), Philadelphia, March 2008.

——, Writing National Cinema: Film Journals and Film Culture in Peru (Lebanon, NH: University Press of New England/Dartmouth College Press, 2009).

Mignolo, Walter, *Local Histories/ Global Designs: Coloniality, Subaltern Knowl-edges and Border Thinking* (Princeton NJ: Princeton University Press, 2000).

Mil Colores website. Available at: http://www.milcolores.info/milc.html.

Millás, Juan José, 'Asunto Volver', *Volver: un guión de Pedro Almodóvar* (Madrid: Ochoymedio, 2006).

Miller, Toby, Nitin Govil, John McMurria, Richard Maxwell, Ting Wang (eds), *Global Hollywood: No 2* (London: BFI Films, 2004).

Mills, Jane, *Loving and Hating Hollywood: Reframing Global and Local Cinemas* (New South Wales: Allen & Unwin, 2009)

Molina-Guzmán, Isabel, *Dangerous Curves: Latina Bodies in the Media* (New York and London: New York University Press, 2010).

Monteiro, Paulo Filipe, 'International Film Financing in Portugal: How? When? And with what Results?', paper given at the symposium *Transnational Film Financing in the Hispanic World* (University of Leeds, 29 June 2009).

Mora, Frank O. and Jerry W. Cooney, *Paraguay and the United States: Distant Allies* (Georgia: University of Georgia Press, 2007).

Moreno Domínguez, José Manuel, 'Diversidad audiovisual e integración cultural: analizando el Programa Ibermedia', *Comunicación y sociedad*, nueva época, 9 (January–June 2008), 95–118.

Mottram, James, *The Sundance Kids: How Hollywood Took Back Hollywood* (London: Faber and Faber, 2006).

Moura, Mariluce, 'A Constructor of Utopias', *Pesquisa online*, September 2006. Available at: http://revistapesquisa.fapesp.br/?art=1778&bd=1&pg=5&lg=en.

Naficy, Hamid, *An Accented Cinema, Exilic and Diasporic Filmmaking* (Princeton: Princeton University Press, 2001).

——, 'Phobic Spaces and Liminal Panics: Independent Transnational Film Genre', in *Global–Local: Cultural Production and the Transnational Imaginary*, ed. Rob Wilson and Wimal Dissanayake (Durham, NC and London: Duke University Press, 1996), pp. 119–44.

——, 'Situating Accented Cinema', in *Transnational Cinema: The Film Reader*, ed. Elizabeth Ezra and Terry Rowden (London: Routledge, 2006), pp. 111–29.

Nagib, Lúcia, *Brazil on Screen: Cinema Novo, New Cinema, Utopia* (London: IB Tauris, 2007).

——, 'Going Global: The Brazilian Scripted Film', in *Trading Cultures: Global Traffic and Local Cultures in Film and Television*, ed. Sylvia Harvey (Eastleigh: John Libbey, 2006), pp. 95–103.

——, 'Towards a Positive Definition of World Cinema', in *Remapping World Cinema: Identity, Culture and Politics in Film*, ed. Stephanie Dennison and Song Hwee Lim (London: Wallflower, 2006), pp. 30–7.

Neumann, Birgit, 'The Literary Representation of Memory', in *Cultural Memory Studies: An International and Interdisciplinary Handbook*, ed. Astrid Erll and Ansgar Nünning (Berlin: Walter de Gruyter, 2008), pp. 301–10.

Nichols, Bill, 'Discovering Form, Inferring Meaning: New Cinemas and Film Festivals Circuit', *Film Quarterly*, XLVII.31 (Spring 1994), 16–30.

Noble, Andrea, *Mexican National Cinema* (London: Routledge, 2005).

Nora, Pierre, 'Between Memory and History: *Les Lieux de mémoire*', *Representations*, 26 (1989), 7–25.

Nuovo, Silvana, Personal Interview with Catherine Leen, 17 August 2010.

O2 Filmes. *I Seminário de Coprodução Internacional*, Rio de Janeiro International Film Festival 2008. Available at: www.cenacine.com.br.

Ochoa, Pedro, *Tango y cine mundial* (Buenos Aires: Ediciones del Jilguero: 2003).

O'Regan, Tom, 'Cultural Exchange', in *A Companion to Film Theory*, ed. Toby Miller and Robert Stam (Oxford: Blackwell, 1999), pp. 262–94.

Orué Pozzo, Aníbal, *Periodismo en Paraguay: Estudios e interpretaciones* (Asunción: Arandurá Editorial, 2007).

O'Shaughnessy, Hugh, *The Priest of Paraguay: Fernando Lugo and the Making of a Nation* (London: Zed Books, 2009).

Pardo, Alejandro, *The Audiovisual Management Handbook* (Madrid: MEDIA Programme, 2002).

Pangea Day website. http://www.pangeaday.org/aboutPangeaDay.php.

Pangrazio Ciancio, Miguel Ángel, *Corrupción e impunidad en el Paraguay* (Asunción: ServiLibro, 2005).

Pelinski, Ramón, *El tango nómade: ensayos sobre la diáspora del tango* (Buenos Aires: Corregido, 2000).

Perriam, Chris, Isabel Santaolalla and Peter W Evans, 'The Transnational in Iberian and Latin American Cinemas: Editors' Introduction', in *Hispanic Research Journal* 8.1 (2007), pp. 3–9.

'Piracy and the Long Term of the Film Marketplace', 22 January 2011. Available at: http://shoana63roach.jimdo.com/2011/01/22/piracy-and-the-long-term-of-the-film-marketplace/.

Podalsky, Laura, 'Negotiating Differences: National Cinemas and Co-productions in Prerevolutionary Cuba', *The Velvet Light Trap*, 34 (Fall 1994), 59–70.

Portes, Alejandro, *Globalization from Below: The Rise of Transnational Communities*, Working Paper Series, Oxford University. Transnational Communities: An ESRC Research Programme; WPTC-98–01 ([Oxford]: Transnational Communities Programme, 1997), pp. 1–26.

Pre-proyecto ley del cine. Available at: http://recam.org/_files/documents/pre_proyecto_ley_de_cine.doc.pdf.

'Pre-proyecto de ley del cine y el audiovisual paraguayo'. Available at: http://www.recam.org/_files/documents/pre_proyecto_ley_de_cine.doc.pdf.

'President Obama "Declares War" on Film Piracy', *NME Movie News*, 24 June 2010. Available at: http://www.nme.com/filmandtv/news/president-obama-declares-war-on-film-piracy/176965.

Programa Ibermedia. Available at: www.programaibermedia.com.

'El Programa Ibermedia anuncia cambios para 2012', *Cine Latino*, 6 December 2011. Available at: http://elcinelatino.wordpress.com/2011/12/06/el-programa-ibermedia-anuncia-cambios-para-2012/.

'El Programa Ibermedia anuncia cambios para 2012', LatAmCinema.com, 7 December, 2011. Available at: http://www.latamcinema.com/noticia.php?id=3862

'El programa MEDIA apoya 12 títulos presentes en las deferentes secciones del Festival de Canne', *CINEinforme,* Año 45 (April 2005), 46.

Ramírez, Marisol, 'Cineastas piden diálogo en torno a la Ley de Cine', *Última hora,* 10 October 2009. Available at: http://www.ultimahora.com/notas/263099-cineastas-piden-di%E1logo-en-torno-a-la-ley-de-cine.

Rêgo, Cacilda and Carolina Rocha (eds.), *New Trends in Argentine and Brazilian Cinema* (Bristol: Intellect, 2010).

Reher, David S. and Blanca Sanchez Alonso, 'Argentina e España: siglo e medio de intercambios migratorios', in *Las multiples caras de la inmigración en España*, ed. David-Sven Reher and Miguel Requena (Madrid: Alianza, 2009), pp. 77–115.

'Remittances to Latin America Stabilizing after 15% Drop Last Year – MIF', *Inter-American Development Bank*, 4 March 2010. Available at: http://www.iadb.org/en/news/news-releases/2010–03–04/remittances-to-latin-america-stabilizing-after-15-drop-last-year-mif,6671.html.

Riba, José María. email interview with Nuria Triana Toribio, 23 and 27 March 2008.

Rios, Diana I., 'Chicana/o and Latina/o Gazing: Audiences of the Mass Media', in *Chicano Renaissance: Contemporary Cultural Trends*, ed. David Maciel, Isidro Ortiz and Maria Herrera-Sobek (Tucson: University of Arizona Press, 2000), pp. 169–90.

Rix, Rob, 'Co-productions and Common Cause', in *Spanish Cinema: Calling the Shots*, ed. Rob Rix and Roberto Rodríguez-Saona, : Leeds Iberian Papers (Leeds: Trinity and All Saints, University of Leeds, 1999), pp. 113–28.

Rocha, Glauber, 'An Aesthetics of Hunger', in *New Latin American Cinema: Theory, Practices and Transcontinental Articulations*, ed. Michael M. Martin (Detroit: Wayne State University Press, 1997), pp. 59–61.

Rodrigo, Márcio, 'O cinema brasileiro mira o exterior', *Gazeta mercantil*, 10 October 2008. Available at: http://www.cenacine.com.br/?p=565.

Rodríguez, Natalia y Prensa MCJ, 'Cinco proyectos de cineastas nacionales escogidos por Ibermedia', 21 July 2009, *Red cultura*. Available at: http://www.redcultura.com/php/Articulos293.htm.

Rolex mentoring scheme website. Available at: http://www.rolexmentorprotege.com/en/index.jsp.

Ross, Miriam, 'Film Festivals and the Ibero-American Sphere', in *Film Festival Yearbook 2: Film Festivals and Imagined Communities*, ed. Dina Iordanova and Ruby Cheung (St Andrews: St Andrews Film Studies/College Gate Press, 2009), pp. 171–87.

——, *South American Cinematic Culture: Policy, Production, Distribution and Exhibition* (Newcastle: Cambridge Scholars, 2010).

Rouse, Roger, 'Making Sense of Settlement: Class Transformation, Cultural Struggle and Transnationalism Among Mexican Migrants in the United States', in *Towards a Transnational Perspective on Migration*, ed. Linda Basch, Nina Glick Schiller and Cristina Blanc-Szanton (New York: New York Academy of Sciences, 1992), pp. 25–52.

——, 'Thinking Through Transnationalism: Notes on the Cultural Politics of Class Relations in the Contemporary United States', *Public Culture*, 7.2 (1995), 353–402.

Rowe, William and Vivian Schelling, *Memory and Modernity: Popular Culture in Latin America* (London: Verso, 1991).

Ruetalo, Victoria, 'Border-crossings and Textual Gaps: A "Globalized" Mode of Production in *Profundo Carmesi* and *Terra Estrangeira*', *Studies in Hispanic Cinemas*, 5.1–2 (2009), 57–71.

Salinas Aguirre, Juan Manuel, 'El cine en Paraguay'. Available at: http://www.paraguaycine.com/cine_nacional.html#3.

Salvador, Agustina, 'Varias banderas unidas para un mismo fin', *La nación*, 27 January 2005, 1.

Sanchez, Victor, Personal Interview with Tamara Falicov, 30 May 2003.

——, Personal Interview with Tamara Falicov, 6 July 2005.

Santaolalla, Isabel, 'A Case of Split Identity? Europe and Spanish America in Recent Spanish Cinema', *Journal of Contemporary European Studies*, 15.1 (2007), 67–78.

Sarlo, Beatriz, *La imaginación técnica: sueños modernos de la cultura argentina* (Buenos Aires: Ediciones Nueva Visión, 1992).

——, *Una modernidad periférica: Buenos Aires 1920–1930* (Buenos Aires: Ediciones Nueva Visión, 1988).

Schatz, Tom, 'The Studio System and Conglomerate Hollywood', in The *Contemporary Hollywood Film Industry*, ed. Paul McDonald and Janet Wasko (Malden, MA: Blackwell, 2007), pp. 13–42.

Schémbori, Tana, Personal Interview with Catherine Leen, 25 August 2010.

Screen Staff, 'Festivals Feel the Political Heat', *Screen International*. 1704, 2–8 October 2009, 10–11.

Secretaría General Iberoamericana (SEGIB) study, 'Programa Ibermedia, 1998–2008, Evaluacion'. Available at: http://www.segib.org/documentos/esp/IBER-MEDIA_PDF.pdf.

Sequera, David, '52 Festival Internacional de Cine de San Sebastián: un altar para el cine independiente', *Cineinforme*, 43 (2004), 7–16.

Shaw, Deborah, *Contemporary Cinema of Latin America: Ten Key Films* (London: Continuum, 2003).

—— (ed.), *Contemporary Latin American Cinema: Breaking into the Global Market* (Lanham: Rowman and Littlefield, 2007).

——, *The Three Amigos: The Transnational Filmmaking of Guillermo del Toro, Alejandro González Iñárritu, and Alfonso Cuarón* (Manchester: Manchester University Press, 2013).

Shaw, Lisa and Stephanie Dennison, *Brazilian National Cinema* (London: Routledge, 2007).

Shohat, Ella and Robert Stam, 'Introduction', in *Multiculturalism, Postcoloniality and Transnational Media*, ed. Ella Shohat and Robert Stam (New Brunswick: Rutgers University Press, 2003), pp. 1–18.

——, *Multiculturalism, Postcoloniality and Transnational Media*, ed. Ella Shohat and Robert Stam (New Brunswick: Rutgers University Press, 2003).

——, *Unthinking Eurocentrism: Multiculturalism and the Media* (New York: Routledge, 2003).

Signetto, Alberto. Video Interview with Pablo Bossi, producer of *El Aura* (2004). Available at: http://www.makingofeuropa.net/makingclip.asp?documentID=924.

Sklair, Leslie, 'Transnational Practices and the Analysis of the Global System', in *Globalization in the Twenty-first Century*, ed. Axel Hulsemeyer (Basingstoke: Palgrave Macmillan, 2003), pp. 15–32.

Smith, Michael and Luis Guarnizo (eds), *Transnationalism from Below* (New Brunswick, NJ: Transaction Publishers, 1998).

Smith, Paul Julian, 'Transatlantic Traffic in Recent Mexican Films', *Journal of Latin American Cultural Studies*, 12.3 (2003), 389–400.

Smith, Robert C., 'Changing Practices of Citizenship, Membership and Nation within the Context of Transnational Migration: Comparative Insights from the Mexican and Italian Cases', paper presented to ICCCR International Conference on Transnationalism, Manchester, 16–18 May 1998.

——, 'Comparing Local-Level Swedish and Mexican Transnational Life: An Essay in Historical Retrieval', in *New Transnational Social Spaces: International Migrations and Transnational Companies in the Early Twenty-first Century*, ed. Ludger Pries (London: Routledge, 2001), pp. 37–58.

——, 'Mexicans: Social, Educational, Economic, and political Problems and Prospects in New York', in *New Immigrants in New York*, ed. Nancy Foner (New York: Columbia University Press, 2002), pp. 275–300.

Smith, Sean, 'Latino Invasion', *Newsweek*, 30 November 2004. Available at www.newsweek.com/2004/11/30/Latino-invasion.html#.

Solanas, Fernando and Octavio Getino, 'Towards a Third Cinema', in *Movies and Methods. An Anthology*, ed. Bill Nichols (Berkeley: University of California Press, 1976), pp. 44–64.

'Spanish Companies in Latin America: A Good Bet? Investments in Latin America Offer Protection against Spain's Slowdown', *The Economist*, 30 April 2009. Available at http://www.economist.com/node/13579705.

Spivak, Gayatri, 'Who Claims Alterity?', in *Remaking History*, ed. Barbara Kruger and Phil Mariani (Seattle: Bay, 1989), pp. 269–92. Reprinted in Art in Theory 1900–1990: An Anthology of Changing Ideas, ed. Charles Harrison and Paul Wood (Cambridge, MA: Blackwell, 1992), pp. 1119–24.

Stavans, Ilan, *The Hispanic Condition: The Power of a People* (New York: Harper Collins, 1995).

Stock, Ann Marie, *Framing Latin American Cinema: Contemporary Critical Perspectives* (Minneapolis: University of Minnesota Press, 1997).

——, 'Migrancy and Latin American Cinemascape: Towards a Post-National Critical Praxis', in *Transnational Cinema: The Film Reader*, ed. Elizabeth Ezra and Terry Rowden (London: Routledge, 2006), pp. 157–65.

——, *On Location in Cuba: Street Film-making during Times of Transition* (Chapel Hill: University of North Carolina Press, 2009).

Strover, Sharon, 'Coproductions International' (1995), 1–3. Available at: http://www.archives.museum.tv/eotvsection.php?entrycode=coproductions.

Swanson, Philip, 'Going Down on Good Neighbours: Imagining *América* in Hollywood Movies of the 1930s and 1940s (*Flying Down to Rio* and *Down Argentine Way*), Bulletin of Latin American Research, 29.1 (2010), 71–84; first published online 15 July 2009, DOI: 10.1111/j.1470–9856.2009.00318.x, pp. 1–14.

——, 'Introduction', in *The Companion to Latin American Studies*, ed. Philip Swanson (London: Arnold, 2003), pp. 1–4.

Tal, Tzvi, 'Viejos republicanos españoles y joven democratización latinoamericana: imagen de exilado en películas de Argentina y Chile: *La historia oficial* y *La frontera*', *Espéculo: Revista de estudios literarios,* 15. Available at: http://www.ucm.es/info/especulo/numero15/tzvi_tal.html.

Tehrani, Bijan, 'Mikel Olaciregui talks about San Sebastian International Film Festival', *Cinema without Borders*, 24 September 2007. Available at http://www.cinemawithoutborders.com/news/130/article/ 1357/2007–09–24.html.

Tierney, Dolores, 'Alejandro Gonzalez Iñárritu: Director without Borders', New Cinemas 7.2 (2009), 101–17.

Tierney, Dolores and Victoria Ruétalo (eds), *Latsploitation, Exploitation Cinemas and Latin America* (Abingdon: Routledge, 2009).

Tomlinson, John, *Globalization and Culture* (Cambridge: Policy Press, 1999).

Treverton, Gregory F., Carl Matthies, Karla J. Cunningham, Jeremiah Goulka, Greg Ridgeway, Anny Wong, *Film Piracy, Organized Crime, and Terrorism* (Los Angeles: RAND Corporation, 2009).

Triana Toribio, Nuria, 'Auteurism and Commerce in Contemporary Spanish Cinema: directores mediáticos', *Screen*, 49 (2008), 259–76.

——, 'Cine en construcción: Building Latin American Cinema in Europe', paper delivered at conference *Transnational Film Financing in the Hispanic World*, University of Leeds, 29 June 2009.

——, 'El festival de los cinéfilos transnacionales: Festival Cinematográfico Internacional de la República Argentina en Mar del Plata, 1959–1970', *Secuencias: Revista de historia del cine*, 25 (2007), 25–45.

——, 'Journeys of El Deseo between the Nation and the Transnational in Spanish
Cinema', in *Studies in Hispanic Cinemas* 4.3 (2007), 151–63.

——, *Spanish National Cinema* (London: Routledge, 2003).

Turan, Kenneth, *Sundance to Sarajevo: Film Festivals and the World They Made*
(Berkeley: University of California Press, 2002).

Vázquez Montalbán, Manuel, *Crónica sentimental de España* (Barcelona: De
bolsillo, 2003).

Vernon, Kathleen, 'Las canciones de Pedro Almodóvar', in *Almodóvar: el cine
como passion. Actas del congreso internacional Pedro Almodóvar*, ed. Fran
A. Zurián and Carmen Vázquez Varela (Cuenca: Ediciones de la Universidad
Castilla-La Mancha, 2005), pp. 161–75.

——, 'Queer Sound: Musical Otherness in Three Films by Pedro Almodóvar',
in *All about Almodóvar: A Passion for Cinema,* ed. Brad Epps and Despina
Kakoudaki (Minneapolis and London: University of Minnesota Press, 2009),
pp. 51–70.

Vertovec, Steven, 'Conceiving and Researching Transnationalism', *Ethnic and
Racial Studies*, 22.2 (1999), 447–62.

Vidal-Villegas, Norma, 'La salida natural para el cine español es Iberoamérica',
El economista (2000). Available at: http://www.americaeconomica.com/
numeros/84/reportajes/ncine.htm.

Vieira, Else (ed.), *City of God in Several Voices: Brazilian Cinema as Social
Action* (Nottingham: Critical, Cultural and Communications Press, 2005)

Villar, Dionisio P., 'Cómo, Por qué, y para qué, se creó la Primera Semana Internacional del Cine', in *Historia de 12 Festivales,* ed. J. M Ferrer and Luis
Gasca (San Sebastián: Festival Internacional del Cine, 1965), pp. 3–7.

Villazana, Libia, 'Hegemony Conditions in the Coproduction Cinema of Latin
America: The Role of Spain', *Framework*, 49.2 (2008), 65–85.

——, *Transnational Financial Structures in the Cinema of Latin America:
Programa Ibermedia in Study* (Saarbrucken: Verlag Dr Muller, 2009).

Waldinger, Roger D. and David Fitzgerald, 'Transnationalism in Question',
American Journal of Sociology 109.5 (2004), 1177–95. Available at: http://
works.bepress.com/roger_waldinger/25.

Wayne, Mike, *Political Film: The Dialectics of Third Cinema* (Sterling, VA:
Pluto Press, 2001).

Wolf, Sergio, 'No Turning Back', *Sight and Sound*, September 2010, 14–17.

Wolff, Janet, *The Social Production of Art* (London: Macmillan, 1993 [1981])

Wood, Jason, 'A Life in Pictures: Guillermo el Toro' (8 July 2008). Available at:
http://www.bafta.org/access-all-areas/videos/a-life-in-pictures-guillermo-del-
toro,466,BA.htm .

——, *The Faber Book of Mexican Cinema* (London: Faber and Faber, 2006).

World Cinema Fund website. Available at: http://www.berlinale.de/en/das_
festival/world_cinema_fund/gefoerderte_projekte_produktion/index.html.

Yúdice, George, *El recurso de la cultura: usos de la cultura en la era global*
(Barcelona: Editorial Gedisa, 2002).

Zaniello, Tom, *The Cinema of Globalization: A Guide to Films about the New Economic Order* (Ithaca: Cornell University Press, 2007).

'Zinema Eraikitzen/ Cine en Construcción', in *Catálogo del 50 festival internacional de San Sebastián/Zinemaldia* (San Sebastián: Festival Internacional de San Sebastián/Zinemaldia, 2002).

Zinemaldia website. Available at: www.sansebastianfestival.com/es/cineenco. php?id=1444.

INDEX

References to notes consist of the page number followed by the letter 'n' followed by the number of the note, e.g. 35n21 refers to note no. 21 on page 35. References to figures are shown in *italics*. References to tables are shown in **bold**.